"Working as a team with other firefighters, to save a person's life, I don't know how to describe it. It's rewarding. It's refreshing. It's heart-wrenching. It brings tears to your eyes. It's absolutely fabulous. It's a great job. It's the best profession in the world." [p. 87]

"Anybody who says they've never experienced fear is lying through their teeth. We've all been scared to death. I've been at it twenty-nine years and I still have that doubt: I was lucky that last one and managed to hang in there, but what about the next one? Maybe I'll just drop the line and run down the hallway. Maybe next time, I'll just bail out." [p. 107]

"The best officers are those who admit they're human. One time I had a chief who always admitted mistakes. I loved him for that. Everyone did. But usually, no. People in command will not admit they were wrong." [p. 140]

―――――

"Totally frank, compelling and highly emotional. . . . Delsohn sought out the toughest and the brightest—proven firefighters respected by both their officers and peers."
—*The International Fire Fighter*

"Conversational, sometimes raw, occasionally profane, but always realistic."
—Gary Giacomo
The California Fire Service

ATTENTION: ORGANIZATIONS AND CORPORATIONS

Most HarperPaperbacks are available at special quantity discounts for bulk purchases for sales promotions, premiums, or fund-raising. For information, please call or write:
Special Markets Department, HarperCollins*Publishers*,
10 East 53rd Street, New York, N.Y. 10022.
Telephone: (212) 207-7528. Fax: (212) 207-7222.

THE FIRE INSIDE

Firefighters Talk About Their Lives

Steve Delsohn

HarperPaperbacks
A Division of HarperCollins*Publishers*

HarperPaperbacks

A Division of HarperCollins*Publishers*
10 East 53rd Street, New York, N.Y. 10022-5299

If you purchased this book without a cover, you should be aware
that this book is stolen property. It was reported as "unsold and
destroyed" to the publisher and neither the author nor the
publisher has received any payment for this "stripped book."

This is a work of fiction. The characters, incidents, and
dialogues are products of the author's imagination and are not to
be construed as real. Any resemblance to actual events or
persons, living or dead, is entirely coincidental.

Copyright © 1996 by Steven Delsohn
All rights reserved. No part of this book may be used or
reproduced in any manner whatsoever without written
permission of the publisher, except in the case of brief
quotations embodied in critical articles and reviews.
For information address HarperCollins*Publishers,*
10 East 53rd Street, New York, N.Y. 10022-5299.

ISBN 0-06-109421-8

HarperCollins®, ® , and HarperPaperbacks™
are trademarks of HarperCollins*Publishers* Inc.

Cover photo: by Alan Simmons

A hardcover edition of this book was published in 1996 by
HarperCollins*Publishers.*

First HarperPaperbacks printing: June 1997

Printed in the United States of America

Visit HarperPaperbacks on the World Wide Web at
http://www.harpercollins.com/paperbacks

❖ 10 9 8 7 6 5 4 3 2

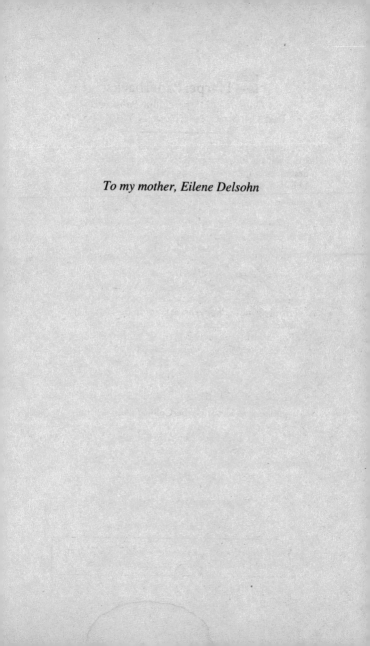

To my mother, Eilene Delsohn

ACKNOWLEDGMENTS

There are many people to thank. Above all, I thank the firefighters themselves. I have never found a more generous group of people. This book could not exist without their cooperation.

I want to thank Rick Horgan, my gifted editor. His honest criticisms, clear thinking, and expertise were crucial to me. Rick's assistant, Airié Dekidjiev, was both extremely capable and kind. My agent, Dan Strone, believed in this book from the start. His enthusiasm for it was infectious.

I am also indebted to the many people in the firefighting community who provided information and referrals. I'd like to mention them here and express my gratitude: Danny Noonan, George Burke, Lori Moore, Marie Grimes, Wayne Powell, Steve McInerny, Harvey Eisner, Georgia Taylor, John Hall, Linda Feldman, Julie Reynolds, Steve MacDonald, Dave Aldrich, Olivia Day, Ed Geils, Larry Cooke, Mike Noonan, Patty Foley, Bruce Angier, Benny King, Charles Stone, Arthur Kenney, Robert Wauhop, Henry Dolberry, Archie Ward, Sue Hasari, Louie Fernandez, Richard Duffy, Mike McCositer, Rita F. Fahy, Reed Bush, Jerry Sanford.

I want to thank my brother, Gary Delsohn, for his unstinting support, and also for sharing his editorial insights.

Finally, special thanks to my wife and children, Mary Kay, Emma, and Hannah. Their tender love has enriched my life.

INTRODUCTION

Growing up in Chicago, I didn't give much thought to firefighters. I looked up to pro athletes, especially football players. My heroes were Dick Butkus and Gale Sayers.

It wasn't until late October of 1993, when firestorms erupted throughout Southern California, that my curiosity about firefighters grew. By then my wife and I had moved to Thousand Oaks, about midway between downtown Los Angeles and Santa Barbara. Just two miles from our house, one of the biggest wildfires was on a wind-whipped rampage. Burning thirty-nine thousand acres and damaging thirty-eight homes, the fire started just off the Ventura Freeway, crossed the Santa Monica Mountains, and raced all the way to the ocean.

A few nights we drove around and watched fires burn in the hills. Mostly we watched the endless TV coverage. As fourteen major blazes spread during one catastrophic week, we could not quite turn away from the powerful images. Residents fleeing; their dreams, mementos, and homes incinerated. Orange walls of flame up to three hundred feet high, and the firefighters rushing in to attack them. They attacked again and again, risking their lives. It was touching and impressive, almost amazing, how brutally hard and bravely they worked.

That's when I started thinking about this book. I wanted to answer some questions if I could.

Why are firefighters willing to do such a dangerous job? Are they adrenaline junkies, chasing the rush? Or do they embody more wholesome traits, like fortitude, selflessness, and commitment? How high do they feel when they save a person's life? How traumatic is it when missions fail, and they cannot save someone? What about that mysterious virtue, courage? When seemingly routine fires turn suddenly lethal, they are lost in smoke-filled rooms, and fear arises, where do they get the nerve to keep on fighting?

Most but not all of these questions were answered directly. Firefighters, for instance, don't talk about bravery much. It isn't their style or part of their lexicon. So they recall events with passion and candor, but unaccompanied by self-promotion. After all, they invariably say, "We were just doing our jobs."

True. But firefighting is an inherently risky profession. In 1994 in the United States, 95,400 firefighters were injured while working. Another 104 firefighters died in the line of duty. That is not to mention occupational illness— the heart and lung diseases, the various cancers they get from inhaling toxic smoke.

When the enemy is fire, even small mistakes can be deadly. Or at least they might sound small to you and me.

Inside a burning building, just standing straight up can kill you. That's because heat and smoke rise up to the ceiling, where temperatures can soar to thirteen hundred degrees. So from almost their first day at training school, new firefighters are told to stay low, where they can find cooler air down near the floor.

In interviewing 108 firefighters—including paid and volunteer; urban, suburban, and rural; structural and wildland—I asked for their gut feelings and unvarnished insights. To help ensure that I'd get them, I didn't use any names. A few firefighters said, "Well, I'll tell you the same things I would if my name was attached." But a lot more firefighters felt it was the best approach. Like most people with interesting jobs, they wanted to relax and tell what it's really like. They just didn't want repercussions from fire bosses.

Their veracity never seemed to become an issue. Trusting my own instincts, I never felt I heard anything but the truth. It might be because of the firefighters I spoke to. I avoided what they call "slackers" and "loads." I concentrated instead on proven firefighters, respected by both their officers and peers. When you and your co-workers know your abilities, there is no need to exaggerate.

Some memories were painful and still fresh. Several were tinged with guilt. I was surprised at the firefighters' frank self-appraisals, even when telling stories with tragic endings. Almost every firefighter seemed haunted, if not by an unforgettable self-doubt, then by something horrible they had witnessed. A few of them got choked up while reminiscing. Each time it involved a child's death, or the death of a colleague. These are the two lowest moments they say they ever face.

To track down my pool of 108 firefighters, I sometimes went through fire department channels, asking to interview their most decorated people. I got names and story ideas from *Firehouse* magazine, the one publication found in almost all fire stations. I relied on personal contacts. My brother's close friend is a veteran firefighter and a captain. My brother-in-law's younger brother got hired four years ago. A firefighter at my gym spoke to me for five hours. I met one female firefighter outside a movie theater. Most of all, firefighters referred me to their friends. A Boston firefighter had buddies in New York. The New York guys, of course, had buddies everywhere. As a nonmember of the club, this was exactly what I'd been hoping for.

Although I interviewed some chiefs and assistant chiefs who came up through the ranks, I mostly spoke with those on the front lines today—firefighters, lieutenants, captains. We talked in empty rooms at their fire stations, in their tidy kitchens at home, while driving in their cars to pick up their kids at school. We spoke in restaurants over bottomless cups of coffee. With their twenty-four-hour shifts and carbon monoxide headaches from eating smoke, firefighters devour a lot of coffee.

When my research began for this book, I had a few vague notions of firefighters. I figured they were type A's. I figured they were tenacious, especially the women, who have to deal with fire and also with the men. I figured their main motivation wasn't the money. But I had no realistic view of their daily existence, why they wanted this stressful job in the first place, and what psychic and emotional costs that job exacted.

There's still many things I don't know about this complex occupation, but even for firefighters the learning never stops. Our society is increasingly high-tech, relentlessly high-tech. As new flammable synthetics proliferate, firefighters must be part physicist and part chemist. On emergency medical calls or prolonged extrications—when people are not just injured but often panicked—firefighters are both doctor and shrink. The modern job is vast and ever-changing. Gone are the days, if they ever existed, when the only requirements were strength and grit.

What I do know about firefighters is that I like them. I admire them. It isn't only a matter of what they accomplish. Firefighters are easy to be around. They have a sense of humor, a spirit of citizenship. And firefighters don't quit. Even in dark circumstances, they keep pushing and trying. This is a form of nobility in itself.

Firefighters are flawed like everyone else, and they'll be the first to say so. But don't let their humility fool you. Their courage is epic. These everyday people are heroes.

1
GETTING STARTED

Many of them were "fire department brats." With fathers or brothers or uncles already firefighters, they belonged to the fraternity even as children. At barbecues and parties they felt the camaraderie. When relatives won medals they basked in reflected glory. One day, they promised themselves, *they* would speed to mishaps on blaring red fire engines. They would rescue people from burning houses. Because this was something more than the family business. It was the highest calling.

Many others never saw the job coming until they were young adults, bored with their nine-to-fives and looking for action. Altruism lured some, while others were simply pragmatic. Married, perhaps with young kids, the steady paycheck, benefits package, and pension plan looked enticing.

"But it doesn't matter why you hired on," says one firefighter. "You can have five uncles on the department and still turn out to be a stiff. You can stumble into it and end up a damn good fireman. All that really counts is what you do once you're here."

For paid firefighters, also called career firefighters, just getting hired means beating out fierce competition.

Although the process varies between each fire department, here's how it generally works.

For twenty-five open positions announced by the municipality, five thousand people might fill out applications. Then comes the written part of the firefighter's test, often a civil service examination, which just about any applicant can take. Essentially a test of general knowledge—math, logic, reading comprehension—some questions may be geared toward firefighting principles. Most firefighters say the current test is easy, but there is scant margin for error. Although a 70 score might be passing, even a 97 could kill your chances.

For the applicants moving on, the standards from this point forward become more stringent. Next they must take a demanding physical test. Rather than how much they bench-press or how fast they run the forty, the point of the test is their firefighting potential. So to simulate the effort of stretching a charged hose line, they drag weighted duffel bags across a gymnasium. To simulate wearing their self-contained breathing apparatus, they wear heavy vests and run through obstacle courses. They scale walls, climb ladders, carry hundred-pound dummies up and down stairways. With little rest between segments, some applicants get dizzy or stop to vomit. But as long as they gear back up and finish the test in time, they can still score one hundred percent.

The written and physical scores are averaged together, giving the applicants an eligibility rating. They can also score extra points for military service, particularly if they served during wartime. With job competition so tight, these five or so extra points can be momentous.

After the written and physical exams, then comes the time when the hiring list is established. But even the top scorers may not end up employed. First the fire department investigates them: For any drug convictions. For all criminal convictions. For discipline problems they had with former employers or their military officers. For any red-flag behavior that might indicate a moral deficiency.

Others disqualify now for physical reasons. At a medical exam, their lungs, hearts, blood, and urine are analyzed. Eyes and ears are checked for subpar vision and hearing. To discourage applicants from keeping things to themselves—like steel pins holding together a fragile collarbone—X rays are sometimes taken.

Finally, when all the weeding is done, the surviving candidates spend about three months at the training academy. For this latest crop of "probies"—probationary firefighters—days are long and unyielding. After running laps or lifting weights, they spend hours in classrooms and training drills, learning their tools and apparatus, building codes and construction, fire prevention, fire behavior, and fire suppression, emergency first aid, the uses of ropes and safety belts, the lifting, lugging, and climbing of various ladders, the hauling and packing of hose, and how to search for prone bodies in pitch-black rooms. Nervous, intimidated, self-doubting at first, they are ultimately surprised by their own prowess. By the last few weeks they're itching to graduate, to stop approximating and do the real thing.

Along with an estimated 260,000 paid firefighters, American lives and property are protected by about 795,000 volunteers. To become a volunteer—and to then be allowed to respond to emergencies—the training requirements differ dramatically. In some badly short-handed volunteer departments, the present resembles the past. You can be sworn in that day and dragging hose that night.

"Sometimes that really still happens," says one volunteer. "But it's rare, and it's probably going to be in the smaller rural communities. As you get closer to cities or bedroom suburbs, the system for recruitment becomes more selective, and there's much greater emphasis on training and safety. In some volunteer departments, the training standards are higher than those in many career departments. Until you've earned the proper certification—by drilling and doing classwork—you can answer phones or help with fund-raising. You can go get people tools. But you can't go inside a burning building."

Some strong volunteer departments even have waiting lists. Nationally, however, volunteer ranks have thinned about ten percent in the last ten years. Among the reasons cited are the greater training demands and subsequent time commitment, the more and more Americans holding down second jobs, the insular nature of some volunteer departments, where females and minorities are not recruited, and the increasing number of sprawling, shapeless suburbs, where residents never develop communal pride.

"Our numbers are dropping," says one long-time volunteer. "But for those of us left, it still runs through our veins. Getting paid isn't the issue. We have chosen a life in the fire service."

I became a firefighter by accident. I was born and raised here in South Florida and I had two brothers. I was working for the phone company, my older brother was working for the airline industry, and my brother John was a bum at home.

One night John said, "I'm going to apply for the fire department."

I said, "You're full of shit, man. You're a big wuss. They ain't gonna take you."

And I'll be damned if he didn't get hired.

Once I saw what he was doing, all the hero stuff, I said, "I want a piece of that action."

Not everyone will admit it, but we *all* want to do the hero stuff. It's like getting your picture on the cover of *Rolling Stone*.

So I went down and applied, and then my older brother went down and applied, and I'll be damned if we ain't all firemen. And we've loved it ever since.

My dad died when I was two years old. In my mind, I've often thought that maybe the fire department was the father I didn't have.

I mean, I wanted to do this my whole life. There were no firemen in my family or anything, but I grew up not too far from a firehouse. I used to hang around there when I was a kid. I'd go and get subs for the guys, or whatever they wanted to eat. When I got older and I got hired myself, I'll never forget my first day on the job. It was almost surreal, like I couldn't believe I made it.

Since then, it has just become the moving force in my life. This is really what I am. I am a fireman.

I was born into a firefighting family. My grandfather came from Ireland, but nobody here in Boston wanted to hire the Irish. There were help-wanted signs in windows of stores: NO IRISH NEED APPLY.

So my grandfather took the civil service examination. It was one of the only places where you couldn't be discriminated against. Then he became a fireman, and that set the mood for what happened the next generation. My father, my uncles, my only brother and I—we all became firefighters. And every one of us joined the fire department in Boston.

As you get older, you see there's more to this job than all the noise and excitement. It's more than riding on trucks and sliding down poles. But that was the magical stuff when I was a kid. I wanted to be a part of it all my life, and nothing has ever changed that. Even when my dad died, I still wanted the job.

My father had gotten injured in a fire. Eventually, a medical board determined that that's what killed him. After the fire, he suffered some complications. He ended up going through a series of operations. Each operation, inevitably, they kept disturbing the injured area. An infection set in and compromised his immune system. He ended up dying of cancer. Before he died, my father suffered horribly.

I was nine years old when he died. I was very shaken up. But it still didn't change my mind about the job. Once I became a teenager, I would go and ride along with my uncles. I saw these guys fight fires and pull off rescues, but I also saw the human end of it, too. These guys all stuck together. They looked out for one another. They ate together and slept together. They worked fourteen-hour night tours together. It had an effect on me. I looked at them and thought, *This is more than a job. There is a mission here.*

My first dream was to be a Catholic priest. I grew up in a real strong Catholic family and my father taught us the value of always looking out for the welfare of other people first. Seek their comfort before you find your own.

At an early age I went off to study to be a priest. The priesthood was not quite for me, but I never lost that feeling of serving others. After I left the seminary, I joined the marines. From the marines I went straight into the fire service. This job has given me everything I was looking for. I can be of service to my community, and I work with a group of people I'd go to hell and back with.

I joined the Chicago Fire Department in 1965. Mostly I was looking for a secure job, and actually I wanted to be a cop.

Because I used to notice this one cop on Twenty-second and Ashland, which is a very busy intersection. This guy would be pulling cars over left and right, all because of this tiny no-left-turn sign. As soon as the cop would get the guy pulled over, he'd go and sit in the car. Next thing you know, he'd get out of the car and the motorist would take off. I was thinking, *What the hell's going on here? Cops don't get in the car.*

Then somebody in the neighborhood clued me in: This guy was making two bucks every time he pulled someone over. I was young, and I was a little conniving son of a gun. So I thought, *Hey, that's the kind of job for me. Stand on the corner, direct some traffic, and make two hundred dollars a day.*

I went downtown to apply to be a cop. A guy from the city said, "How about being a fireman?"

I had never been in a firehouse in my life. But I told the guy, "Why not?"

If you worked for the city, I knew that you had benefits, you had insurance, you had something stable.

While I'm waiting to hear from the cops, not even really thinking about the firemen, I'm hanging out in a tavern one day. The guy behind the bar says to me, "Hey Don, why don't you take the fireman job instead?"

I says, "For what? I want to be a cop. I want to carry a gun, make all that money."

He says, "Yeah, but a fireman, you work one day and then you get two days off."

I says, "What? Get outta here!"

I did some investigating, and son of a gun if it wasn't true. So even though I wound up passing both tests, I waived the job with the cops and ended up being a fireman. All because I wanted to get that time off.

I had just gotten back from Vietnam. I was in a specialized unit over there. It was a recon platoon with twenty-two guys, sometimes twenty-four. Our mission was to make contact with the enemy.

We'd be told, "Look, we think there's a base camp in here. We'd like you guys to go in and see what it is. And we'd like you to make contact."

That was our big thing: making contact. Finding the enemy. Surprising him. Ambushing him.

I was there a year. Three months after I came back, I joined the fire department. It happened that quick because I had taken the test for the city two days before I was drafted into the army. Then my name had passed while I was in Vietnam.

Coming back, after being there, wasn't really that big a transition for me. I guess it all depends on the individual. Everyone comes back from war in different ways. Some people come back shell-shocked. Some come back and they're nervous wrecks. Other people come back and fake these conditions. And then some people come back and are able to say, "Well, that was a very bad time. I saw a lot of bad things, and friends of mine died. But I have to go on. I've gotta keep living."

For the past seventeen years, I've been in the same rescue squad. There's always been many military guys here. A lot of us survived in Vietnam, and I don't think it's coincidence. Because a certain type of person is drawn to the rescue squad. Guys who want to get dirty. Guys who are gung ho. Guys who don't want to come to work and do nothing. They want to go from call to call and wade right in there.

Our rescue is very busy. We average about forty-two hundred runs a year, and we respond to every call on the first signal.

I love it. I love the challenge. I love the closeness you get in a busy firehouse. And it may sound crazy, but it's the truth: This is the closest you'll ever come to actual combat.

Until my twin brother got on in 1977, we never had a firefighter in our family. At the time he got hired, I was working at a country club in Youngstown, Ohio. Between shining shoes, cleaning the locker room, and helping with dinners at night, it seemed like I was working twenty hours a day. They were talking about sending me to Cornell University to go to club management school, but I began having second thoughts. I would come home at night dead tired. Then I'd have to be back at work at 7:00 A.M.

Meanwhile, my brother the firefighter was working one day and taking two off, drinking, playing golf, enjoying life. On top of all that I started asking myself: *Do I really want to spend the rest of my life kissing ass?*

Because that's really what country club management's all about. Pleasing the rich.

My brother said, "Why don't you become a fireman?"

I applied and bingo! When I told the country club what I was doing, they were in shock. The fire department? They thought that was demeaning. One guy said, "That's not a suit and tie job."

I said, "Maybe I'm not set for a suit and tie."

No doubt in my mind I made the right move. I can't imagine *not* being a firefighter.

I grew up in an Irish Catholic family. My folks are from Dublin, Ireland. So what are you going to do?

Either you'll be a cop, which my brother used to be, or you're going to be a fireman like me. We also have one brother who's very successful in business. We call him the black sheep.

I also grew up in a firefighting environment. My best friend's dad was a fireman in Los Angeles. In 1971 in the Sylmar earthquake, he received the Medal of Valor. He dug a man out of a ditch with just his hands. Their family had the medal on the wall, with a picture of my friend's dad digging this man out. I saw that and thought, *Okay, I want to do that. I want to be the guy that people call for help*.

It wasn't easy, though. There's so much intense competition to get this job, you have to be dedicated.

Actually, you have to be obsessed. Before I got on, the city was only giving out so many applications. If you weren't in line, you just weren't going to get one. So just to make sure I got the application, I stood in line for three days and never left. I slept in a sleeping bag on the sidewalk. Just me and several hundred of my close pals.

They were giving out the application on Monday, so I got there on Friday afternoon. But some guys couldn't do that. They had other jobs. So they would have their girlfriend wait in line for them, or their mom, or their dad, or their brother. That's just how it works. From the minute you try for this job, you start to compete.

My father passed away in June of 1989. He had thirty-eight years on the job. From 1963 through 1978, he was a deputy chief in the South Bronx. Anybody familiar with the fire department in New York will tell you those were the high-fire years. Ridiculous amounts of fires. Pat Moynihan described it as a level of domestic destruction unprecedented in history. He said the only thing he could liken it to was Dresden.

My father was an extremely respected chief. He kind of ran the show during the really busy years there. And if it was true that he was highly competent, it was because he recognized his dire responsibility. He knew those guys were out there putting their lives on the line, and really breaking their asses. He wanted to make sure he was up to the challenge, too. It was my father's job to keep them safe.

Sometimes now I'll go to these coalitions. They have them on Medal Day, when the fire department gives out its annual awards, or else on Memorial Day. People will sit around, usually in uniform, and it will run the gamut. Retired members show up, senior guys are there, chiefs are there, probies are there. If I go to one in the Bronx, a buzz goes through the room, I kid you not, because I'm my father's son. It looks like a priest at confession. I have chiefs waiting on line to speak to me.

It's ridiculous. These guys are wearing eagles, which means deputy chief, and they are making the effort to seek me out. But what they want to do is talk about my dad. They wanna tell me about their experiences, and they are always effusive in their praise. What I emphasize to them is that the feeling was mutual. He loved them, and they made him look good, and he watched out for them.

When he was with our family, my father never talked about the danger. He played it down, especially with my mom. But we all knew when he was hurt. He constantly had a bad back. He used to lie on the floor as therapy. He had to sleep with a board beneath his bed. I remember that. I remember him coming home smelling of fire. Same thing happens to me now. There's just nothing you can do. You can take a shower, but the minute you exercise you can smell the smoke again. It just comes out of your pores.

I remember parties. He was very young, a captain then. I was maybe five years old. One time they all went to a big party at a place called Gilco Beach out on Long Island.

These guys are pounding beers, and suddenly they decide it's time to go surfing. I'm talking about a bunch of guys from the Bronx. They couldn't even swim.

After the party was winding down, my dad was the guy who wouldn't let it end. He invited everybody back to our house. Thirty firemen and their wives and girlfriends, impromptu. I'm sure my mom loved that.

Those are all very warm memories for me. And looking back on it now, I don't think I ever had a chance. There was no way I couldn't end up a fireman. I don't mean he pushed. He never pushed. But boy, did my father brag about his men. He bragged about them nonstop, but all the good officers brag about their men. And all the guys who were there say the same thing. It was the greatest time of their lives.

Our house burned down when I was twelve years old. We lived in a suburb of Buffalo, in an every-third-house-is-the-same kind of neighborhood. There were five kids in our family, one girl and four boys. There was a church near our house.

One day, my older brother and sister, myself and my mother were all in church. My father and two little brothers were back at home.

When we came out of church, we could hear sirens coming from every direction. We tried to protect our mom. We were saying, "Don't worry. It doesn't look like our house."

But I could make out the smoke. It was billowing out through the window in our back bedroom.

There was an early snow that day, an unexpected snowstorm in November. So it took us forever to drive around to our house. My father was standing in front. It was a snowstorm and all he had on was shorts. He looked like an Indian; he was all red.

My father didn't like talking about it much. But my little brothers were only five and eight, at that innocent age. You could ask them about it, and they would tell you exactly what it was.

They said my dad was in bed. They came into his room and one of them said, "I smell breakfast. What are we having?"

My father said, "What do you mean?"

He got up and looked out the hallway and he saw the fire coming right down the hallway. He went back into the bedroom. He knocked out the window with his hand. He went to throw my little brothers out that window. But the windows were too small, and he saw that he couldn't get them out there. So he grabbed their two heads in each of his arms. He put them behind his back, ducked his own head down and ran through the fire. My little brothers said it was kind of strange. They said there was like an opening of no flame. It went right to the front door.

When he got to the front door—this thick wooden front door without any windows in it—my dad couldn't get it open. He thought there was some kind of pressure holding it closed. I don't know of a pressure that would do that, but that's what he said he was thinking. So my father backed up again, and ran headfirst through the door. Afterwards you could see the remnants of the door. It was hanging off the hinges where he had busted through it.

Our house was totally burned. We were in the house across the street, watching. Our house was burning down, and I kept seeing these firemen running inside.

I remember thinking, *I can't believe these people.*

I was just in awe.

There was nothing left of our house after the fire. It ended up getting bulldozed over. We lost everything we had. Clothes, toys, keepsakes, a lot of our personal stuff we could never get back. As a matter of fact, when I go in a fire now, I always try to save things like baby books, family albums, a picture of a grandmother on the wall. You can always go to the store and buy a new lamp. But you can't get pictures of your kids when they were babies.

The fire was devastating. I was a kid. I didn't really know how anything worked. When your house burns, what do you do? Where do you go? I had never been exposed to anything like that. I felt total fear. What's going to happen to me? What's going to happen to our family?

You don't realize that things can get rebuilt. That things get better. And you certainly don't realize how many people will help you. There was this one guy who owned a toy store. He saw in the paper that there was a fire; a family lost their home. This was a month before Christmas. And this guy drove up with a truckload of toys. "Here are some toys. Your kids are going to have a Christmas this year."

Even though we had insurance on our home, it wasn't like now, where they automatically up it each year with inflation. So we really lost a considerable amount. But there was this guy in town, the volunteer fire chief. He was also a builder, and he knew my dad, and he came back to us after the fire was out. He built us another house.

He built it on our old foundation, except he built it bigger than it was before. It used to be a ranch, but now my parents live in a two-story house. You know how much the fire chief did this for? The exact amount of the insurance money. Not one penny more. His name was Billy Belinson. I was twelve years old and this guy was my hero.

About five years after that, the volunteer department started a junior firefighter program. But at first I didn't think I could be a fireman. I was never really athletic or anything. I always pictured a fireman as a real tall guy with arms as big as anvils. This big guy, you know? Just walking around. And that just wasn't me.

But I still had these memories. When they were rebuilding our house, most of the guys were also volunteer firemen. I would come home from school and I would be around them. They were like most firemen. They liked to laugh a lot and they liked to goof on each other. And I noticed when their fire alarm would sound, you'd see all their nail aprons just drop to the ground, and they'd hop into the pickup truck and be gone. They'd come back and start right back on our house. I wanted to be like them.

So I became a volunteer at the age of seventeen. Today, I'm a paid firefighter in Buffalo. I tend to get kidded sometimes, because sometimes I get more emotional than other guys. I don't know why exactly. Maybe it was seeing my house burn down. But I just look at things differently sometimes. I'll hear some guys saying, "It's just my job. It's where I work. It's the same as if I worked on a garbage truck."

I'm always saying, "No. Kids don't wave at you on a garbage truck. They don't have bagpipes at your funeral. People don't hug you and thank you for saving their life. This is a totally different thing that we are into."

I was a volunteer when I first came on. I was not getting paid anything to go out and risk my life. My father was shocked by that, but he was also proud. I grew up in Washington, D.C. But I wasn't out on the street like a lot of my friends. I never got caught up in crime or doing drugs. I was doing something positive with my life.

Still, it took a while for my father to accept it. He said he would stand behind me, but I knew he was scared. One time he said to me, "Everyone else will be running out of the fire, and you'll be running in. Why do you want to do a job like that?"

I said, "Dad, while those people are running out, I *will* be running in. But I'm running in for a good reason. I'm gonna save someone's life doing this job."

My father died the same month I became a paid firefighter. My mom and my grandparents *still* don't know why I do it. In my grandmother's case, it was two or three months before she stopped calling me crazy. She would ask everyone, "What's that boy's problem? Is that boy going crazy?"

She just had a really hard time getting used to it. Part of it was, she and my grandfather had just gone out and seen *Backdraft*.

They came back and said, "Are you nuts? You *want* to deal with stuff like that?"

I said, "That's right. This is what I want to do. I want to be a hero."

Even today I think my grandma's still scared. Every morning before I leave for work, she says a prayer for me. She prays I'll make it back home.

I grew up around the firehouse. My grandfather was a volunteer fireman. My father's a volunteer, still to this day. He's seventy-five years old.

I think several motives drive volunteer firefighters. It's often a family thing, like it is in mine, handed down from generation to generation. Out in the more rural areas, it's a focal point of the town. Anybody who's anybody is in the volunteer fire department. Most of all, we perform a community service. We protect our own neighbors and their homes, and that gives us tremendous satisfaction.

Plus, it's a cheap form of excitement. I've been a volunteer for twenty-something years now, and I still have to admit: I can be sitting home just talking to my wife, and all the sudden the beeper goes off for a house or building fire. If we get there and it's a good one, I still get my gun off.

I was a personal trainer working at a gym. One morning I was driving with my girlfriend on the freeway. We were in the slow lane. Two of our friends were driving right behind us. Suddenly, from our left, a car came flying by us and almost hit us. He was probably going close to ninety. A few centimeters more and that would be it. We'd probably be dead.

About three miles down, I got off the freeway at the next exit. We were on our way to a sporting goods convention. As I was pulling up behind this car in front of me, I noticed it was the same car. My window was down and I yelled at the guy. "You stupid fool! You almost killed us back there!"

The guy got out of his car immediately. He was maybe twenty, wearing a baseball cap backwards. Looked Italian. He started walking back, so I got out, too. The guy just kept walking toward me. I remember looking at him the whole time, looking at his eyes. It was weird. His eyes were huge. They were open so wide that I could see the white parts. I mean all the way around, not just on the sides but also the top and bottom.

I thought he would just come up and stick his chest into mine. So I put my hands up straight, so he wouldn't run into me. Right as my hands went up against his chest, I felt something hit me in the lower left groin.

I grabbed on to his shirt and pulled him down onto the curb. I was gonna stand up and get over him. Just as I started to, it felt like he hit me again—this time in my back. I put my hand back there and looked at it. I had blood on my hand. I figured I fell on a sprinkler head. But when I turned around, he was holding this knife. That's when it dawned on me that I'd been stabbed.

My friends pulled up at that moment and I said, "That guy stabbed me!"

The guy turned and ran back to his car and he took off.

At that point, I thought I'd only been stabbed in the back.

There wasn't much pain. More of a feeling of wetness.

My friends and my girlfriend came over, then a gentleman walked up and asked what was going on. Turns out he's a doctor.

He pulled up my shirt and said, "Yes, you've been stabbed. One, two, three, four—you've been stabbed four times in the back."

I just thought, *Wow. This guy tried to kill me.*

The doctor said to sit down on the side of the road. Then his wife walked up with a cellular phone. She called 911, for the fire department and also the police. While she was making the call, I looked down at the curb and there was a pool of blood.

I said to the doctor, "Where is this coming from? Is my back bleeding this bad?"

He said, "No. Actually, your back is hardly bleeding at all."

I said, "Look at this pool of blood here in the gutter."

So he took another look. It turned out the blood was dripping from inside my shorts. He pulled up my shorts and blood was spurting. There was a four-and-a-half-inch slice. It went from the edge of my penis into the crease of my leg.

The doctor said, "I'm going to be honest with you. It looks like your femoral artery has been severed. I'm going to have to reach in and pinch it off."

I took a deep breath and said, "Okay."

He reached in with his forefinger and his thumb, and literally pinched it off. He just stood there squeezing the artery for me. But then he saw something else. I'd also been stabbed in the chest. That was four times in my back, once in the groin and once in the chest. I couldn't believe it. This was a bright sunny day. Two in the afternoon. This guy tried to stab me to death.

Somehow, I was staying pretty calm. Probably because my girlfriend was out of control. She was screaming and yelling and running around. I kept trying to tell her I was okay. What happened to me was actually very serious, but I didn't know it yet. It was more of a psychological stress. Seeing all that blood and everything.

When the fire department arrived I was in a daze. I just wanted to lie down. The fire department guys asked me what happened. They asked if I'd lost consciousness. Did I have any pain in my neck, or any pain anywhere else they should know about? I told them no. Just what I felt from the stabbing.

They rolled me onto my side and tipped me onto their backboard. They taped me down to the board and put me in their ambulance. Then they shut the doors and took off and started talking to me.

There were two of them in back with me. The guy right next to me asked me what my name was. From that point forward he started calling me Brad. I don't know why, but it made me feel more relaxed. It made me feel like I was not a victim. It was more like a conversation between two friends.

The other firefighter was taking my pulse and blood pressure, working on my artery, putting the saline solution on my wounds, and starting an IV. While he's doing this, he's reporting everything to his partner. His partner is taking it in, even though he's still having this talk with me. It left a strong impression. We were all in a crisis and they were real smooth.

At the hospital they gave me drugs and then I was unconscious. They did emergency surgery, I found out later. I was in there for six days, just happy to be alive. But when I got released I got depressed. There was a lot of pain and rehab work, but I was also brooding about my future. I wasn't really fulfilled in my current job.

I kept thinking about how good those firefighters were. The doctor was very good, too, but he didn't have the warmth that these guys had. I kept mentioning this to my mother and father. One day my mother said, "Why don't you do it? Why don't you become a firefighter?"

Right at that moment, it sounded really good.

I started by going to thank the two guys who treated me. I figured they could answer some of my questions. They weren't in the firehouse, but just by chance that day, the chief was in. I asked him how to get started. He said I needed schooling, in things like fire science and emergency medical training. He also said it wouldn't happen overnight. There was a lot of competition for the job.

But he also said before I left, "If this is where your heart is, I think you should go after it."

I ended up back in college, taking fire classes. Then I started out as a volunteer. At age twenty-eight, I got hired on as a paid firefighter. Both paid and volunteer, it's been fantastic. It's everything I hoped for. I have a positive impact on people's lives.

<u>TRAINING</u>

In the New York Fire Department, our training academy lasts twelve weeks. It was only six weeks when I went through it, but it was more of a formality back then. What you really needed to learn, you learned in the field. Today the academy isn't run that way. We keep them here twelve weeks and the standards are very high. They either know their stuff or they don't graduate. We make that very clear, early.

One thing that hasn't changed is our facility. It's still out on Randalls Island, right next to the New York City Sewage Retrieval Plant. It smells that way, too. This whole place, in fact, is very Spartan. We call it the Rock.

As training instructors, we're using a semimilitary approach. We have 150 probationary firefighters in school right now—we call them probies—and they are divided into two platoons. Each platoon has three squads of twenty-five. Each squad has a squad leader. Hopefully, the squad leaders are men of veteran status, guys who have served. They bring the type of experience we need, because we are out here drilling every day. The probies learn how to march. They learn chants. They learn how to do about face. We have roll call procedures. It's very simple stuff, but to the average person who's never done it, it's kind of odd. But the veterans understand it, so we give them the position of squad leader. And I always tell the probies, "I don't want you busting on the squad leader. It you bust his balls, you bust my balls. And if you're busting my balls, I'm busting yours."

So there is a certain military aspect. We don't get carried away with it, but it's there.

The academy is where they learn to be firefighters. Most of them come in here knowing nothing. And that's how we prefer it. Because those who come here from other fire departments, or from the volunteers, can be a pain in the ass. They think they *do* know something. But what they know and what we do here in New York may be very different.

It's not a big problem, though. We just wear them down. And even if they come in with some prior knowledge, they're all good guys and all very eager to learn.

We have many objectives. One is to develop a sense of teamwork. We try to wear down their individuality. Because teamwork in this job is absolutely essential. They have to know their own job at a fire, but also every man's job on their company. If they don't put forth an integrated effort, sometimes that's how people die.

So teamwork is very important, and so is camaraderie. We want to instill in them esprit de corps. We want it running deep. So right at the beginning, I tell them they're part of a brotherhood. I refer to them as brothers. Some of the other officers don't do that, because they feel they're *not* brothers yet; they haven't established themselves. It's a valid point. I tend to knight them with brotherhood too soon. But that's how I operate. I call them brother this and brother that.

I say, "You take care of yourself, you take care of your brother."

I push that hard and they respond to it. Not every guy. Some are a little reluctant; they're too cool or whatever. But it doesn't last. Even the cool guys want to be part of a team.

Once they're in a squad of twenty-five, we give them nicknames. We got the Palefaces and the Mooseheads. There's one guy in one squad whose name is Parrot, so we'll call them the Dead Parrot Society. It's mostly that kind of nonsense, but they establish a squad camaraderie and pride.

We also teach them that they can't leave people behind. If twenty-four of their twenty-five guys have finished a drill, and that drill has just run over into their lunch break, those first twenty-four guys would love to just go to lunch. No good. If one guy's not done, they're all not done. That's foreign to some guys, but again, we wear them down.

As probies, we let them know where they stand in the hierarchy. Most probies don't have any problem with the hierarchy of rank. We even have a page in our training manual that shows the collar insignias: The chief of the department has a circle of five stars, the assistant chief has four stars and on and on. That, they understand. What the probies have problems with, what always needs special attention, is the hierarchy of seniority. Some of these probies see themselves wearing the same clothes as the senior firefighters, so they see themselves as their peers. But they are by no means their peers. It's just like in the military: Out in the field, the average senior firefighter is worth five probies, maybe ten probies. The average probie is little more than a guy who is carrying tools and hopefully doesn't get himself killed at fires.

Some of the probies have to be told this quite bluntly. My intent is not to make the probies feel small. I just want them to have great respect for the senior firefighters. They are the guys in the front lines. They are extremely important, and they deserve that respect.

Our attrition rate is very small. Out of 150 people in a new class, we might lose three. Normally, they leave of their own volition. We don't have to tell them, they tell us. Some guys go back to their better-paying jobs. Or maybe a guy is afraid of heights. When I was a probie, in fact, we had a cop who entered the fire department. When it got time for him to climb an eight-story ladder, he said, "No. Going back to the cops. Ha ha."

Fear of heights.

In some cases, the semimilitary nature scares them away. It's not a bunch of college kids, you know. I'm not saying it's nasty and crude, but the brothers can be tough. There's a brutal honesty in the firehouse, and that is learned immediately in the training school. Some guys aren't ready for that. They want to go back to civilian life. Wear a suit and tie.

Other guys drop out because of the danger, especially today. For a stretch here in New York City, two months didn't go by when there wasn't a dead firefighter on page one. We've had six line-of-duty deaths in just the last year. That has had an impact on our entire department, including our training school. It has made training here extremely dramatic. Because even more poignantly, the last line-of-duty death was a probationary firefighter. He was in the field just three months.

Three years before that, another probie died in the line of duty. He was a young man with amazing credentials: the son of a four-star chief, and a paratrooper before he came to us. When something like this occurs, every probie in the academy's shaken up. So we spend a lot of time talking about it. We encourage long talks, with probies asking questions and officers giving answers. We counsel them and console them and try to reassure. But there's no way around it. Whenever we lose a brother, it's very emotional.

In the course of their training, we strongly stress the things that can do them harm. We tell them this job is not easy; the potential of getting burned is always there. This is painfully true in New York City, because of the way we fight fires. On TV, or certainly in the movies, you'll see firemen standing outside pouring water into the windows. That is not the case here. In New York, most fires are fought with an aggressive interior attack. The key idea there is to get ahead of the fire. If you yield to the fire, if it has twenty minutes of free-burning headway, that means you're playing catch-up. And that means you will probably lose the structure. So the aggressive interior attack is very similar to the military: you get real close and meet the thing head-on. That might require being in a room where there is high heat, and by that I mean at least one thousand degrees. We want our trainees to be comfortable with that concept.

"You *are* going to put yourself in harm's way," we tell them. "You can expect to."

To make sure we get their attention, we sometimes use colorful language. We want the probies to know how dynamic fire can be. It's really a slow explosion: the intensity of fire doubles with every seventeen-degree rise in temperature. So, in a sense, fire is a living, breathing thing; one that is out to get them. And we use that. We use it a lot.

"Fire is your enemy," we tell them. "That red devil comes licking up your ass, the fire escape's gonna look like the gates of heaven."

Or we'll say, "Stay low you go, stay high you die."

That's another key precept, because heat and smoke and fire will rise to the ceiling. It's always gonna be cooler down by the floor.

One of the classic dangers we teach is passing the fire. There's two ways of passing fire: vertically or horizontally. I'll start with horizontally.

We have a term called "the floor above." Let's say a five-story building has a fire on the third floor. If you're the second-due ladder company, you're gonna spend most of your time on the fourth floor. That's the "floor above," and anytime you are there, it means you're passing the fire vertically. That's dangerous. These tenement buildings here are old and very leaky, and fire and smoke and heat always go upward. So let's say the engine company's one floor below you. They make their advance into the fire apartment. If something goes wrong, the fire can then burn into the hallway. Then it will burn immediately up the stairway. That's the floor above, and that's where you are. Without having that stairway as an escape route, you might run out of air. You might get lost in the smoke. You might get exposed to the actual fire.

As for passing the fire horizontally, let's say the fire is in the kitchen. But you're gonna search the bedrooms, and the kitchen is in your path. If the fire allows you, if it's not too intense, you make it through the kitchen. But if the fire gets worse while you're searching bedrooms, now you can't go out the way you just came in. So maybe you go out a window that has a fire escape. But sometimes it's too smoky and you can't find a window. Sometimes you find the window, but it has no fire escape.

This is where knowledge of building construction comes in. They get a lot of classroom hours on that: the various types of buildings in New York City, which types have fire escapes, and where they are. Because whether it's vertical or horizontal, passing the fire is something they *will* do.

So we tell them to size up the building before they go in. Size up the construction. Size up the means of escape. Size up the extent and location of the fire. Size up how good or bad your water supply will be. Once they do get inside the fire building, we tell them to stay fluid and stay alert. A fire situation can change in an instant.

We teach them about collapses. Guys get killed in collapses. It doesn't routinely occur, fortunately. But when it does, it tends to take large numbers. Firefighting is labor-intensive. There might be five or six firefighters in one immediate area. If there's a wall collapse, a ceiling collapse, or a roof collapse, now you have five dead guys.

So once again, we tell them to do their size-up. Usually, the collapse potential is the concern of the first-due officer, and then succeeding officers who come upon the scene. The officers, in turn, will warn the interior forces of signs of collapse. But we still want the firefighters to recognize the signs. One of them is a traveling crack in a wall, a crack that's actually moving and you can see it. Another is groaning sounds. There's also what we refer to as "lack of water runoff." The hose line will put out about 185 gallons a minute, and that's a tremendous load to add to the weight of the structure. Sometimes that water isn't finding its way out of the building. It's just adding weight. That can cause a collapse.

We show them all the techniques they'll use their entire career, like using hoses and nozzles. The key to handling the hose, believe it or not, is not the man on the nozzle. The key is the backup man. Now, the man on the nozzle always gets all the credit, but the backup man is the one who makes him look like the hero. He stands immediately behind the nozzle man. He will be close enough to the nozzle man to perform an intimate sexual act, and he will take up the back pressure from the hose. He has his bit of hose line in his hands, and he keeps it low and leans forward into the nozzle man. They work together. If the nozzle man leans left, he will lean right. If the nozzle man leans right, he will lean left. For one guy to do it himself, it is virtually impossible to control. The hose line has too much damn power. At 185 gallons of water a minute, coming out at anywhere from forty-five to seventy pounds of pressure, that's a lot of force.

We tell the probies this, and it still doesn't make a difference. The first time they feel that power, every single probie is surprised. A couple times, I've gotten a face full of water. They aren't prepared for the force and they lose the hose, and I'm talking big strong boys. They're always so apologetic, but I expect it. In fact, the first time they do it, they lose it routinely. Now this thing's whipping around and it's dangerous. Because somebody could get hit upside the head.

As for the nozzle man, he can't have too little hose line. I see probies with just the nozzle in their hands. That's wrong. You need about a foot of hose in front of you, and you have to open the nozzle slowly and evenly. The nozzle has a pull handle you pull toward you. We call this "give me water." If you open that handle too fast, you'll probably lose the hose and now it's flying again.

The other big rule is, Don't open the nozzle too soon. You want to hit fire, not smoke. If you hit smoke but you're not reaching the fire, all you're doing is cooling the smoke and creating steam. Steam is not like radiated heat—the heat from the fire. Radiated heat travels in straight lines, like light travels in straight lines. So you can almost hide from it. But steam is ubiquitous; it's everywhere. If your ears aren't covered, or the back of your neck, you are going to feel it.

So we tell the nozzle man: "Don't open the nozzle until you can hit fire itself." It means they have to get close, and this can be scary. Some probies don't want to wait. They're sort of like the soldier who cannot hold his fire. They open the nozzle a half mile away, instead of when they are right on top of the flames.

Their first real taste of fire comes in the smoke room. Out of everything we do here, that's what makes them most nervous. They're nervous and they're questioning their own abilities, but when they come out, all of a sudden they all get religion. They realize how nasty it really is.

The smoke-room door is at the end of a hall. The door is closed. Inside it, the room has propane-set fires. At the one-foot level, the temperature is maybe three hundred degrees. It's eight hundred degrees at five feet, and at ceiling level it's twelve hundred degrees. We give them their weapon, a charged hose line. And under the direction of several officers, they will advance the hose line into this burning room.

This is when I scare the hell out of them. It's really kind of funny. Instead of turning them loose, I start talking to them, and I take my sweet-ass time. Because their tendency is to just run inside the room, open the hose line and put water on the fire. *Goddamn! Let me put this thing out!*

But I make them wait. I make them take their time.

Because I won't let them open the nozzle until I feel they're set. I'm trying to hone their technique, but I'm also instilling in them some mental toughness. You control the hose. You control the fire. Not the other way around.

So I say to them, "Are you ready, nozzle man? Are you and your backup man talking? Are you both squared off?" I can see them through their masks. They're looking at me and they trust me. The concern is on their face: *It's hot in here. When is he going to let me open this thing?*

Then, finally—it seems like a real long time but it's only about twenty seconds—I say, "All right. If you're ready, I'm ready."

So they finally do put some water on a fire, and it's remarkable: suddenly, they get salty after that. Now they're walking around with their turnout coats open, their masks hanging down a bit. They put out some fire, so they think they're firemen now. All of a sudden, they address me as "Lieu." Previous to that, I'm either "Sir," or if they feel real comfortable, "Lieutenant." But after they come from the smokehouse, I routinely hear a bunch of "Lieu's" that day.

It's kind of cute, you know?

Two days before graduation, they get their assignments. That is a real big day. We put them in the auditorium, and all 150 of them are waiting with bated breath. Actually, some of them already know where they might be going, because some of these probies have what we call "weight," or to use another, crasser term, some guys are "hung." That means their daddy was a chief, or they have an older buddy who's big in the union, so they find themselves getting assigned to busy houses. That's where they all want to go—to busy houses. It's just more fun. These guys are young and full of juice and they want to do the job.

Sometimes they'll ask me if I can help. They'll say, "Can you get me into this Engine?" Mostly, I can't, but occasionally I can swing it for one of my all-stars. And I *do* have all-stars. Sometimes a probie's got everything: the attitude, the strength, the aptitude, and a certain level of confidence. With a kid like that, I can really do a favor for one of my officer buddies. They'll call me up and say, "We got an opening. I think I'm getting a probie. Who do you got?"

So I'll tell them about my all-star and set up an introduction.

Twelve weeks after it starts, the academy ends with graduation day. It's a fabulous moment for the probies. They've made it through the gauntlet. But it is just as fabulous for the instructors. Probies come up to you and want you to meet their parents. Some of the probies have children, so you hear the babies crying. It's really quite touching to me. It's touching for all the instructors. On graduation day, I have seen tears come to the eyes of even the most experienced instructors. The bond we form with the probies is very emotional. It's very paternalistic. After we send them off, we worry about them.

On graduation day, I always make it a point to stand near the front. Each probie gets called up there, and Mayor Giuliani gives him his diploma. Then they have to pass me. To a man, or a woman, each one will hesitate, grab my hand and shake it and say, "Thank you."

Just like that scene from *An Officer and a Gentleman,* some of them tell me, "I'll never forget you. Good-bye."

I don't know how else to say it. It's very moving.

The academy was memorable for me. It was ten weeks of hell. It's every day and it's all day. Technically, it was supposed to be eight to five, but you were kidding yourself if you thought you were leaving by five. You left whenever they felt like letting you go.

First thing in the morning you report for inspection. Then you take off your uniform, go outside and do your physical training. You do running, push-ups, sit-ups, and pull-ups until you can't do anymore. You're given ten minutes to change back into your uniform, and you spend the next few hours in the classroom. Then you eat lunch.

After lunch, the afternoon is spent drilling on what you were just taught in class. You're wearing your full gear and you're sweating bullets. Then you go home. Well, now you have notes you need to transcribe—the notes that you scribbled while your instructor was talking. They have to be typed and put in some kind of order, because everyone has a notebook that they are responsible for. In addition, you have to study the material that you were given yesterday, for the test you're going to get on it tomorrow. If you fail two or three quizzes over the course of the academy, you're fired.

While all this is going on, you are dog-tired, and after

the third or fourth week you really start to feel drained.
On certain guys, you can just see the stress overwhelming
them. Those are the ones who don't make it.

**The first week of training, you don't even want them
to know your name.** If they know your name, it means
you already messed up.

I remember my first day. I went in thinking, *Just be a
poker-faced mute. Don't show any emotion. Don't say
anything that you don't have to say.*

Meanwhile, I was just waiting for that first guy to
make a dumb comment, or not have his belt on straight.
Because once they find their guy, they'll hone in on him.
And you are thinking, *Thank God. They finally found
their guy and now I can breathe.*

I'll still never forget our first laying-hose drill. There
is a large black hose that's usually mounted on the side of
the fire engine. It's called a hard suction. It's about eight
to ten feet long, and that's what you hook the hydrant up
to the fire engine with. My job in this drill was to guide
the fire engine to the spot where the driver should park,
so we could hook up the hard suction. Well, I guided him
and he stopped, and I came up about eight to twelve
inches short. That was bad enough. But I had two training captains standing right there—the training captain for
our particular group, plus the head training captain for
our entire class.

The head training captain says to me, "I don't think
we have to worry about *you* being here next week."

I blurted something like, "Jesus Christ!"

He said, "Jesus Christ can't help you out right now.
And don't even worry about that house burning down . . .
just because you screwed up."

I felt about one inch tall.

We had this ominous training instructor who was a captain. Even the other instructors called him "the Wedge." He was an older captain, maybe twenty-five years on the job, but the guy was incredibly built. He had these big wide shoulders and this tiny little waist. That's why they called him the Wedge.

We'd be out in the drill yard, and it was pure concrete and extremely hot. The Wedge would march out every day in his pressed white shirt, his tie and uniform perfect, his eyes completely hidden behind mirrored glasses. He would start doing push-ups on the concrete. Boom, boom, boom, boom—like a machine. He was not even leading us through them; he was just doing them. Just to build up his muscles, you know? Or maybe it was a psychological deal. Whatever it was, it worked. He just kept getting stronger and we were all getting more awed. We'd be doing our thing in the drill yard, but we'd all be watching the Wedge from the corners of our eyes.

If one person screws up during rookie school, they don't yell at that one person. They yell at the group. Right off the bat, they want you to learn to function as a team. Because that's how it is as soon as you get in the firehouse. *Everything* we do is as a team, whether it's pulling the hose off the engine, or "It's my turn to do the dishes, your turn to cook," or "What are we all watching tonight on TV?"

The worst label you can get in the firehouse is the "one-dog, one-bone motherfucker." If you get a new guy in the house and everyone's eating spaghetti, and this guy brings in a sub sandwich for himself, it's definitely pointed out to him. "Listen, you one-dog, one-bone motherfucker. We're all together, this is us, we're a team.

Whether we're eating dinner or going across a roof, it's only going to work if we're side by side."

I didn't really appreciate it at the time, but our instructors had a saying they used every day. They would tell us, "Life on the grinder is good."

The grinder meant the asphalt they worked us like dogs on. And life on the grinder *is* good. The stress you face there is tough, but it's nothing compared to a real emergency scene.

Once you get out in the field, there's quite a bit of pressure. You pull up to a house. There's fire out the windows and people trapped inside. All the neighbors are watching to see what you're going to do. Some of those neighbors are also screaming at you. You're only taking two minutes, but they know the people inside. To them, it seems like forever.

To see if you can handle that kind of pressure, they use various kinds of discipline at training school. For instance, we use brass couplings to connect our fire hoses. These are big heavy couplings, up to eight pounds. Let's say there was a coupling on the training ground, and you ran over it with the fire truck. You then had to carry that coupling everywhere you went. You ran with it in the morning. You had it with you in class. You took it everywhere, until someone else ran one over. Then you gave that coupling to him.

One guy ran over a ladder. He barely touched it, but that was enough. They weren't gonna make him carry a huge ladder, so they figured out something else. They made him carry around this two-foot step ladder that someone found in the office.

It's kind of humiliating, but it does get you out of the habit of making dumb mistakes.

The hardest part for me was the smoke exercise. In Seattle, as in most fire departments, we use the self-contained breathing apparatus. Of course you're going to wear it during fires, but what if you have a malfunction? Then you gotta take it off. And then, without panicking, you gotta be able to eat and breathe real smoke.

So that's how they do the smoke room here. You go in without a mask. All you have on is your turnout coat, helmet, and gloves. They light a mattress on fire and let it smoke.

That was harder for me to deal with than even the ladders. At least with the ladders, you don't have to look down. You can pretend you're at ground level, or whatever you need to do in order to work on the ladder. But in the smoke room, there's no tricks you can play. There's nowhere to go and you *gotta* breathe.

The very first day we did it, I knew it would be a tough moment for me. And then it was. When I got inside, my mind said, *Hey, let's go. It's time to get out of here.*

But you have to fight it off. You have to think, *Hey, do I want this job?* If the answer is yes, then you have to keep your head in that smoky, hot, disorienting environment.

Some smoke-room days are better than others, too. It all depends on who goes out and buys the mattresses, and where that person buys them. Some of the mattresses can smoke up real bad. But it is just that simple: if you want to fight fire, you have to cope with smoke.

My first two weeks of training I was freaked out. I had gone to school, I had a lot of book knowledge, but I had no real hands-on. There was just so much to learn and it was nonstop.

My biggest challenge was to conquer the mechanical machinery. Now this may be strictly from a female fire-fighter's point of view, but I had never started a chain saw before. I had used handsaws and regular saws, but you just pushed a button to start them. And I have to tell you, man, for the life of me, I could never start one of our damn chain saws. My legs were strong. They were very strong. They were my savior. But I didn't have that upper-body strength that guys have. Some guys could take that chain saw with both their arms. They could just go, *ploom,* the macho way. I couldn't do that. I had to use my foot and my body weight, and I used to get so frustrated I'd go nuts. I didn't want to be laughed at, so when I thought no one was looking, I would go out and practice every Sunday. Then I'd glance up and see the captains looking at me through their windows. I'd be muttering, "Damn. Just leave me alone."

Now it's nothing to me. Give me anything to pull and I'll just start it. I'm real determined, you know?

What stands out for me was the flashover drill. In a real flashover, the room becomes so hot that all the objects inside achieve their ignition point. Almost at once, flames will then flash over the whole room.

To get us ready for that if it happened on the street, they had us standing within one room of a burning structure. They let it get so hot that it was about to flashover. Now, the fire is all around you. It's over the top of your head, and on each side of you. Even the floor would catch fire sometimes.

They always got you out before there was trouble, but

first they let you see what it felt like to get trapped. Because a trapped firefighter who panics is going to die. The guy who stays cool has a chance to work his way out.

I really enjoyed that flashover drill. That gave me a real nice rush of adrenaline.

2
ROOKIE DAYS

On the brief helicopter ride there, the rookie felt the same way he did before every fire. Slightly apprehensive. Tremendously pumped up. Eager to do well in front of the veterans. At age nineteen, he had been fighting fires for less than fifteen months. He didn't want to make any glaring mistakes.

The wildland fire was nothing unusual—about twelve acres of dry brown chaparral brush, burning high on a rugged hillside in Los Angeles County. Once the eight-man crew left the helicopter, they worked above the fire with shovels and axes, creating a fire line by cutting and scraping away all vegetation. If the fire below them spread to their line, it would stop burning there for lack of fuel.

That was the theory, anyway, but as fire suppression theories often do, this went awry when nature intervened. Suddenly driven by gusting winds, the fire intensified and burned rapidly uphill. The crew was trapped while it was still cutting the line.

From where the rookie stood on a steep incline, surrounded by brush up to fifteen feet high, he didn't see the fire roar up the canyon. But he heard crackling noises and saw thick smoke, and he knew this bone-dry hill had plenty of unburned fuel. He also knew that fire can run uphill faster than people.

He did not retreat immediately, because the veterans didn't. Then, as the fire jumped toward their position, the danger grew more clear, and the veterans started screaming, "Get out! Get out!"

That's when he turned uphill to make his escape, but he could not get traction. His crew had made such an efficient fire line, the ground beneath him was sand. For every step he took forward, he slid two steps back downhill. As the wall of flame swept over him, burning his skin right through his protective clothes, his thoughts flashed on his pregnant wife. *I am going to die. I will never see my wife and child.*

That was unacceptable to him. He would not submit. Severely burned on his face, arms, hands, and legs, he kept climbing and crawling uphill, until he reached the ridge line and went into shock. Then, in his pain and confusion, he *wanted* to die. Lying on a dirt road with open wounds, he asked his comrades to kill him. They poured water on him and called for the medics.

A helicopter rushed him to a burn center, where they cut him from his charred clothes and dripped morphine into his vein. About 45 percent of his body was burned. His doctors thought he would die, then expected him to live, then thought he would die again. The next six weeks were a blur of pain medication and skin grafts. At some point, finally, he was told the awful news: The fire had killed two members of his crew. Although he knew both men well, he was especially close to one, and even looked up to him as a father figure. This firefighter was thirty-three.

His doctor said he probably would have died, too, if not for being nineteen and superbly fit. But the rookie felt he pulled through for another, more powerful reason. He desperately wanted to live for his wife and unborn child.

The hospital released him after three months. The next month, his wife gave birth to their baby girl. The baby was fine. The baby was fantastic. The baby made him forget his abject pain. He would pick up his baby and feel joy.

Two years after nearly burning to death, today his recovery is still incomplete. Following twenty reconstructive surgeries, he says he will probably undergo twenty more. He still wears a mask on his badly burned face. Made of clear plastic, with holes for his eyes, nose, and mouth, the mask massages his skin and keeps his scar tissue flat. It took some getting used to for him and his family. Strangers, he says, will sometimes stop and stare.

Still, he shows no bitterness, no trace of self-pity. The son of a police officer, he grew up around leathery men. Moreover, he knew the risks when he joined the fire department. For him, as for many other young firefighters, taking those risks was part of the attraction.

Even though his department has put him back on light duty, he predicts he's a year away from fighting fires again. He says he has no mixed feelings about returning to battle. He longs for it, in fact. Still just twenty-one, he can't conceive of a life without fighting fires.

"I love the adrenaline rush," he says. "I love running out of a helicopter with fire coming up at you. I miss that feeling. I want it back."

Not every young firefighter is thrown into such hardship. But rarely is it easy for any of them. They struggle with fire, with inexperience, with being accepted by older peers, with their confidence in themselves. So they take it call by call. They endure. Two steps back, one step forward.

A probie never complains. A probie keeps his mouth shut, his eyes open. A probie is never idle. A probie is always learning or drilling or cleaning.

That's why you're still called a probie: for one year after you leave training school, you're on probation. If you're not doing your job to their expectations, you can be terminated at any time. So there's always that looming threat of losing it all.

You don't even have a name. You're "boot" or "probie" or "num-nuts" or "Hey, you." Your first day in the firehouse—especially your first few hours—all you get is "Hurry up, get ready, come on, let's go!"

Then, for one whole year, a boot is the first one out of bed in the morning. He makes the coffee, puts the flag up, brings in the paper. At dinner, he is the last one to sit down and the first one to finish. He's the first one into the dishes, or as we call them, suds. At night he is the last one to go to bed. First he must lock up station and take the flag down, make sure everything is put in its right place.

This whole time, you're also being tested and scrutinized. How do you perform in an emergency? How do you get along with the other guys?

In the fire department, a year is a long time.

When I came on there was still a lot of hazing. Everyone got it, but I was a legend. They gave me the nickname "Sweetums."

At the academy, I'd been voted by my peers most inspirational. I was twenty-three years old, this real high-spirited guy. My first day of work, we had our mandatory fitness drills for an hour.

Then our captain says to me, "I want you to go upstairs, get showered and get ready. Report back to me in twenty minutes."

So I buzz upstairs. There's all kinds of commotion. Guys are taking off their sweats, putting on their uniforms, taking showers. But there are only two showers and they're both real small. So I look at these showers. They're already being used. One guy is one shower, and *two* guys are in the other one. I'm just standing there.

Everyone's going, "Come on, let's move it, boot! Let's get in the shower!"

By this time, I know they're screwing with me. So I have two choices. Either I stay out of the shower and they call me a sissy, or I let them know I gotta pair of balls. So I figure, Okay. You guys wanna play, I'll play.

Well, the guy that is by himself doesn't know that this is a joke. He's an older guy, an engineer, about sixteen years on the job. So I'm butt-naked, this brand new boot, and I open up the door and I'm ready to step in there.

This old engineer goes out of his mind. "What the fuck are you doing? Jesus Christ, what kind of guys are they hiring? Holy shit!"

He's going on and on and everyone's laughing. Then someone says, "Hey, man, you got in the wrong shower. That's the shower for engineers and captains. *This* is the firemen's shower."

That's the one with the two guys inside it, right? And now they're saying, "Hey, if you wanna shower you gotta come in here."

Fine. Plenty good. I opened up the door and stepped right in there. You know how firemen gossip? The entire department knew it before I got dried off.

That was eleven years ago. To this day, I hear it every so often. "Hey, Sweetums, you want to take a shower?"

In our department—I guess in a lot of departments— there's this big ritual. The first day a new probie comes to the firehouse, he's got to meet everyone. This time, the new probie came to our rescue company. We had a bunch of characters there, including me. Even though I was an officer, I'd go along with anything for a few laughs. A lot of times, in fact, I would be the one who was stirring the shit.

So this new probie comes in and we've got the whole thing planned. They bring the guy up to the third floor of the firehouse. All that's basically up there is the locker room, and my office. They knock on my door and bring him inside. As he's walking in, I'm sitting at the desk with my chair rolled right up to it. When I roll my chair out, I got no pants on. All the probie can see is my shirttail hanging down. Then the firemen who brought him in go out the door. They make sure they close the door behind them.

Now you have to understand, our rescue company is held in high esteem. So that's what I'm telling this guy as I'm making chitchat.

I'm telling him, "You know, it takes a lot to be a rescue fireman. You really gotta be willing to go the extra mile. We got a real proud history over the years."

I notice now his hand is on the doorknob. He's trying to turn the doorknob and get out. But he can't. The guys are holding the door shut from the outside.

This guy is getting nervous. He thinks he's come to a company run by a crackpot. But I'm still laying it on him real thick—our rescue did this, our rescue did that—and all without my pants on. And this was not a small guy. He was a strapper. He could have broken me in half at any time he wanted. But all he wanted was out. He wanted out so bad, you could actually see the sweat coming down his face.

Whenever a rookie comes in, the veterans are leery. He's a stranger in their house. They don't know what kind of person he is. They don't know if he'll be fired. They certainly don't know if he can be relied on. When things turn bad, can he drag their ass out?

Sure, they know the basics when they come in. But the basics are just things to build off of. You learn the basics in Pop Warner Football. It's not the same game in the NFL. Things change constantly here. Can a rookie learn to adapt and think on his feet? Do they really want to learn, or do they have an attitude? "I already went through this stuff at training. Don't give me any shit or I'll file charges on you."

As for how the rookies look at the veterans, they look at them as pricks. At least for the first few shifts.

There was a point, it was early on, when I wasn't sure that I was cut out for this job. It wasn't the fires or any of that. It was the veterans on our squad. I had a real hard time taking their shit.

I was a real aggressive kid. Went to an all-boy Catholic high school. Played football. Never took shit from anyone. I mean, you give an Irish guy shit, it was fist city. Well, you can't fist-city here. You start getting in altercations, you're out on the street.

The saying back then was, "Rookies are to be seen and never heard." As a rookie, you're thought of as not knowing anything. So why *would* you say anything?

We had one old captain who told us, "Hey, in the scale of life, you rookies are lower than whale shit."

When this is all you've ever wanted to do—be a fire-man, and now you are one, and this guy's calling you whale shit—it's a little hard to hear.

It seemed to me there were two kinds of older guys. Some gave you shit just to see how you'd react. If your temper was too short, that probably meant you wouldn't do well at a fire. Because when under stress, most people revert back to their real self.

Those guys didn't bother me. They just wanted to see if you could stay calm.

The other guys were just chumps. They would haze a rookie because they *could*. Those were the guys who were hard to accept. There was one guy, in fact, whose ass I wanted to kick. I was ready to chuck it all and pop this guy. But an older firefighter, the guy assigned to train me, told me how dumb that was.

He said, "You'll lose your job and you'll lose your dream. What will you have accomplished?"

Hazing isn't common anymore. Not with all the new laws about workplace harassment. That's a good thing. In my view, there was never a place for it.

In between calls, a probie can't sit around. You're sup-posed to work on projects all day long. Like taking apart the chain saw, for example. You take it apart, you clean it, you put it back together. It teaches you how the thing works. Then, if you go to a fire and it doesn't operate right, maybe you can get the chain saw going again. That's how probies score points.

Once a firefighter has been on for one year, he receives a second shield that goes on his helmet. It means you're no longer a rookie. Now you're a firefighter. So if we see

...eone running around at a fire without their helmet
..ield, we know he still has probationary status. That
means we don't want to give him too big a job.

It really depends on the officer and the probie. If a
probie knows what he's doing, his officer might give him
the nozzle early. Or at least the backup position on the
nozzle. It's like, "Okay, let's find out what you got."

They want the probie's nervousness gone right away.
This way it isn't allowed to keep on building. Too much
nervousness can get people hurt.

We had a young fellow who died here. He went to a ladder company with two or three other probies. But this guy
was unlucky. He went a long time before seeing any real
action. So the other two or three probies were busting on
him. Calling him virgin and all that stuff. When he finally
got in on his first real fire, that was the fire that killed him.

**As a junior firefighter, you typically get the nozzle when
things are under control.** The fire is basically out, and
they're letting you see how it feels. But one time, I got on
the nozzle when things were still bad. The fire was on the
top floor of this vacant building, but the fire was stubborn.
It wasn't going out, and one by one the veterans peeled off.
They had all been beaten up and had to regroup.

Our captain, Harry Young, finally came in. He and I
were the only two people in there. Everywhere I looked I
could see fire. It was right above us. It was in every direction, this rolling orange glow. But Captain Young just
kept directing me.

He would say, "Okay. Now hit it to the right. Hit it to
the left. Hit it right in front of us."

After a while, the others came back in and the fire was

extinguished. Captain Young told me later, "We were trapped in there, you know."

With my inexperience, I never realized. But his coolness got us through. He knew the situation and we just hung in there.

When I got hired on, there were only a few other probies coming in. But for economic reasons, the department liked to wait until they got a large group. Then they would send them all through the academy.

With only a few of us, that wasn't possible this time. But they needed extra manpower right away, so they sent me straight to a firehouse. I had no formal training at all. Just what the guys had time to show me at the station.

I was thinking, *My God. What's going to happen when I get my first fire?*

What stands out from my first fire was all the hard work.

You know what my reaction to that was? I wasn't sure I was *willing* to work that hard. It's like when you have your first child, and your whole life is suddenly turned upside down. Are you willing to accept this new responsibility? If so, how well will you handle it?

My first day on the job, I've got this crisp, brand-new, bright yellow uniform on. Man, I was really proud. I couldn't help but smile.

About two in the afternoon we get a fire. So we're driving up to wildland country now, and we can see this large black column of smoke. That usually means the fire is already big, but I didn't know that yet. I'm too green to know anything. I'm just thinking, *Wow, I wonder what my first fire is gonna be like?*

We go up this real steep hill in the fire engine, and the smoke is deeper and denser. It's banking so low to the ground, it looks like fog. My captain looks at me with my brand-new uniform on.

He says to me, "I want a line right here. I want to stop this fire *here*."

I look back behind us. All I see is this fire crowning through the trees. It is this huge wall of flame. And I say to myself, *What the hell have I gotten myself into?*

We were out there until about midnight. My wife called the station and said, "Tom was supposed to be home."

They said, "Tom's at a big fire."

My wife said, "He is? This is his first day on the job."

I don't remember feeling any self-doubt. I was too cocky for that. I was young, I was single, I'd be hanging out in a bar talking to girls. Someone would ask what I did.

"I'm a New York City fireman."

"Wow. Oh, wow."

I did that a lot when I was a rookie. Hell, I remember doing that while still at training school. I hadn't even been to a fire yet! I was riding on the shoulders of all the guys who came before me.

ROOKIE MISTAKES

Now that I'm an officer, a major part of my job is restraining young firefighters. But I was the same way when I started out. One time I went on a boat fire. The boat was small, but fully involved. Right next to the small boat there was a yacht. Both boats were tied up at a dock.

We attacked the smaller boat, but then I saw something from the corner of my eye. Looking into the window of the yacht, I thought I saw what looked like a dim light burning. I thought, *Well, maybe a curtain or something caught on fire. Maybe it got exposed to the fire on this little boat.*

So I walked onboard the yacht and into the cabin. I didn't tell anyone what I was doing. I didn't even have a hose.

There was a one-gallon glass bottle sitting there. It looked like a Clorox bottle, but the liquid inside was a brownish green. There was a wick coming out of the bottle and it was burning. It was a Molotov cocktail. The person who torched off the small boat was planning on torching this, too.

So I pick up the bottle. It has this burning wick, and I don't know what's in it, but I'm guessing gasoline. So I hurry up and carry it off the boat. Everything turns out fine. But now that I think back, I should have just called for someone to douse it with a hose. Because who knows when this thing is gonna explode and kill me?

But that's the way you are when you're young and stupid. You think you're bulletproof.

As an officer, you walk a fine line with your rookies. If they get *too* gung ho, you gotta hold them back. But if you're constantly holding them back, they'll just end up gun-shy. That can cause problems, too. Many times people get hurt because they *don't* advance. They keep hesitating and hesitating. Then they finally advance when the fire is too far gone.

So, as a captain, I have a theory. Either you make your advance and put it out, or you gotta get out of there. You can't fuck around with it.

I'll tell you one example. On the rescue squad one morning, we came up on a real bad fire on Forty-second Street in Times Square. It was a big commercial building, four stories high. Down in the cellar, there was a porno palace burning up.

We get inside and crawl to the back of the first floor. Then we crawl down these narrow stairs into the cellar. It's pitch-black, smoky, hot as fucking hell. I've got two of my rescue guys with me, both of them seasoned, and two young firemen from an engine company. They had come in with a hose line and followed us down the stairs.

Now the two young guys start to open the line. And nothing's happening. Five minutes, maybe ten minutes, the fire is just as hot, possibly hotter. I can *hear* the fire burning, and now we are down in some cellar in a big commercial building at six in the morning. Nobody's lives are in there except for ours.

Here is where experience came in. Back in 1966, though I was too young to be there, I knew there had been a fire on Twenty-third Street where twelve firemen got killed. The first floor collapsed and fell into the basement. And I'm starting to realize, *This is like that situation.*

So I figure I better check the conditions above us.

I crawl up the stairway. It is so hot at the top of the stairs—and these two young guys are working underneath it—I go straight back down and take off my mask. This way I know they can hear me.

I say, "We got to get outta here. Let's go."

When I say "Let's go," the young guy on the nozzle shuts off the hose. He just shuts it off. As soon as he does, suddenly it gets hotter. Without any water on it, the fire is like, "Fuck you."

So I yell over the fire to turn the nozzle back on. By now, I'm starting to choke without my mask on. So he puts the nozzle back on, and that cools off our immediate area. Now we gotta get back upstairs, and here's where things start to happen.

The fire's still burning around us. It's pitch-black smoke. The two kids start backing their way upstairs with the line. The line gets stuck on something. One kid gets caught on the line. I fall over him. All these clusterfuck things are starting to go down.

We don't have time for this. So, finally, my own two guys and I just back up the stairs with the line. Now all of us are out and they shut the cellar door. We're standing on the first floor and I see the chief.

I tell him, "It's just too much. We better get out of here."

He's a wizened guy and he says, "Okay."

So we pull everyone out and we get on the street. I swear to God five minutes later the first floor collapses. The fire had burned too long. They never got in there and stopped it. So the fire had just eaten through everything.

If we had still been down there playing around, we'd have been trapped. The first floor would have collapsed and that would have been it. They'd never have gotten to us. You'd have four guys killed, easily.

It turned out my hunch was correct and we got out in time. But that was what any senior officer would do. That's our responsibility. When you're working with young guys and you realize something's wrong, you gotta get them out. You can't let your pride, or their pride, get in the way. You get too much self-pride and it can fuck up the whole thing.

Whether or not they admit it, everyone makes their foolish rookie mistakes. We had a fire once inside a vacant building. While we were searching inside, I was crawling around the floor and bumped into a guy. Through my mask, I asked him how he was doing. I got no answer. He just kept looking at me. So I'm saying to myself, *Okay then, screw you.*

After the fire was out, I came back inside and looked around. I saw the same jerk, and realized it was me. I'd been looking into a mirror.

As a boot, you're all fired up. I was so fired up it was unbelievable. My first night I'm sleeping in my T-shirt, shorts, and socks, so I can be quick as possible once the tones go off. So then the tones go off. Before I'm sliding the pole, I'm already wide awake. I turn around and see these blurry-eyed guys. They're walking out of bed, going, "Oh, shit."

On that very first shift, we had a second-alarm structure fire at a sweatshop. I was on a truck company, and we went up on the roof to cut a hole. We call that ventilation. We're allowing all that pent-up pressure—from heat and fire and smoke—to escape up through the roof. This makes it more bearable for the firefighters inside. It also lets them see more clearly, so they can find the fire, attack it, and make their rescues.

Anyway, when you are up on a roof, you're taught to always walk in single file. Your "sound guy" is leading the way to determine which path is safe. He is sounding things out with a six- or eight-foot pike pole. The pole has a spike on the end. If he hits the roof and the spike goes through, it means don't walk there. You'll probably go through, too.

I was third in line up there, behind the sound guy and the guy who's got the saw. So I can't see where I'm going. All I see is the back of the guy in front of me. I'm pumped up to the max, because I'm a boot. I say to myself, *Hey, I'm gonna step over here and see what's going on.*

So I step out of line, and sure as shit, my foot sinks through the roof. My captain, right behind me, sees it coming. He grabs me and pulls me out. Later on, he chews my ass something fierce. But I had it coming. Idiotic mistake. First day, last day, is what it could have been.

We call it the rookie syndrome. As part of their self-contained breathing apparatus, every firefighter has an air bottle on their back. It provides you about twenty minutes of air time, fifteen minutes if you're working hard.

Unless, of course, you're breathing like a rookie. The first fire they go to—I don't care who they are—they will be the first bottle to run out of air. And it's gonna be by a long shot. We call them Aqua-Lung, they're breathing so hard.

You see things happen. That's how you learn. Sometimes you learn by seeing things go haywire.

It happened to me two or three times. You go into a building and there's no smoke. There's no indication that there's anything going on in this building at all. So you just walk in. You're bullshitting with your friends, your fellow firefighters, when you're all supposed to be looking for signs of fire. Everyone's laughing and not paying much attention. It looks like a false alarm. All of a sudden, bingo, there it is. Everything gets black, and you don't remember how many floors you went up. You didn't look close at the building when you walked in, so you don't know how many floors are over your head.

Where is the fire escape? Where are the windows and doors?

Later on you think, *I will* never *do that again.*

I was like any rookie: eager to learn but not very knowledgeable. At my first fire, I stood up and nearly burned my ears off. I wanted to prove myself, show them I could get in there and get right after it. But I didn't duck, and that heat tore me up. It dropped me right to my knees, and eventually to my belly. It taught me a lesson. Now I don't run into fires standing up.

It was kind of funny afterwards. My sister saw my ears and said, "What the hell are you doing? You've only been to one fire."

We had a restaurant fire my rookie year. It was a combination restaurant and bar, and the place was fully involved. So I got a two-and-a-half-inch hose line. That's a pretty big line, and I'm solo on this thing, and I'm hitting the hell out of these flames. My officer comes over.

He says, "What the hell are you doing? The fire's out."

I say, "Look inside here. Look at all the fire I've been hitting."

It was night, and the lights in this place were flickering like crazy. What I had done was put about one hundred thousand gallons into a red bathroom. With all the lights blinking and everything, I thought it was fire.

Right out of training school, I was sent to this specialized squad in Chicago. We scuba dived in Lake Michigan, pulled people out of rivers, made extrications from car wrecks. We did everything. We were the elite, and I was in my prime. I was twenty-five years old, six foot five, and 255 pounds. A real gorilla.

I still recall my first run, because it was funny.

It was in the afternoon. The bell rang and, boom, we get on the squad. I don't know where we're going or what it is.

But I know what the captain just told me.

He said, "When you get off that rig, you better have your nose right up my ass. And you better have your pole, your axe, and your hand pump."

So we jump on the rig and we're screaming down to the run. This is the first time I ever hear the sirens. It sounds like ten thousand decibels. I'm thinking, *Oh, my God, I'm really a fireman.*

We pull up and jump off the rig. I got my pole, my axe and my hand pump. I got my brand-new boots, brand-new coat, brand-new helmet. And this was in October. It was still a nice day out, about sixty degrees. But I'm all done up like December.

I follow the captain inside, and I notice that nobody else has their fire gear on. Back then, on some days, you just wore whatever old clothes you had. Because your turnout gear would get dirty and torn, and the city would never give money for you to buy new stuff.

So the other firefighters are all in their salty old clothes, and they're walking in real casual. We're going into this tough school on the south side of Chicago, and I'm the only geek with all his fire gear on.

We walk into the school room. Some kid had caught his arm in a folding chair. He couldn't get it out, so the teacher called the fire department.

The first engine was already there when we arrived. Their captain, this crusty old guy, pulls out a screwdriver and a little crescent wrench and starts working on the chair. He's lying on the floor, but every few seconds he stops and peers up at me, this six-foot-five gorilla, with my pole, my axe, and my hand pump, my new coat, helmet, and boots. He's looking at me like "I see it, but I don't believe it."

My first night on the job, I wasn't there twenty minutes when we had a working fire. I never even got close. I really felt left out. There were three other guys in line between me and the nozzle man.

It was typical rookie stuff: Yeah, kid. Maybe next time.

I worked at a busy engine when I first came on. We averaged about six thousand runs a year. It was a good assignment, too, because we were working where we were needed the most. The people didn't have money. They didn't have insurance. A lot of the kids never had a real chance.

I worked with a guy who took one kid down an aerial ladder.

The kid said, "This is the third time I've been down an aerial ladder."

The kid is five years old and he's gotten burned out three times.

My first night we had about thirty-five runs. We had about five abandoned car fires, some rubbish fires and other bullshit fires. But then we topped off the night just a few blocks down from the firehouse. It was a six-story apartment with a fire in the top floor. It was my first apartment fire and I was scared shitless. Flames were blowing out the sixth-floor window, and I was apprehensive just walking *under* the flames. But I had a really good crew. I never got close to the fire. When you were brand-new, those guys would take care of you.

So that was my first night and it was just amazing. All I could say was, "Wow." I was in awe.

At fires in midtown Manhattan, you get these tremendous crowds. But over in the ghetto, where fires are a matter of course, people walk by and don't even give you a second glance. You can have a big working fire, a third alarm, and the only people you see there are fire buffs with cameras. You know: all white guys from the suburbs.

Early in my career, I was still on probation and working in midtown Manhattan. We had a fire one time right there on Fifth Avenue. As we pulled up, we looked and there's this guy who's out on a tenth-story ledge. He looks like he's ready to jump, and the smoke is billowing out, and there's a huge crowd of people watching all this.

I didn't know whether to shit or go blind.

I'm with this older officer, Jack Braggan. We shoot up through the building on an elevator. We take a roof rope with us. We're the second-due company in, so we're going to the floor above the guy on the ledge.

So Jack, real nonchalantly, starts tying a knot in the roof rope. He looks at me and just smiles and goes, "Well, you ready, kid?"

I said, "For what?"

Jack said, "We're going out there. I'm going to lower you out the window, and you're gonna get that guy."

I wasn't so concerned about going out the window. All I could think of was those five hundred people out there watching.

With my luck, I figured I'd get this guy then drop him.

We went to the window. Just as I was stepping into the knot, ready to drop out the window ten stories up, I got called back in. The engine company down below had knocked down most of the fire. So the ladder guys were able to crawl in and get this guy from the inside. I didn't say a word when they called me back in. I just thought, *Thank you, God. Now there's no way I can fumble this guy.*

My very first fire was a big furniture store. It's a good fire, really involved. And the big chief, the main guy, says, "Kelly, get on in there!"

There is fire coming out all the windows. The glass in the windows is breaking. I'm looking at the chief like, You sure you want me to go inside this thing?

So me and my captain go in. The captain yells at me, "Just go far enough into the smoke where the chief can't see you! Don't go in any further!"

Meanwhile, I can hear that old chief outside: "Get in there, get in there!"

Anyhow, we get in there. We're putting the fire out. Pretty soon, the roof collapses. This big old air conditioning unit comes crashing through the roof. It lands about five feet from where we're standing. And it's my first fire, you know? I'm going, *Whoa. That crazy bastard chief almost killed us!*

LEARNING FROM MENTORS AND VETERANS

After a pretty decent fire my first year, we all came back to the fire station. One of the older firemen went to the cabinet and took out four Tylenols. I was watching him.

He just threw them in his mouth, and shot them down with a cup of coffee.

I said, "What are you doing?"

He laughed. Then he said, "Smoke headache. You'll get used to it. It's just one of the things we get."

And you do. Even if you wear a mask, at some point that mask comes off. That's usually when the heavy smoke is gone, but the building is still full of carbon monoxide. It's a colorless, odorless gas, and it gives you what we call a carbon monoxide headache. It can last for days sometimes. That's why you'll always find lots of aspirin in any firehouse.

You learn how to fight fire from watching experienced firemen. It's also a good way to learn how a firefighter *behaves.*

Let's say you've never been in the service, never been to war. So you're seeing things now that most people will never see during their lifetime. Right out of the gate, you have a car accident with major traumas, or you're pulling two dead bodies out of a burning building. While you're at the scene, you're watching the older people to see how they are reacting.

Then you go back to the fire station. You watch the guys as they start to talk about it. They're heavy-hearted, but they don't dwell on it. They can still eat their dinner. They can still have a laugh. It's just something new guys must learn. You swallow it and move forward, no matter how tragic it is. You can't let those calls drag you down, emotionally or physically. You're only getting started. There will be thousands more of those calls awaiting you.

I would watch these guys as we pulled up to a fire. The hotter the fire looked, the colder and cooler they got.

It was like they went into this other mode. It was real interesting.

When I first came on I was very lucky. I worked with mostly old-timers. I was twenty-two years old and these guys were World War II vets. I've always said it's a great thing for a young kid to work with old-timers. If you gotta crew with all young guys, everyone is trying to outdo each other. The old guys were never like that. They had more discipline than younger guys. They had more respect. Many of them were veterans, so they were neat and prompt and organized. When you're around people like that, it starts to rub off on you.

We all like to think we're pretty tough today, but I know we weren't as tough as the old-timers. We had one old guy named Bob Hartwig. You know what Bob Hartwig did at a fire? He put a twenty-four-foot ladder on his shoulder, and people were climbing down it. How tough was that guy?

At another fire, I'm watching this other fireman waiting outside a window. Someone inside the fire passes him a baby. Well, the guy inside in the fire room, handing out the baby, is this Bob Hartwig. That was routine for him. He was the guy who went in and got the baby, then never said two words about it later. He was a World War II vet, a marine, a tough old goat. I loved him. And he was the best cook I ever had in the firehouse.

Once in a while, my mom and dad would come by and see me at the firehouse. I'd be embarrassed about it. I'm a fireman, and my parents are coming by to check up on me? Then one day this old couple came to the back door of the firehouse. They had to be in their nineties. One of them had a cane. They ask, "Is Bob Hartwig here? We're his parents."

That was the last time I was embarrassed about my parents. I was like, "Hey, if it's all right for Bob's parents to come, then it must be cool."

Bob was always real nice to my mom. My mother was sickly, and at the end of a shift, Bob would give me some food to take home to her. He'd tell me, "Here, have your ma taste this."

Then I'd call her every day when I got home. Her first question would be, "Did you have any fires?" The next thing out of her mouth was, "What did you eat? What did Bob cook today?"

Bob made a lot of different things, but his clam chowder stood out. You know the white kind? New England? Excellent.

I remember an early fire I went on with him. I was pure rookie, doing everything I could to impress these guys. I'm keeping my mouth shut, answering every phone, doing the dishes. So we get a fire. I go running up to the third floor, all-out and gung ho. And I'm in good shape, right? But I get that first blast of smoke and I go reeling back, because back then we didn't wear masks. I turn around and see Bob, this sixty-year-old man, just walking up the stairs. He tells me, "Slow down, kid."

Then they leave me in the hallway and walk into the apartment that was on fire. Once he got inside there, you know Bob worked like a horse. And I learned that from those old guys. Relax. Relax. The fire's not going anywhere.

The ironic thing was, I won an Award of Valor a few years ago. While the mayor is giving me my award, Bob Hartwig was standing behind me. He was retired by then, but he was the honor guard for the military. When the city presents our awards, the VFW guys always do the flags and guns.

It was a strange sensation. I was so proud that Hartwig was there, but at the same time I felt funny. Here is a man who did tenfold what I ever did.

But Bob was real nice, like he always was. He just said, "Hey, kid, nice job."

Bob Hartwig. Great human being.

My mentor was Joe Penda. He always stood up for me.

I joined the fire department in 1968, the era of hippies. I had long hair and all of that, so the older guys were always ribbing me. "Hey, here comes the long-haired, hippie, commie, pinko bed wetter."

Then Joe Penda would jump right in.

He'd say, "Hey, forget about his hair. As a fireman, you couldn't make a pimple on this guy's ass."

Joe Penda. He had an Irish brogue like he just fell off the boat, but he was actually brilliant. He later became a borough commander, and he got there by scoring first on every test he ever took. But I worked with him when he was a fireman, and I gotta tell you, Joe Penda had leather lungs. I don't think I ever remember seeing him put a Scott mask on, and that in itself used to flabbergast me. Not that I was not an aggressive young fireman. I was extremely aggressive. I would go where a lot of guys would not. But I hated the smoke. So I always wore my Scott. I just felt much more at ease when I had it on. When it came to making rescues, I felt I could go anywhere with that damn mask on.

Joe didn't need it. He felt more comfortable without his mask on. You could cut the smoke with a knife it would get so thick, and he'd just be real relaxed, breathing in and out through his nose.

My mentor just retired. His name is Ben Apicella. You meet one or two guys like him in your career, you're very lucky.

There still is not a day when I don't think of him. I miss him, but I'm happy for him, too. He just retired with a pacemaker and now he's off to Florida for the winters. That was after thirty-five years in.

He was the officer on my engine, a rough-around-the-edges Italian guy. Ben led by example. Like getting to work every day one hour early. We don't start getting paid until 8:00 A.M., but he was getting in at seven every day. So we followed his lead. The whole shift would get in at seven each day, with him.

But Ben wasn't super-straight. He wasn't Mr. Rulebook. He was a fireman's fireman. When I became a captain, he told me something I'll never forget.

Ben said, "Do what's right for your crew, and don't let the upper echelon bullshit you. This job is done on the back step of the engine."

That's *precisely* where the real job is done. All the politicking and all the other bullshit is exactly that.

The bottom line is what happens at that fire. That's our bread and butter.

When I first came on the department in San Francisco, I worked on an engine right in the city, down on Fifth and Mission. Our engine officer there was the toughest guy who ever lived. He would rather breathe smoke than clean air.

The funny thing was, he really wasn't a mentor. He didn't like to teach. The way that you learned with this guy was watching his moves. And he would take you everywhere with him. He enjoyed taking normal human beings into terrible places, and then watching them disintegrate. It would get so hot and smoky and rotten in there, I'd be hanging on to his belt, puking up lunch, and he'd be laughing. I would be thinking, *I'll never make it in this business. I just don't have what this guy does.*

I spent about five or six months with this guy. It's been child play ever since.

TROUBLING ROOKIE CALLS

My worst one came on Christmas Day. It was the first suicide I ever made. A young guy, twenty-five. Blew his head off with a shotgun.

I walk in and he's down at the bottom of a staircase. Down in the basement. There's brain matter everywhere. And I remember stepping in the brain matter. It's very slick. I can't get it off my shoe. I remember that. And I remember the pungent smell of blood.

Later on, at the firehouse, we joked about that. I mean, that was funny as hell, that I couldn't get this guy's brains off the bottom of my shoe. It's really sick, you know, but that's how we deal with those things. We make up dark jokes, we tell funny stories. But it's only funny to another firefighter. Because they've been there.

I went to the morgue when I first came on. I wanted to see a person who got burned, so I wouldn't be shocked when I saw one in the field.

The guy working at the morgue said, "Here. This is a person who's burned."

I lifted off the cover. Whether it was a lady or a guy, I don't know. But the skin was all tight, like burnt leather, and the skin was all pulled back. The jaw was wide open, like it was screaming, *"Ahhhh!"*

I actually heard that person scream in my mind. Then I put the cover back on, and I didn't hear it anymore.

I said to the guy working the morgue, "Did you hear that? I heard that person screaming."

I guess it was my emotions taking over. But I'll never forget seeing that person, and what fear they probably went through their last few moments. That really brought me down to earth. Even to this day, I think it still makes me try a little bit harder, when we pull up and they say someone is trapped.

I remember my first fire victim. It was a good fire. It charred out the whole apartment. After it's over, everyone's overhauling. That means pulling down the ceiling and walls, to find and put out any hidden fire that's left. Then the captain of the squad looks over at me.

He says, "Give them a hand with the body."

I'm thinking, *What the hell is he talking about? What body?*

I'm looking around and I don't see nothing.

He's getting impatient. He says it again. "Come on! Give them a hand with the body!"

I say, "Okay. Where's it at?"

He says, "Right over there."

So I look on the floor and here's this mound of charcoal. It wasn't the body. It was the embers and all the burnt wood and other debris. The body was underneath. It turned out she was a woman, burnt beyond recognition. I'm looking at this thing. It's the first time I've ever been face-to-face with a body in this state. I don't know what the hell I'm supposed to do.

This guy on the other end says, "Okay, we got her

over here. You grab her legs. On the count of three, we get her in the body bag."

So one, two, three, I lift. Guess what happens? The leg falls through my hands; that's how bad she was. I got her flesh in my hands, but the leg bone itself fell down.

Now we can't get her in the bag because the leg is dragging.

He says, "Then grab her other leg, okay?"

I'm doing this and I'm saying to myself, *Please, Lord, don't let me throw up right here. Wait until these guys get the bag out of here, and I'll get sick in the corner.*

It was a sobering experience. But since that time, there is nothing I can see that will even faze me. At fires and shootings and car wrecks, I've seen the human body in every conceivable form. I've learned to leave it at work and not take it home. For me, it's always been easy. Maybe there's something psychologically wrong with me, but I just don't carry it with me. I didn't cause these terrible things to happen. I can only make things better, and sometimes I can't do that. No matter how hard you try, you can't save everyone. Death is there. It's just there. If you want to put it that way, death is a part of life.

My roughest early call was when I was seventeen. I was just an Explorer, which is kind of like a fireman in waiting. You are not allowed indoors for insurance reasons. You're kept outside, where it's safe, and even then you're working on the perimeter, setting up lighting, or taping off a place to keep people out, or running and getting equipment off the rig.

But that's not what happened on this particular call.

It was a regular house fire. A good working fire, but no big deal. Nothing unusual. But it was in a real poor part of downtown, and what's prevalent down there is security bars on the windows. I mean, all the windows. And that would become a big factor later on.

This fire was ripping. It was blowing out a couple of windows, and threatening to ignite the house next door.

That *would* be a big deal. You've already lost one house and you don't want to lose two.

Me and this firefighter were standing outside, right between the two houses, manning a hose line. He's on the nozzle and I'm right behind him. The house to our left is the one that's involved. We've got our hose on the house to the right, keeping it cool. Even though I'm an Explorer, this fireman trusts me. And depending on your abilities, sometimes the firefighters will give you certain tasks.

So he says to me, "Hey kid, you take the nozzle."

That's the ultimate compliment. Excellent.

Then, out of the corner of our eyes, we see a flash.

We look over to the house that's already involved. We see a little boy, probably nine years old. He is in the window and screaming for help. So far that room is not on fire, but you can see smoke in there, and you can feel the heat coming out of the walls.

We didn't have portable radios, so my firefighter tells me to stay there. He tells me to keep the hose on the house, meaning the house that is not yet involved.

Then he says to me, "I gotta go tell the cap that we got somebody inside."

So he runs around to tell him. Right then, the heat inside the kid's room blows the window out. This introduces more oxygen into the room, and now the room is on fire. The window is gone; the bars are still there. The kid is at the bars looking at me. I got to be no more than five feet away. He catches fire. He's screaming and he has his hands on the bars. I turn my hose on the kid. I'm trying to keep him as cool as I can. Then he disappears. I can't see him.

Now I'm trying to find him with my hose line. I got it up on my shoulder, like I've been trained. But I'm breaking all the rules of fighting fire. I'm putting a hose from the outside into the inside, when there are guys inside who I'm probably burning with steam. But I didn't even think about the guys in there. I only thought about this kid.

I still can't see him. So I put the hose down. I grab these bars. But steel gets hot, and even though I have gloves on, they're not firefighting gloves, because I'm not inside. I'm just an Explorer. They are just leather gloves. So I grab the bars with both palms, and I burn both palms and let go real fast. They end up finding the kid. He was burned beyond recognition in just a minute or so.

I was a mess. My captain knew what I'd seen because the fireman told him. So I went to the fire department psychologist. In talking to the guy, we realized that I grew up knowing his dad. I'm not real big on shrinks, but he was extremely helpful. So was my whole family. When something like that happens, you must have supportive family. If I didn't have that, I would probably be an alcoholic or something.

It still isn't over for me. It's fifteen years later now, and that call still wakes me up in the middle of the night. Not very often, but still. It will wake me up tonight, just because I talked about it today.

The most crucial thing I learned was how fast it can happen.

That really rung out in my mind: how fast somebody can die in a fire. I mean, you're going to fires right around the corner and it's hard to understand, even to this day, how quick it takes place. The people say they saw smoke and they call the fire department. We get there and we can't even get in. And the people are already dead.

We had a call one evening when I was a probationary firefighter. It was a busy Friday night. The truck company in our station was already out. They were running all over the place, fighting fires and going to false alarms. We worked on the engine, so we were in the station by ourselves.

A block away from our station, somebody pulls the pull box. We go down there and look around. There's nothing there. But there are a lot of people on the street, so we think someone has just pulled a false alarm. We're just about to call in on the radio, report it that way, when somebody sticks his head around the next-block corner.

He starts screaming at us.

So we drive up that way and we turn onto the block. Here is a brick row house, three stories, with fire blowing out all the second-floor windows. As we pull up, there's a couple of people standing in front of the building. Their clothing is smoldering. They had jumped out the window from the floor above the fire. There's two or three more people like them, lying on the sidewalk. So now we know we have a serious fire. And we're there all by ourselves. The truck is still out working another call. So there's no one to put up ladders and get people out.

We start stretching hose into the building. With or without a truck, that is our job on the engine company: get the hose line into the building, get water in the line and put out the fire. The faster you put it out, the better it's going to be for anyone in that building.

At the same time we started stretching into the building, our officer had sent one of our guys to the roof to make sure it was ventilated. This, again, is normally done by the guys on the truck. But we gotta spare this one guy to make sure there's some ventilation.

Now we're all in position. We're just waiting for water so we can attack the fire. Unfortunately, it was cold out, and the driver tried the front hydrant and it was frozen. He had to go to the second hydrant. That was all the way down on the next block. Then he had to go to a *third* before we ever got water.

It wasn't our fault the hydrants were frozen. But precious moments were lost. It wasn't our fault that here was a fire, fully involved, and the most anybody did was go around the corner, pull the box, but then not stay long enough to indicate where the fire was. Even with all those people on the street, nobody said a word. We call that kind of thing "delayed notification." And the end result is the same as with the frozen hydrants: precious moments lost. Another time delay. And this is truly a matter of life and death.

While this is going on, the mother of some of the children in the building shows up in front. She tries to race into the building, which is on fire. Here I am, as a probie, the last guy on the line, wrestling with this woman who is hysterical, who desperately wants to get inside this building, because she realizes her family's still in there.

And you've got to picture the scene here. It wasn't just this woman. There are hundreds of people out there, losing it, because they realize there are children in there, and here's the fire department on the scene, and the best thing we've done so far is stretch hose line into the building. We haven't put out a bit of fire.

Fortunately, finally, the police department showed up and they held on to the woman. We managed to get back in there, we finally got water, we put out the fire. But the outcome of the whole thing was tremendously tragic. Seven children inside the building perished.

This is what it was like to be a young firefighter. I mean, total chaos. And here you are thrown into the middle of it.

We had a car accident my second year on the job. My first multiple fatality.

Sometime after midnight, a small Honda traveling east crashed through the center divider and into the westbound traffic. In our city, we don't have the concrete center divider. We have a real thick metal cable that runs lengthwise, and there is chain-link fencing that runs along with it. It can be very unforgiving. We call it the guillotine. And that's exactly what it turned out to be right here. Of the four guys in this Honda, it decapitated one guy sitting in the backseat.

That wasn't our only victim. We were the first engine company on-scene, and we had bodies strewn all over the place. On the other side of the freeway, this car had caused a really terrible pileup.

My captain got off the rig and told me, "Okay. You're our triage guy."

Which means that now I'm God. I walk around and sort through the patients. I determine which of them can be salvaged. I determine which can't.

In this case we had twelve patients, and I triaged them all. Within about thirty seconds, maybe a minute, I determined who needed hospital care immediately, or if they could wait, or if there was no point in sending them at all. That's just how it is. If somebody isn't breathing, you readjust their airway. If they're still not breathing then, you gotta move on. You have eleven other people who need your help.

It's a pretty large responsibility, especially when you've only got two years on. But if you know your job, you can handle it. These people are counting on you for their lives. You can't say, "Hey, I can't deal with this." That's not fair to them. You signed on to help them. That's the whole reason you wanted to be a fireman. Now at this moment they need you more than ever. It isn't time to be young.

3
FIREFIGHTS AND RESCUES

In order to achieve a common purpose, firefighters must blend their individual talents. So they work together in teams referred to as companies. Consisting of a company officer, a driver/operator, and anywhere from one to three firefighters, the standard companies are the engine, the truck, and the rescue.

When new firefighters graduate training school, what company they go to is decided by their higher-ups. Some probies with clout can influence these assignments, but even they can forget about working the rescue squad. Although the engine and truck are equally important, rescue work is by consensus the most prestigious. Besides responding to all major fires, the rescue company rolls to the highest-profile disasters: airplane crashes, subway derailments, industrial accidents, building collapses and so on. Many small departments don't have a rescue company—the heavy equipment they use makes the cost prohibitive—and a large city like Philadelphia has just one. So rescue assignments are tight, even for gifted veterans. Probies need not apply.

A handful of probies, however, will be sent to trucks. They will probably be bigger and stronger than their fellow graduates. Among their many duties, truckies are in charge of forcible entry; they bust through steel doors with sledgehammers and axes. They are also responsible for overhauling. Once the main body of fire has been extinguished, they pull down ceilings and walls with pike poles and axes, to examine them for hidden pockets of fire. If any fire should go undetected, the firefighters may leave and the building may reignite. This is a major black eye for any fire department, and truckies are entrusted to see that it doesn't happen. As one engine man said in deference to them, "Those big guys love doing that demolition stuff. No one tears apart a room like those guys can."

Most new firefighters are sent to engines. There are more engine companies, for one thing, than truck and rescue companies combined. San Diego, for instance, has one rescue, fifteen trucks and forty-two engines. This is because you need water to extinguish fire—often a lot of water—and this is the primary role of the engine company. The fire engine itself carries the hose lines. Then its personnel stretches those lines inside burning buildings.

And for all the field's technological progress, for all the brilliant work done by trucks and rescues, the core of firefighting hasn't changed. It is still, as firefighters say, "putting the wet stuff on the red stuff."

This is another reason most probies start out on engines. The fire department wants them to understand the red stuff, to see it up close and learn its predilections.

Sometimes at a structural fire an engine and truck arrive simultaneously. But when an engine pulls up first, as it frequently does, it usually won't wait for a truck to appear. It will make its initial attack by dragging in its first hose line. If the building has occupants, that line will often be placed between them and the fire. After confining the fire so occupants can flee, the engine company will try to extinguish it.

"The first engine on a scene is very important," explains one firefighter who's worked both engines and trucks. "Just like it says in our textbook, they're the ones who take the line inside the main entrance. So if they don't handle it right initially, it becomes a bigger fire. You can end up with three alarms, when it really should never get past a one-alarm. That's why everyone wants to be the first-due engine. Being first due is the meat and potatoes. Getting first whack at the fire, before anyone else does. That's the whole thing right there. The balls of the job."

Not necessarily, according to truckies. In addition to forcible entry, overhauling, and working with the ladders their fire trucks carry—why truck companies are also called "ladder companies"—truckies perform search and rescue. At times they'll follow the engine inside the front door. But when terrified people are ready to jump out windows, truckies climb aerial ladders and haul them back down to safety. As diverse as truck work gets, human life is its top priority.

Another key task of the truck is ventilation. By cutting holes in roofs or breaking windows, truckies let smoke and heat escape from the structure, thus drawing them away from both victims and firefighters inside. Roof ventilation in particular can also prevent deadly backdrafts. This is because a fire needs three things—oxygen, fuel, and heat. In a building sealed tightly, without any ventilation, the fire will first burn freely and then begin to smolder. It still has fuel and heat, but it needs a fresh supply of oxygen.

"Now, if you just run up and open the front door, you will cause a backdraft," explains a roof man. "The fire gets oxygen and it just explodes. It can blow metal gates across the street. It can blow firefighters across the street. But if you open the *roof* first, the air currents act like a chimney. The fire blows out the roof, instead of the front door. Then our people down on the street can move right in."

On many structural fires, this includes the rescue company, the specially trained crew of accomplished veterans. Rescue company members refer to two kinds of searches: primary and secondary. A primary search is done immediately, before the fire is under control, while heat is still high and smoke still blindingly thick. Time being of the essence for both rescuers and victims, these primary searches are quick and aggressive ones, with emphasis placed on locations where victims are commonly found. These include front doors and back doors, stairways, and any other principal means of escape; underneath beds and in closets, where children often cower; directly behind closed doors and beneath closed windows, where people struggling with locks may have gotten overwhelmed.

In a secondary search, the fire has been restrained if not yet fully extinguished. Smoke is beginning to clear, and rescuers can now see where they are going. In case they were somehow missed in the primary search, all the likeliest places are checked again, sometimes by someone else on the rescue company, the better to afford a fresh perspective. But this secondary search is also much more expansive. When looking for small children, for example, *any* place they can fit into will be probed. One prime area to explore is in their hiding places. On secondary searches, kids have been found, alive, hiding inside a toy chest or under stuffed animals.

So that, briefly, is a sketch of the engine, the truck, and the rescue companies. Among the three, all separate yet all vital, how do they view one another?

Perhaps unsurprisingly, there is a friendly rivalry that exists.

"Oh, yeah, it never ends," says one firefighter who

went from engine to rescue work. "The truckies think the engine men are midgets. The engine men think truckies got their heads up their asses; all they are is big mules that can swing an ax. And the rescue just sits back and laughs at all of them. But you know what? That's all firehouse talk. Once you get to a fire, it doesn't matter what company you're in. Everything you do is interconnected. You all depend on each other."

WHY THEY DO THIS JOB

I'm still not really sure. We know how dangerous it is. We know it can take our lives. But we still go rushing into these infernos.

I'm kind of a jacked-up guy. I need a job like this.

I think all firefighters are crazy. Take a look at your typical structure fire. All the sane people are running out. Who's running in?

After you work here awhile, you understand the importance of *not* going in. In a fire, your chances of surviving are very small. If someone doesn't go in there and get you quickly, you are going to die. And if you don't succumb to the smoke, if the fire kills you, you are certainly going to die a violent death. In my lifetime I have seen some ugly things, but there is not anything as destructive as fire. I once came upon a girl whose face was split down the middle like a hot dog. Her face had just exploded from the heat.

I don't ever want to see that happen again. That's why I keep going in. There could be somebody in there still alive.

I've always worked in busy firehouses. I like the action, but there's another attraction. Busy houses are usually located in poor neighborhoods. There's no political bull-shit. There's no window dressing. It's just people needing help, and actually getting it.

Most of us are in it because we get genuine satisfaction from helping people. I mean, many of us could get jobs that pay more money. We could get jobs without any real danger.

And then we go on these medical calls, first thing in the morning, and people throw up on us, or we get crapped on. If we didn't like helping people, why would we do it?

I'm an adrenaline junkie. I get high off this stuff.

Firemen crave excitement. It's a fact. Just like a drug addict will shoot up to experience that high, firemen want to feel that adrenaline flow. The feeling of climbing on that apparatus and heading off into an unknown situation, something that may be totally bullshit or may be life and death . . . it's a real rush.

I've been on nine years and I still get rig boners.

Every time we go code three—red lights and siren and driving through traffic—that stuff is still bitchin' to me. I love it, and so do the guys I work with. That's why you joined on, and that feeling never leaves you.

The longer you have in, the more extreme the call you need to get that sensation. When you're a rookie, a guy with a two-inch cut is a real hot call. Now I'm a twenty-year veteran. If an arm ain't hanging off, it ain't a big deal.

All my life I've loved to go fast. I drive motorcycles. I drive a Corvette. But I've never done anything more exciting than driving that fire truck. And the more I heard on the radio that people were trapped, or the fire was intense, the faster I drove. When we had the killer rig with the eighteen-wheeler? I used to make turns on nine wheels!

The *best* time to drive the truck was late at night. During the day, everyone's out and doing their business. At night the city shuts down and it's kind of eerie; it's just you and the cabbies. But that's city life, you know? While the rest of the city sleeps, a fire engine is screaming to a call.

On the way to the fire, you're already excited. In fact, I used to get into arguments with my bosses, the ones who would not blow the sirens continuously while we were en route to a fire. Because a siren pumps you up. It gets you ready to face the ultimate challenge, and that's what fire-fighting really is. Your heart is racing, you're scared. But once you knock down the fire, and then you're back outside and picking up lines, it's almost like you want to beat your chest.

It's not like an everyday job, where you're waiting for the next phone call, to take care of some piece-of-shit paperwork problem. We're waiting for that gong to go off so we can enter somebody's worst nightmare. Then we try and give it a happy ending.

It sharpens your senses. When you're in a structural fire, it's very encapsulated. You hear the roar of the flames. You hear firemen grunting. You feel each droplet of sweat under your mask. It makes you feel alive.

It's just you against the fire. So you have no choice but to overcome your fears. Fear of claustrophobia. Fear of death. Fear of the dark. People don't realize how dark it gets. Inside a burning building, the smoke is so black you can't even see your hand.

Winning a battle like that, in those conditions, it's good for your self-respect.

People see all this fire and chaos and they are over-whelmed. They'll tell us, "Hey, I wouldn't do your job for all the money in the world."

So, yes, that's a part of it. The average citizen on the street thinks you're hot shit.

It's one of the last pure battles. It's not like the cops, with the drug war. There's people out there who feel drugs should be legalized. Our job is never that gray. We are the knights in shining armor. Fire is the devil. Who's gonna win?

On the morning of Halloween night, our shift had just started at 7:30 A.M. Forty-five minutes later we got an alert. A four-family dwelling was on fire.

I was working on Engine 21 at the time, with a good friend of mine whose name is George Orzezh. As we rolled up on this place—a small apartment building—we saw a man and woman on the lawn. The father was bleeding. He was in his underwear. The mother was in her nightgown. They were jumping up and down, screaming that their two kids were still in there.

The fire was on George's side of the street, so he got off the rig and ran inside. I got off the rig, ran around the rig and came in behind him. The building was a four-flat, with two dwellings downstairs and two dwellings upstairs. The fire was in the downstairs, on the right side. The kids were supposed to be in the back of that apartment.

We worked our way through the living room and the dining room. There were still pieces of furniture burning there, but mostly there was heat without a whole lot of flame, because the fire had already used up all the oxygen.

It was smoldering now, like the white, hot coals in a barbecue pit.

As I came down the hall toward the back of the apartment, George came running back out the other way with a seven-year-old boy held in his arms. I continued forward, down the hall and into the back bedroom. The smoke was so heavy in there, I couldn't see. So I did our normal technique when looking for people in smoky conditions: I felt around for the bed, found it, and gave it a push to see if I'd get a bounce. If there's anyone on a bed, their body will bounce.

The first bed, I got nothing. The second one I felt a bounce, so I ran my hand across it real quick. I felt a little girl, about three years old.

I grabbed her, and I got her in my arms, but in my

haste and excitement to find her, I had lost track of where
the door was. Fortunately, by now, my sergeant was
standing outside the bedroom door. I heard him calling
my name from out in the hallway.

I said, "Yeah! Which way is the door?"

He said, "This way. Come to my voice."

I got to his voice and out to the hall. We were going to
try and egress the same way that we came in—through
the living room and the dining room. But at that same
exact moment, the firemen outside were doing their ventilation. It happened very suddenly. They broke the windows out, more oxygen came in, and this superheated
room burst into flames again.

The guys doing ventilation had done the right thing.
We have a policy here in Detroit: You don't ventilate
until you have water in the hose line. Because as soon as
you ventilate, you are going to make the fire worse.
That's one of the purposes of ventilation—to feed the
fire, so it will show itself. Then as soon as it lights up,
you open the hose and you put it out.

So those guys used proper procedure. They waited
until there was water in the hose. Then they ventilated.
The mistake that got made was by the guys on the hose
line. When they stretched the line, they should've brought
it through the front door of the building; the same door
we came in. But they stretched to the side of the building
and came inside a door there. In those few seconds they
lost, the room ignited again and there was no water. It
was just a bad call. I don't blame anyone. We've all made
our own bad calls.

We were halfway through the dining room when
everything lit up. Furniture, carpet, walls—it was like
someone took lighter fluid and squeezed it into the pit.
The heat was so strong it drove me to my knees. My
sergeant hit his knees also. It was a pretty bad scene. I

have a three-year-old kid in my arms, she is unconscious, and we are in a room that's suddenly on fire. A second ago it was smoldering. Now it's raw flame.

I pulled the girl as close to me as I could, and while I was doing that, I looked up and saw the front door through all the fire. I'm not gonna say I found it because I have so much experience, or because I'm so good at what I do. I found it because it wasn't my day to die.

I jumped off my knees when I saw the door. My sergeant must have seen it at the same time. He jumped back up, too. We didn't speak. We just looked at each other like, *There's the door! Let's get the hell out of here!*

Just as we got through the door, more flames mushroomed out the apartment behind us. By then, there were plenty of firemen out in the hallway. They said they could not believe what we just came through. It looked like a wall of flame.

Out on the lawn, I snatched off my mask to see what condition the kid was in. Her forehead was burned. So was most of the hair on the top of her head. Otherwise, considering, she looked good. And I still remember that moment vividly. It was cool outside. Late October air. We released so much heat into this cool air, the steam was rising off the three of us. The little girl, my sergeant, and myself.

They took all three of us to the hospital. The little girl lived. As matter of fact, she had a full recovery. The blessing, I believe, was that she was so young.

My neck was burned and I missed a month of work. It took two weeks for my burns to heal, and then about two more weeks for the skin to grow back. Until it grew back, they wouldn't *let* me return. The skin on my neck was too tender. I couldn't put anything on it, like my mask.

Several months later, I was privileged to receive the Medal of Valor, the highest award for bravery that year.

They also gave one to George, for pulling out that seven-year-old boy. It was the first time in the history of the Detroit Fire Department that they gave the Medal of Valor to two people.

I always love it when we save someone. I always love it when we win. But that was singularly, to date, the moment I am most proud of on this job.

HOW IT FEELS TO SAVE A LIFE

It is the ultimate high. Nothing else comes close.

I remember my first night out of the training academy. Watching all the firemen, I felt like I wasn't one of them. Even though I *was* one, I felt like an observer.

After I made my rescue, that feeling changed. I distinctly remember feeling, *I'm one of these firemen now.*

It's real weird stuff, saving somebody's life. Hard to articulate, because it's a *feeling*. I don't really know what else to compare it to, other than your first love, or maybe your first child being born. You get these butterflies in your stomach, and you get all welled up and you want to cry.

A lot of it is luck. And you'll hear that a lot when someone's pulled out of a fire. "Geez, I was lucky. I happened to stumble on them."

They're telling the truth; it's not just being modest.

With the smoke and the heat, you can't always tell what's what. Children, for example, are notorious for going under beds, or behind beds, or in closets, because they feel that's where they'll be safe. So one firefighter will look in all those places, and end up saving a kid. Another firefighter will pull out a doll. I've seen it happen. Both firefighters searched in all the right places. One guy had the luck.

Many times, rescues are made where the people aren't in much danger. They're hanging out of windows, but they're hanging out where the fire is not gonna spread. But they don't realize that, and they may jump. So we have to take the risk and go and get them. Basically, we're saving them from themselves.

I've been on a couple CPR calls where the person was dead when we walked in their home, and they were up and talking to us by the time we pulled up to the hospital. That's not the doctor that saved them. That's us that saved them. It's the best feeling in the world—the one that you stole back from the grim reaper. He had his rig backed up with the doors open, and we reached in and plucked someone back. Of course, he's probably a little pissed at us right now, and he'll come one day for us, but this one we denied him.

Unfortunately, it doesn't happen that often. It's not like that TV show, *Rescue 911,* where everybody they save comes to the fire station and meets the fire guys. That's a load of shit, because nobody on that program ever dies. It's a fantasyland fire department. They save *everyone*.

But every once in a while in real life, you do get to

save someone, and that's all it takes. Making the difference in one child's life—or any person's life—will get you through years of shit.

I had an elderly gentleman once who was having an aneurysm.

The large vessel in his brain was about to burst. There didn't seem any way that he would live, but we brought him back to life in the back of our ambulance. We rushed him to the emergency room. ER took him up to surgery. A few hours later, we went back there on another call. So I checked on the old man. The guy was awake and talking and doing pretty good. I can't tell you how great that felt.

Ultimately, he died about one week later. But it didn't take away from the feeling I had had. See, I have these three rules. One is, You don't spit on the floor of my ambulance. Two is, You don't get sick and throw up back there. The third rule is, You don't die in my ambulance when I am back there with you.

That's how I see it. If I know I've done everything I can do, and that patient is still alive when I deliver them to the emergency room—not only alive, but in better condition than when I first got to them—I feel good.

When that life depended on me alone, I sustained it. After that, I can't control their fate.

For me, the best incident is what we call a live rescue.

They're not only alive when you get them out, they stay alive. The very best is saving a kid. Kids who perish in a fire had no chance at life. So to give back to a little kid his chance to have a life? That's hard to top.

I've worked in different places, and for me it's especially nice if you're working in a small town. Usually, in a big city, you don't hear from them again. I guess it's just . . . life goes on. But in smaller towns, you can see the kid walking to school, or you might know their uncle, or you might see the kid's name in the sports section. Maybe he scored ten points in a basketball game.

You don't tell anyone, "Hey, I saved that boy's life." You just sit back and smile.

We pulled out this little girl whose name is Shamika. After the fire she could barely walk. Her hands were all swelled up and burned severely. Now she's come a long way. After six or seven operations, she's able to use her hands and she's walking properly. She's a very nice little girl, tough little girl. In all honesty, I can't imagine going through what she went through.

I just talked to her the other day. She's doing well. She keeps telling me she's getting straight A's, so I think she really is. You know, she and I come from totally different backgrounds. She's black, I'm white. She's from the city, I'm not. But I think we'll have a bond the rest of our lives.

Working as a team with other firefighters, to save a person's life, I don't know how to describe it. It's rewarding. It's refreshing. It's heart-wrenching. It brings tears to your eyes. And then you get credit, of course, and anyone who says they don't like credit, I don't think is telling you the truth. Everyone is smacking you on the back—people out on the street, fellow firefighters—and everyone is saying you did a great thing. It's absolutely fabulous. It's a great job. It's the best profession in the world!

When one of us makes a successful rescue, our chief goes on our radio to report it to dispatch. The chief gets on there and he's giving his size-up: two-story wood frame. The fire started on the second floor, extended throughout. We used so much hose, we used so many ladders. Three victims were rescued by firefighters. First victim was rescued by . . . and he says your name over the radio.

That, for me, was a super rush of pride. All over the city, you know everyone's hearing it. Because it isn't just firefighters. Everybody in scanner land hears that report. Every person, every old lady, every newsroom in the city—anyone who has a scanner will hear that you rescued someone.

In my case, when I saved a woman, I thought that was pretty much it. I never knew it would turn into such a big deal. I thought it would be the usual thing: Put the hose back on the rig, go back to the fire station, clean up and then cook lunch. That's not what happened. Shortly after we got back from the fire, the news people came to the station. Then these other firefighters were calling me, even some guys I didn't know, saying, "Way to go, beautiful job." That afternoon, for lunch, we went to the Broadway Market to pick up meat. This little woman came up and said a prayer for me. She had seen me on the news and said, "You're the guy!"

When I got home from work, I had a ton of messages on my machine. The woman's mother called, too, and I called her back. When I asked how her daughter was, I noticed that she didn't sound optimistic. But she thanked me for going in there. She thanked me for giving her time, so she could go in and say good-bye to her daughter. That's what she appreciated the most. Having the time to say good-bye.

All the medals I have, except for one, are for dragging other firefighters out. I've rescued seven brothers in my career, and I've never gotten a thank you from any of them! In their heart, you know they're grateful. But firemen aren't real big on paying each other compliments. And saving one another is part of the job.

It does get pretty dramatic when it happens. I mean, your adrenaline pumps when anyone is trapped. But when one of the brothers goes down, man, the whole place goes crazy. One of the signals we have is a helmet thrown out a window. That means a brother is trapped. Which means it's more than a fire. Now there is a family member in there, and you just kind of go berserk. You dig deeper inside yourself than you ever have before. Nothing else will suffice. You gotta get in there.

I've been on the Boston Fire Department for twenty-five years. In that period, I've experienced quite a few gruesome deaths and real bad accidents. In time, you get over it. Maybe you go out after work that night and have a few beers.

It stiffens your lip a little. In the months and years to come, you learn to let it go.

That's usually how it works, but not every time. We had a tragedy here this June I'll never forget. We lost one of our own, and I was involved in that. In fact, I had gotten lost in the building myself.

It was a warehouse on top of a pier in the Charlestown section of Boston. A little after midnight, we received a call for a building fire there. I happened to be driving Rescue 1 that night. Going over the top of the North Washington State Bridge, I could see we had a small fire at the end of a pier. I said to myself: *Oh. We'll be out of here in fifteen or twenty minutes. It's no big deal.*

So we got out of the truck and grabbed our tools and masks. Engine 8 and Ladder 1 were already there. As they started to stretch a line inside the warehouse, we followed them in. Even though we knew we had a fire, from that vantage point we still saw no indication. We were standing right in the middle of the warehouse. It was as clear as my kitchen.

Without any warning whatsoever, this whole place turned to thick black smoke. The smoke came down from the ceiling. It was so thick you couldn't see the hand in front of your face. I dropped to the floor, trying to get on my face piece. I got it on and turned on my air supply. Otherwise, I'd be choking.

It was so dark you couldn't see anyone now. Nobody from the Ladder, the Engine, the Rescue. There was probably thirteen of us, but you couldn't even see one. All you could hear was mumbling and grumbling and groaning. I was still down on my hands and knees. When I looked underneath me, I saw the fire coming up from the floorboards. That was when we determined to leave the building. Anything that turns sour that fast, there is something definitely wrong.

When I turned around and yelled for the rest of them, they were gone. I got no reply at all. Everybody was already on their way out.

Normally, your training and experience always tells you: If you bring a hose line into a building, you follow that hose line right back out the door you came in. So I started scrambling around the floor, searching for the hose. I knew it was off to my right, but I didn't know where. So I go off to the right and, geez, there's the line. I start to follow it back, and meantime this place is really turning rotten. The fire is up through the floor, and I'm following the hose, and suddenly it hits me: I'm going in circles.

I thought, *I'm in real trouble here. I should be going in a straight line, and I'm going round in a circle.*

Then I thought, *Stop! Get your head together and try something else.*

So I got another plan. I'd follow the hose line the other way, back to the nozzle, and start all over again. But in the next split second, I realized that I had no time to do this. I didn't know how far back the nozzle was, and this place was burning up. That's when I got worried I might get trapped. Because I still couldn't find anyone.

I thought, *I'm lost. I'm trapped in here. I'm gonna die in this place. All the rotten, lousy, friggin' vacant warehouses there are, I'm gonna die in here.*

That was the last thing I remember going through my mind. Then one of the fellows I work with grabbed my shoulder.

He said, "Come on, you stupid son of a bitch. You're going the wrong way."

We turned around, hand in hand, followed the line, and went out the front door. Outside the building, I turned around and looked back and started shaking my head. I couldn't believe it took off the way it did. Even to this day, they haven't found the cause. But I think it still seems suspicious. How does a pier take off like that, at midnight, if there aren't any combustibles involved?

Assuming now that everybody was out, we went back to the Rescue to get the K-12 saws. We had seen an overhead door, and thought we could make another entry there. But as I went to start the saw, the deputy chief's driver came running up to us. He said the deputy chief wanted us right away. Two men from Engine 8 were reported missing.

Once we got the order to go back in, we put down our saws and grabbed our steel cables. They have hooks on the end, for hooking to outsides of buildings. You use them for guidelines when you go inside. You keep your hand on the cable and never let go. That way, if you gotta leave, you know you're coming back out.

The cables are about fifty feet in length; I think we grabbed a couple hundred feet of them. A building this deep in size, we figured we needed that much. Then we went back to make another entry. The entire pier, not just the warehouse, was burning at this point. Underneath the pier, also, was fully involved. It had gotten some wind, and that wind was like gasoline. It just went up like, *poof.*

We didn't know what to expect once we got inside. We didn't know if the fire had penetrated the floor entirely. But we were going in there anyway. We had to make an attempt to find the two guys. Anybody on this fire department would do it. This is a ballsy department in my opinion.

Five of us went inside from the Rescue Company, but there was an instant problem. The fire was overlapping the door we just came in. An engine company tried to knock it down, but there was too much fire. So now we had fire behind us, and we knew we'd soon have heavy fire in front. It was determined that we could not stay inside.

We were informed outside that both men from Engine 8 had just been found. They were located in another part of the building. Both men were still alive and on their way to the hospital.

We were also informed at this time about Lieutenant Minehan. They said he was missing. His entire company, Ladder 15, had gone in the same door we had, to look for the two missing members of Engine 8. Like us, they had encountered great fire and heat and determined they had to leave. But as they turned to go, the lieutenant got separated from his crew. And he got lost in there.

I looked at the warehouse burning. I prayed he wasn't inside. Maybe he'd gotten out some way we didn't know.

Then they asked our Rescue if we could get in there again.

If they got a couple of lines in that front door, we said we would give it our best shot.

So they got some lines in there, and they started hitting the fire and knocking some of it down. We took the cables again and in we went. But we were not able to penetrate very deep. The fire by then had burned right through the floor. For the third time that night, we were driven out of the building. That's when I looked at the water.

I said, "Maybe he was able to get out a window. Maybe he jumped in the harbor. He could be hanging on to a pier. A piling or something."

Right away, we had divers in the water. It was probably 2:00 A.M., but with that amount of fire beneath the pier, the water was all lit up. You could see pretty well. There was no sign of Stevie Minehan.

We ended up there until first daylight. By then, it had already been determined that he was lost. But then, around 7:00 A.M., the commissioner asked if we could get in there again. So we went in again and took a look. Most of the fire was pretty much knocked down, but the walls had collapsed. Sections of the roof had dropped on top of the pier. Parts of the pier had dropped into the water. There was scattered debris all over, pieces of roofs and walls. We lifted the debris, looking everywhere. We were in there two hours when one of the Rescue members hollered to me.

He said, "Hey, I found him."

I went over and looked and there was Stevie. He was the farthest point in the warehouse that you could possibly be. It meant we would never have found him anyway.

That made us feel a little bit better. If we had found him right inside the front door, we would have felt terrible. This way at least we didn't miss him, you know?

Before we had gone in to find him, we had been told not to touch him if we did. Because if Stevie's own company wanted to remove him, with our assistance, they would have that option. *Only* if they didn't feel up to it, would we bring him out ourselves.

The commissioner and the chaplain came in. The chaplain gave Stevie his last rites. Then the commissioner called in Ladder 15.

He said, "You guys want to take him out?"

They said, "Yeah, we do."

So they took him out and we gave them a hand. He was later pronounced dead.

It turned into a very big story. Not only in the city of Boston, but in all the surrounding cities and towns. His funeral was carried on all the TV stations here, and the public was extremely sympathetic. They raised quite a bit of money for his family. The outpouring was unbelievable. I think it was because of the way he died. If Stevie was inside there to save a civilian, or if he died because his fire truck flipped, it wouldn't have been the same. But he died trying to save two other firemen. He knew they needed help and he went in.

Stevie's death hit close to home for me. We are a very tight family in this department. Even to this day, if we go on a rescue call and run into Ladder 15, I stand there and look at their truck. I look at the front seat. I still think, *Where's Stevie? He should be there.*

Steve was in the wrong place, wrong time. He wasn't even at the fire at the beginning. He was what we call "covering" for another station that night. But Steve knew this other fire was going down. So rather than pulling their truck into this station, they took a position down the street. If the warehouse fire struck another alarm, this way they'd be ready to go.

That is how he was—a real go-getter. And once the shit hit the fan, his company got right in there. They went in to find these guys who'd gotten trapped, and Steve Minehan wound up getting trapped himself. The last thing everyone heard on the radio was Stevie's voice on his own radio.

He said, "Ladder 15 to firemen. I'm trapped."

After he died, the media really jumped on the racial angle. Here is a white guy, Irish Catholic, and he was in there looking for two black firefighters. Because it was Boston, they really played it up. I never thought they should. We are the fire department. We don't care what color our firefighters are. We don't care what color the citizens are. We just go in and save them.

That warehouse was vacant. Yes, he went inside there to find two firefighters, but those two men and their crew went in there when it was empty. That's a big issue for us across the country. When property is at stake, but no human lives, is it worth risking our firefighters' lives?

We hear it all the time. "It's a big, vacant warehouse. Why would you want to go in there?"

You have to go in. There could be someone in there. A homeless person or something. You know for a *fact* it's vacant?

There's another reason we must go in. If we don't go in there and put that fire out, that building burns, and livelihoods burn with it. I've been to many warehouse fires, restaurant fires, small-company fires, where the workers show up the next morning. They thought they were going to work. And now they're not. Literally, they go home unemployed. Now how do they get by?

But if we get in there fast and put the thing out? We've had it that way, too. People come by while you're packing hose.

They say, "Thank you for saving our jobs."

That means a lot to us. You can just see the gratitude on their faces.

Back in September of this past year, we had a fire lieutenant die in the line of duty. He had about thirty years on. He died in a carpet warehouse. He was not more than ten feet inside when the roof collapsed and killed him. I'm not sure anyone actually sent him in; he probably went in of his own volition. But it made a lot of people in this department stop and think: there is *no* building worth risking the life of a person.

That's why we always need to err on the side of safety. I don't mean just sit there and watch it burn. But we can always make an exterior attack, ventilate it, and when things clear up, we can reconsider our position. But sending people into a building to save the insurance company from having to pay a bigger claim? There's no firefighter on earth that needs to pay that price.

As an officer, if I think an operation is a bad one, but it's only going to cost property, I'll probably follow orders. Maybe I don't know the big picture my bosses do.

But if someone tells me to put another firefighter at risk, I won't do it. I can't. And by "at risk," it could only be my perception. Maybe one of my bosses sees it differently. That's fine. But I'm staying with my position. They can see it differently with another officer.

If it's a vacant structure, we'll treat it as such. We're still charged up to do the job. But we take our time. We make sure no one gets hurt putting out a piece of trash, which is basically what the fire has turned it into.

When a building has people inside, that's a different story. We will clearly take more risks. When they tell us, "Reported people trapped," you can see it in our eyes en route to the fire. If we don't come through for them, people may die.

It was a Sunday morning. It was summertime, so we had our windows open. I was sleeping at home, about to wake up and go in to the firehouse. A few minutes before six, I heard someone screaming outside our bedroom window.

I recognized the voice and stuck my head out the window. My next-door neighbor was yelling to me for help.

There was fire in her house and her mom was in there. I knew her mom and she was eighty years old.

I yelled, "I'm coming down!"

I didn't have a shirt on, but I had slept that night in some cut-off sweats. So I bolted out of the room, told my wife to call 911, threw on my work shoes and ran downstairs. By the time I got outside, I could see smoke seeping out their windows.

I asked her, "Where's your mother's bedroom at?"

She said it was in the front part of the house. I asked if the front door was open. She said yes, so I ran to the front door. It all happened fast. I didn't think about getting hurt. I just ran into the building. I know how fire is and time is a major factor.

Smoke was starting to push out the front doorway, so I got in the crawl position and crawled inside the front entrance. Then I crawled up five or six steps to their first-floor apartment. Once I crawled in their door, I could feel the heat and smoke building up.

About eight feet inside their apartment, I saw another doorway. That's where the fire was concentrated at. As I went through that doorway, I kind of stood halfway up.

All I could see was the woman on the bed. Even though she was unconscious, I knew she was alive. I could see her body twitching, still reacting to the flame.

As I made my way toward her, the flames were already starting to jump up the sides of her mattress. She was right in the center, so at first I tried to put my arms around her, in a bear hug position, and pull her off the bed that way. But with the flames now coming through the mattress, my hands and arms were starting to burn. She was slipping out of my hands, because my skin was melting.

So I tried something different. I pulled her arms toward me and got a lock on her wrists. With that grip, I started dragging her off the bed. At one point she slipped from my hands and we both fell into the curtains. They were on fire, and I felt the burning sensation right on my buttocks. When I stood back up, I started feeling woozy from the heat. It was almost as if I was in a drunken state. But I wasn't going to stop. We were already halfway out.

I grabbed her wrists again. I kept dragging her body across the floor. The room was becoming more involved in flames, but there was more fire than smoke, so I could see enough to spot her bedroom door. Just before we got there, her hip hit a chair that was sitting by the door. She got jammed between the chair and the doorway. The doorway, by that time, was on fire, and that did some damage to me. I got burned on my back, my upper arm and my shoulder.

I pried loose the chair and untangled the woman, then I continued dragging her through the apartment. I was close to passing out when I got through her front door, so I just took her out to the hallway steps, jumped over her body and ran downstairs. By then, there were people assembled down there.

I said, "Come on! Help me get her down the stairs!" No one came up, so I went back up myself. I dragged her down the steps, then a couple guys helped me drag her out to the lawn.

First, I opened her airway. Her breathing was barely there, and I didn't want it to stop. Her tongue was black from smoke. I mean black like shoe polish. Then I did some compressions on her chest, a couple respirations into her mouth. She started breathing at more of a normal pace. Then my wife ran up with the woman who lived below us. Together, they started peeling off her burnt clothing. By that point she was breathing on her own, even though she was unconscious. That was a good sign. Firefighters were already showing up, and I thought she could hold on until paramedics arrived.

I stood up at this point and walked back and forth. That's when I started feeling extremely hot. I actually felt like I was on fire, so I asked my next-door neighbor to hose me down. But when my neighbor hit me with his garden hose, I screamed for him to stop. The water was hitting my burns and it hurt like hell. So I yelled out to my wife. I told her to run upstairs and call 911 again.

I said, "Tell them we're going to need a second ambulance."

While we waited for the ambulance to come, I realized that I was in pretty bad shape. The adrenaline had worn off and the pain was sinking in. My body started shaking uncontrollably. I was going into shock.

The firemen told me to sit down on the sidewalk. Once I did, I saw the damage I'd done. The skin on my left arm was hanging off and melted. On my left hand, the skin melted there had fused together my fingers. My fingernails had also fallen off.

I thought that was pretty much it—I thought my left arm and hand were burned up. But it turned out I had burns over 30 percent of my body. Actually, I had burns almost everywhere, but only 30 percent were third-degree. Most of that was sustained by my upper body, because I went into there without a shirt.

The first thing they did at the hospital was put in a catheter. Then they tried hooking me up to the IV, but my arms were so burnt they couldn't get into the veins. Instead, they stuck two IVs into my femoral artery. So I had these two big needles going in next to my groin.

They then proceeded to take me into the scrub room, which is just a steel bed with hoses all around it. They started washing and scrubbing off my burnt skin, probably the worst thing I've ever felt in my life. I think I can take most pain pretty well, but I screamed at the top of my lungs when they took me in there. Everybody screamed. You could hear each person they brought in. You have to scream. You have to let it out.

After I was scrubbed, they rubbed this cream called Silvadine all over me. Over the cream, they wrapped me up like a mummy. They told me I would swell up, and I swelled up like a balloon. One eye was completely shut. The other one, I could barely see out of. The swelling came from the burns, and also all that intravenous fluid.

They listed me in critical condition.

For the next three days, they did their scrubbings two or three times a day. After my fourth day there, they took me in for my skin graft operation. The doctor said since I was young and in real good shape, they would try and do the whole thing in one operation. It lasted somewhere between eight and twelve hours. They stripped the good skin off my legs and lower back, and they grafted it onto the places where I had third-degree burns. Then they stapled the skin so it would remain in place. When I came out of surgery the next morning, I had about fifteen hundred staples on my left side.

When I woke up from that, the guys I work with were there. So was my wife. I couldn't talk with this tube going in my throat, so I just scribbled notes. I told them I was fine, but I wanted to know when this doctor was taking this tube from my throat. I really wasn't fine, though. There were areas on my left arm where the skin grafts didn't take. Those areas had formed large open wounds. I couldn't sleep that night or several nights after. Not only from the burns, but all that sweating you do when you're all bandaged up. I have to tell you, some nights it felt like torture. There were some moments, you know, I wished I was dead.

I was also dealing with the psychological thing. I mean about my burns, the way I looked. I kept thinking about that day when they'd let my children see me. Our oldest daughter was nine, our son was almost five, and our little girl was two. I had already dropped about forty pounds, and I had been gone three weeks. I was afraid our two-year-old wouldn't know me. All that stuff was playing on my mind.

Finally, about three or four days before I got released, they let the children come. My smallest child ran right up to me. I picked her up and she knew it was her dad. Wow, did that feel great.

At first, with those open wounds, it didn't look like I'd

be going home too quickly. The doctor said he was guessing about six weeks. I couldn't wait that long. After twenty-two days, I said, "I want to go home. I've shown you people that I can walk. I can exercise. I can handle it. Let me go home."

So they gave my wife some lessons on how to treat me at home. She was just wonderful. She would change my bandages and bathe me. She would help me eat. We hung in there together, but it got hard sometimes for both of us. I was off work for nine months—a real up-and-down time, emotionally. I was still self-conscious about my looks. There were times I doubted why my wife was with me. I didn't want her to be with me out of pity. When you get burned like that, all those crazy things go through your mind.

It took awhile for my head to get straight. Sometimes out of frustration, I'd go off the deep end and punch a wall. It was pretty bad, but my wife just stuck with me the whole way through. I needed that from her. I needed that sense of security.

The rescue effort I made was actually successful: the elderly woman survived. She stayed in the hospital for about six months, then her family put her in a nursing home. Unfortunately, she died in the nursing home about four months later. This entire time, there was never a knock at our door from her daughter and son. They never said one word. Never even, "Is everything okay?"

At first, that was hard to deal with. Especially for my wife. She saw her husband get burned, and this family was so cold.

I told my wife, "I understand how you feel, but you should stop being upset. I don't regret what I did."

I never have regretted it. It doesn't matter who was inside that building, how old the person was, or how the family was afterwards. What I did was right. I took the extra step. I'll always be proud of that.

For that particular rescue, I wound up winning several big awards. I got first prize that year from *Firehouse* magazine. I received the Lambert Tree Award, the highest award from the city of Chicago. There were state awards and national awards, and an international award from the International Association of Fire Chiefs. For that ceremony, they flew my wife and myself to California. They took us to Disneyland and Universal Studios. They put us up at a nice hotel.

It was great. All of that kind of recognition was. We have a real good fire department here in Chicago. I felt honored to carry on that tradition.

COURAGE, PEER PRESSURE, AND FEAR

We had a truck crew up on a roof. It was a chickenshit, nothing fire, but it burned away the roof they were standing on. The first guy went through the roof with his sounding tool. He fell right into the fire. The guy behind him tried to go in after him. This guy who fell in was his friend. Plus, this second guy had been in Vietnam. He was a tunnel rat there. So he was no stranger to brave acts.

He *wanted* to go in the fire and get his friend, but his captain saw him and grabbed him before he could. It was the right thing to do. We would have had two men down instead of one.

I was on the ground when it happened, advancing a hose line, when we heard we had a fireman go through the roof. I saw our guys, in record time, cut through and rip open a commercial metal door. They just ripped those doors apart and ran in and got him. He was dead at the time, pulseless, nonbreathing. So they administered CPR and brought him back. Although he survived, he never returned to the job. He burned up his hands too badly. He couldn't perform his firefighting duties.

So that was the bravest thing I've seen so far: one guy ready to dive in a fire to save his friend.

We just lost four firefighters here in Seattle. It happened on a Thursday night. You know where the real acts of courage are? They're in the men and women who went to work Friday morning, knowing that four of their colleagues just died the night before.

Courage is not a topic we talk about. The opposite, maybe. If you find somebody who is a coward, that will be discussed. Often, in that person's presence. Fortunately, there aren't too many firefighters like that.

When you roll up on a scene, a good firefighter will reach down for what he needs. In order to get the job done, he is willing to put aside his own health and welfare.

A bad firefighter is going to back off. All he's concerned about is self-preservation. You can see it at a fire. You are coming off your rig. There might be a few companies already on the scene—and you will see some firemen lagging back.

You just walk right by them. You don't even pay attention.

As a captain, a lot of times I should really be hanging

back. Not standing out in the street or anything, but going a little slower, observing things. But when we force that door, I always find myself wanting to lead the charge. Everybody wants the respect of their peers.

The peer pressure is real. Junior high school doesn't have the peer pressure we do.

Because everyone wants to be known as a good fireman. "Hey, he's a good fireman"—no one can say much better about you. And you have to understand, that has no correlation to what kind of person you are. You might be divorced three times, a deadbeat on bills, or a lot of other things. But he's a good fireman, you know? And that, to a fireman, is really what matters. We're very, very competitive. Everyone wants to do it better than the next guy. Nobody ever wants to be known as the slacker, the bum, or God forbid, the coward.

We had a fire in a five-story apartment house. We could see people jumping out the windows, trying to make this tree.

My job was to cut through the fence on the side of the building. After I got it open, some other guys were gonna come through with ladders.

Guess what? I couldn't get the saw started. I mean, I got it started and then it conked out. I'm thinking, *My God! Come on! Get this thing started!*

So now I see the guys coming with the ladders, and I still can't get it started, and I'm in panic mode. I'm looking, double-checking everything, and one guy goes, "Give it to me!"

I said, "No! I gotta get this thing!"

Then I looked down. I had inadvertently kicked the on/off switch. I kicked it back up, boom, got it started, cut through the fence and we got the ladders in. But just in the nick of time.

I always felt bad about that. Even if just for that moment, I wondered if my peers considered me incompetent. That's why I never gave that guy the saw. If I did that, I'd be dead. My reputation would be destroyed.

One time, on the truck, we dragged a woman out of a four-story apartment building. We arrived there expecting to do ventilation, but our engine company was still out at another call. So we get to this fire and everyone's standing outside, yelling that people are trapped. So we just went running in there. We didn't even have time to put our masks on. And in the process of pulling this woman out, I threw up three times from taking too much smoke.

After she was on her way to the hospital, I spent the rest of the fire sitting on the curb with my head between my legs. It felt like a herd of buffalo running through my head. I had carbon monoxide poisoning from the smoke. I should have gone to the hospital, but I was only three years on the job. And back then we had this big thing about sucking it up: "You can handle it, man. That wasn't so bad."

I wound up not getting treated, and I had headaches and nausea for three days. But that's the way we are in the fire department, especially when we're young. We sometimes let our image dictate our actions.

Firemen love to gossip. If you get a reputation for being a bum, word travels fast. So when you go out to fires, you will work yourself into the ground. Just so nobody else thinks you're a puss.

A minority of guys get carried away. We call them cowboys. They want to look so brave to other firemen, they get to a fire and start doing stupid things. They're running wild in there, running in no direction. They're dangerous to themselves, and to everyone else who comes in contact with them. Because you always want an escape route at a fire, but they rush in helter-skelter, and suddenly they're in a place with no way out. Now you and the rest of the crew have to go in and get them.

I don't feel any peer pressure. The only thing I have to prove is to myself.

Anybody who says they've never experienced fear is lying through their teeth. We've all been scared to death.

I've been at it twenty-nine years and I still have that doubt: *I was lucky that last one and managed to hang in there, but what about the next one? Maybe I'll just drop the line and run down the hallway. Maybe next time, I'll just bail out.*

If you're not scared in some situations, we're gonna take you to the doctor.

You're supposed to be scared. Especially as an officer. If you're not scared for your men, what can happen to

them, then you're really fucked up. If you're in denial—
hey, man, nothing can happen—you shouldn't be allowed
to command other men. Because *anything* can happen
inside a fire.

So a little fear is good. It keeps you right on the ball.
The key is to not let your fear paralyze you.

**We once had a big training exercise in a building that
was about to be destroyed anyway.** At the same time a
crew was working inside, the point of the exercise was to
ventilate the roof.

First we torched the place off. Then they opened the
roof. But the Santa Anas were blowing hard that day. So
once the roof got opened, the Santa Anas blew all the
gases and smokes into this attic space. It built up heat,
and built up heat, and pretty soon it just exploded.

Two of our guys were on the crew inside. They were
manning the nozzle. The two backup guys on the nozzle
were our guys, too. When the backup guys saw this shit
storm coming at them, both of them ran. Didn't say a
word to the guys on the nozzle.

Well, the two guys on the nozzle were busy and never
saw anything coming. The first nozzle man, in fact, never
saw it coming until it hit him. The fire melted his helmet
right onto his head. It burned him all over his body, even
with all his protective clothing on.

I went to see him about two or three weeks later.
That's how long it took before he could have visitors. He
hadn't even walked yet, his legs were burnt so bad.

I brought him a six-pack of beer. Smuggled it in. We
had a few beers.

He said, "I gotta walk, but they won't let me."

So I got me a doctor smock and a clipboard, and I got
him up and started to walk him around.

He said, "Oh, man. This feels so good to walk."

But pretty soon his legs were bleeding through his bandages.

I said, "Come on. We better get you back now."

He said, "Thanks. It really felt good to walk." Then I got out of there before the doctors came back.

He got burnt so bad, he never came back. All because those two guys had bailed on him.

I've never seen that before at a real fire, but I have seen guys who are timid. They pussyfoot around, when they really should go in and hit it hard. On the other hand, there are guys like me. Guys who might be *too* gung ho. So far I've been lucky. But maybe, someday, it will fuck me up.

If you're worth anything at all in the fire department, you're *always* gauging yourself against the next guy. You use it as motivation, and that helps you excel.

But there were two guys I worked with who honestly scared me. Their names were Pete Bondy and Glenn Harris. Excellent firefighters. If something ever happened to me at a fire, I'd want Pete Bondy and Glenn Harris coming in after me. That's how I felt about them.

But like I said, they scared me. They'd go into these situations and do these things, and you had to do them, too, if you were their partner. Before we'd go on a call, I'd watch them and think, *Can I take what these guys can?*

I have a funny story about one of these guys in particular. Pete Bondy had scars all over him. Scars and burns from getting banged and beat up. He had a tremendous tolerance for pain. He had a tremendous tolerance for heat. We all swore that the nerve endings in this guy's body were deeper down in his skin. There was only one time I was able to stay with Pete, and that's when they first invented the Nomex hood. With the Nomex hood, your ears and neck wouldn't get burned so bad.

One day Pete comes up to me.

He says, "Hey, look what Jack just gave me."

And this guy is holding a freaking Nomex hood. I'm thinking to myself, *Unbelievable*. Now *what do I do to stay with this guy?*

There was one fellow in the fire department who was looked up to as this great firefighter. He would go into these really tough places and do these tough things. And that's great. But his pride of always wanting to be the first one in, of always getting the first water on the fire, could sometimes cause us problems.

For example, one time we have a pier going. It's twelve hundred feet long, maybe a hundred feet wide, encased in a building. It's burning pretty good from one end to the other. Well, the chief wants to go into a defensive mode of firefighting. You just stand back and put the master streams on the fire.

But he's got this guy with a line in the front door, saying, "Give me a few more minutes. I think I can handle it."

Well, now the chief can't put the master streams to work, because it's going to cook these guys in there. The chief is telling the guy to get the hell out of there, but the guy won't leave the building. He thinks he can put out the fire with this one line he's got. Meanwhile, the pier is burning down. So this is a place where pride, this macho stuff, got in the way.

Whatever engine company arrives first, the fire is theirs to put out. The worst possible blow to anyone's pride is to have another company put out your fire. You never want other guys coming out of a fire, saying, "Here you go, man. Here's your line."

We've got a very experienced rescue squad. Frequently, at a fire where there is no one to rescue, we'll follow the hose line in, to assist the engine company fighting the fire. Sometimes we'll get a company that's a little green. By green, I mean they don't go to a lot of fires. It's just not a busy house. So having that lack of experience, they might not move as quickly or have the same savvy as us. So when you get up behind those guys, you talk to them. You talk them into the fire.

You just say, "You got it, babe. Come on, don't worry, you got it. Shut it down. Let's move, let's move."

Sometimes in that situation, if the other guys are spent, or they're out of air, we'll take the line and we'll go ourselves. Sometimes we don't make any friends that way. But we're not there to make friends.

In the old days, we tried to steal lines off everybody. If we pulled it off, I pity the poor sons of bitches we took the line from. We had no shame. We'd use any trick we could. Like, "Hey, your captain wants you out in front. Don't worry, just go. I'll hold the line for you."

Then the guy would go out and his captain would go ballistic. "What the fuck are you doing here? Get back in there and get that line."

It was like a soldier with his gun. Even if you were dying, you never gave up your line.

Everyone wants to be the guy on the nozzle. There is

nothing else like it. You are the guy with the weapon in his hand. You're the guy who's going to put this thing out. Yeah, you want the nozzle. That's the place to be.

I still have this captain who tells us, "You don't give the nozzle to anyone. You hold on to the nozzle. That's *our* nozzle."

Because guys will come up at a fire, and they'll be saying, "Pass me that nozzle, will you?"

You'll be saying, "Fuck you! This is our nozzle. We pulled it in here. What do you want me to put out with it? *Show* me where you want the nozzle. I'll take it there for you. But don't be touching my nozzle. That's *my* nozzle."

I don't know how it evolved, but that's the glory job if you work on an engine. You're setting the pace. You have the power. If you feel hot in some direction, you can turn that nozzle and hit it with the hose, and you'll feel better about it. If you think it's getting real hot over your head, you can stick it straight up in the air and let it all shower down. It's a pride thing and a control thing. But it's not like guys will go in there and punch each other out. It's a positive thing. They're fighting to go in and take care of business.

You've got pride between companies and pride between whole departments. Not taking anything from anyone else, I still say New York has the best fire department in the world.

Nobody does the kind of volume we do. And you always got so much spectacular stuff going on. I didn't coin the phrase, and the rest of the country won't like it, but we've been called the rock and roll stars of the fire service.

I was assigned to Rescue 3 in upper Manhattan. It covers the Bronx and Harlem, and it also responds to any major emergency in New York City. One evening in September, almost at midnight, we got a call on a plane crash at La Guardia Airport.

It wasn't my first one. Before I was a firefighter, I was a New York City police officer. We went on a plane crash then at Kennedy Airport. The plane came short of the runway and crashed on landing. Every passenger died; I think about 60 people. So this time, I wasn't sure what we would encounter. We were advised on the way that people were in the water, but we didn't know their condition.

On Rescue 3, we have a small lifesaving boat. We also have exposure suits, for the elements in the New York City water. In this specific area where the plane was, the currents are swift. As a matter of fact, there is a part they call Hell's Gate. It's a notorious place where they lose a lot of boats.

That was the kind of stuff that was going through my mind, because I already knew I was going into the water. That's how we do it here. We have six firefighters on the rig. The officer and the driver sit up front, and four men sit in back. So right away in the back of the rig, we make up the assignments. Two guys will go into the water. They are the entry team. The other two guys will stay nearby and watch you. They're the safety people. This way everyone knows the plan, so we can jump off the rig and go into action.

We were one of the first pieces of apparatus there. But when we got to the end of the runway, there was a twenty-foot drop into the water. There was also a pier.

The plane was crashed in the water near the pier. It was a
Boeing 737, a pretty big plane. The pilot had tried taking
off, but he didn't think they had enough power. Once they
tried to abort, it was too late. They couldn't stop the
plane. It skidded off the runway and into the East River.

Naturally, there was a lot of hysteria. Passengers were
screaming. There were passengers on the wings and in
the water. The plane had torn in half. It looked like a bent
piece of pipe, with the tail section bending down into the
water. The main fuselage was separated from that, and
the only thing holding the plane up was some pilings.
They looked like telephone poles stuck in the water.
Fortunately, that's what the plane fell on. Otherwise,
many more people would have been killed.

Our particular unit does not have scuba gear. We more
or less do surface-water rescues. So with this twenty-foot
drop, we lowered a portable ladder and climbed down
that to the water. I didn't feel the cold with my exposure
suit on, but I could smell fuel. Everyone could. That was
a fear for our supervisors there: they thought the fuel
could ignite.

But they were worried about it more than us. We had
victims. We had to take the risk.

I swam right to the tail section, while another firefighter went to the wing. The tail-section door was par-
tially open. I opened it up the rest and went inside the
cabin. I started searching the rubble with my flashlight. It
was a wreck, a mass of mangled steel and mangled
chairs. The tail section was also submerged in water, so
the cabin had maybe a foot of water inside.

The lower part of the tail was in the water. That's
where I was, so I had to walk up. Going up what used to
be the aisle, I called out for victims and searched with my
flashlight. When I got near the top I saw two people. A
mother and daughter. Obviously both dead.

I thought that was it. I thought nobody else was in there. But I yelled again anyway. And I heard a faint cry for help.

I held up my flashlight and I could just see a face. The closest I could get was seven or eight feet away, but I could see it was a woman. She couldn't move. The floor of the plane had actually met the ceiling, and she was totally pinned inside her chair. As it turned out later on, she had a broken arm and a broken shoulder, broken ribs and a broken leg.

Her name was Mrs. Crews. She was about sixty years old.

I said to her, "I see you. We're gonna get you out of here."

Then I got on my handie-talkie. I told my lieutenant out on the pier, "I have a victim pinned in the rear of the plane."

I said I was going to need a lot of tools. For sure the Jaws of Life.

Within ten minutes, Chris Blackwell, another fireman, joined me from Rescue 3. So did Mike Milner from Rescue 4. Standing inside together, the three of us decided we wouldn't leave her. We told her that. Because now there was all this talk on the handie-talkie. The officers thought the tail section might break off, then sink in the water with all of us inside. The woman could hear those radio transmissions.

So we told her not to worry. We weren't going anywhere without her.

She said, "Oh, thank God. Thank God."

As the rescue went on, the tail section kept taking more and more water. Our chiefs were telling us to abandon the rescue. We kept telling them we weren't giving up; it was just a matter of time before we would have her out.

It turned into quite a bit of time. Even though we got the Jaws of Life, there was no way we could operate it inside. The Jaws run on gasoline and there were too many fumes. It would have been a disaster. So what they wound up doing was pretty smart. They shot a tower ladder over the water, with this power unit on it, so they could power the Jaws from outside.

As we started cutting debris to get to Mrs. Crews, we were also administering psychological first-aid. And she was very good with that part, too. She never panicked. She kept her wits. She told us she had a son in the marines. He was a drill instructor. I told her he would be proud of the way she was acting.

I said, "You're the one who's keeping us calm. It's supposed to be the other way around."

We just kept working and teasing her like that.

In reality, it was tense for everyone. For one thing, she was sitting behind where the mother and daughter died. She could see them, too. One time, she asked me how they were doing. I told her not too good, only because I thought she already knew. She was one seat below them, and their blood was dripping down in her direction.

Though I kept it to myself, by then some doubt was creeping into my own mind. The plane kept taking more water. There was still a maze of metal between her and us. The chief officers kept screaming that we should abort the rescue, and we kept stalling them. We kept saying "one more minute," and it would turn into another fifteen. It was becoming a race against time. So we just kept cutting away with the Jaws of Life.

When we finally got close enough, we switched to the Ram Tool. We used it to push the bulkhead off of her, then we used it to cut the back of her seat. But even then, she wasn't free. When we tried pulling her out, her foot was caught in a twisted sheet of heavy aluminum. I had to crawl down in there and use a hacksaw.

Once we had her completely loose, we knew our position was still precarious. To get her off the plane, we only had a two-foot clearance to work in. The rest of the cabin was filled with water; it was up to our chest now. So we held her over our heads, the three of us, and we were able to carry her like that.

When we got her to the door, next we had to get her onto a raft. And we were in a pretty swift current here.

So I told the other guys, "Whatever we do, we cannot drop her."

She was all broken up and she was older, too. We didn't want to drop her in twenty-five feet of water.

We got her on the raft with Lieutenant Tom Williams' help. By then we were exhausted, dripping with diesel fuel. So other people took care of her from then on.

It was a great day for all the rescuers there. In a Boeing 737, the only two deaths were that mother and daughter. But much of that credit must go to the passengers. They didn't panic and jump into the water. They waited in the plane until help arrived. Had more people jumped in with the current so fast, you're looking at multiple drownings.

The next time I saw Mrs. Crews was later that afternoon. Chris Blackwell and myself went to visit her at the hospital. Usually when you save someone, you never get to see them again. But this was really nice. She had asked to see the guys who got her out of the plane.

That was probably the high point of the whole thing. She kissed us and hugged us. She said she didn't think she was gonna make it, until she heard my voice. And once we told her we wouldn't leave, she said she knew for sure she'd get out alive. This is what she told myself and Chris. It was real emotional for us.

Later that year, I received the highest award in the New York City Fire Department. It's called the Gordon Bennett Medal. They only give one a year, and who do you think showed up on Medal Day? Mrs. Crews came all the way from Virginia. She was the one who called me up onstage, then she gave a little talk about what happened. That was really something. Nobody even told me she was coming.

We still exchange Christmas cards. Sometimes she'll call our house when I'm at work, and she and my wife will talk. When her son the drill instructor was in the Gulf War, my kids wrote letters to him and he wrote them back. One time he sent my young daughter a Marine Corps patch, and she was all excited. He also wrote her a letter saying what a good job we'd done in helping his mom. I'm very proud of that letter. This is an instructor in the marines.

Firefighters aren't in it for the glory. When you go on a call, your goal is not to get thanked or win an award. You just want the people out safely. You just want to do a professional job.

But looking back on it, this was the ultimate experience I could have. The rescue was successful. The woman and her family were wonderful to us. I was awarded by the New York Fire Department, the biggest and, I think, the best department there is. I was just very fortunate, I feel.

It was about ten at night. We had just finished dinner when we got called to an explosion at the Consolidated Edison plant. The plant runs along the west side of Manhattan. It's three or four blocks long and it generates electricity. The by-product is this superheated steam—about five hundred degrees—which they pipe throughout the city and heat the skyscrapers with. On this night, they had an explosion in one of their steam lines. They had a major steam leak and still had workers inside.

I was the captain of Rescue 4 in Queens, so the plant was just a few minutes from our quarters. It was eerie when we arrived. The escaping steam was making this ear-piercing noise. It sounded like a 747 with all of its engines going at one time.

As a rescue squad, we are normally sent to emergencies of this kind. We search for victims and then try to remove them. This time we followed some Con Ed employees into the plant, to an area where some people had last been seen working. One man was already dead, but we didn't know that yet.

The area we went into was large and open. It looked like the boiler room of a very, very big ship. Obviously, from conditions, this was also where the steam had been released. Initially, I didn't think we could get in there. It seemed beyond our capabilities. But once we worked our way in, we felt we could handle it.

There were six of us in the Rescue. I took one firefighter with me to conduct the search. I told the other fellows to stay in the safe area outside. They'd be our safety team if anything went wrong.

The two of us searched the first level and didn't find anyone. So we climbed the staircase up to the second level. The firefighter with me went searching around the far end of this second level. Visibility was very poor. There was nothing there but open grating, so there was nothing stopping the steam from going from level to level. As he continued walking, it was like he disappeared into a steam cloud.

Right about then, I realized something had changed. Conditions had gotten much worse. If I stayed there much longer, I would start burning up. Everything in my body was telling me to leave.

The only problem was, our firefighter was still inside the steam cloud. If I went to try and find him, it would be like going into a fog bank; I could very well miss him. So I decided to stay right where I was. That firefighter was my responsibility.

It seemed like eternity, but he returned maybe thirty seconds later. He must have felt the same increase in heat: As he hit the open area where I was, he actually turned around to go back the way he came.

That wasn't good. It was like a blast furnace in there now. He needed to get to the exit.

He couldn't hear me with the noise in there, so I kept motioning with my arms. When he realized I was pointing to the exit, he just ran and went diving down the stairs.

Once I knew he went down, I ran for the stairs and dove down also. There was no hesitation at that point. I had to get out of there. I was burning up.

The other firefighter had also gotten burned, but he landed at the bottom of the stairs, which was probably the best spot. That's where the other fellows from our squad were. So all they had to do was reach in and drag him out.

Then they looked up the stairs to see about me. I was halfway down the stairs on a metal landing. According to their accounts, I'd only made it that far when I dove down the stairs. Then the air pack on my back had somehow got jammed in the railing.

All I know myself is that I dove for the stairs. And the next thing, I was stuck. I was struggling to move forward but something was caught. I could move my arms and legs, but I could not progress.

I thought I was dead. There was no two ways about it. I was being baked alive by the heat coming up beneath me. All I could think was, *Dear God, please take me.*

When you're being cooked, you don't want to hang around for very long.

Fortunately, I passed out at that point.

As I found out later on, the firefighters were trying to rescue me. They came up the stairs to get me, but they were being burnt also in these conditions. So one firefighter would make a mad dash in, pull me a little, and have to get back out. They did it like a relay, all three of them rotating, trying to get a hand on me and grab me. Finally, with this action, they managed to free me. Once I was freed up they pulled me out of the heat.

Right outside the steam area, I regained consciousness immediately. But I couldn't breathe. I was going into shock. My mind was still functioning, but I was piercingly hurt. I couldn't help myself, or even stand. So they had to pick me up and carry me out of there, and that turned into a tragedy of errors. We were buried inside this huge complex, and there was nobody there to give us directions. Our guys couldn't make any contact on their radio. Not with that roaring steam drowning everything out.

It took a long time to find our way outside. But once we did, the air temperature was in the upper thirties, and I could feel the cooling effect on my body. They brought me into an ambulance. The EMS people started working on me. They cut away my clothing and they poured water on me. I must have still been in some kind of shock; everything seemed to be moving in slow motion.

We ended up at New York Hospital's burn center. They put me on a respirator and started the intravenous. Then people started coming to visit me there. The fire commissioner, the police commissioner, Mayor Dinkins—all the dignitaries came in. When *they* all start showing up, it means you're in a bad way.

I remember being conscious while they were there. I

remember writing down notes to all their questions. But all this time in the back of my mind, I was saying to myself, *Where are the drugs? I wish they would give me something to knock me out.*

Some good friends of mine had gotten the word what happened. They brought in my wife. When she walked into the emergency room, there was nothing but firefighters in there, even a few she recognized. Nobody would look at her. She said it was the worst feeling in her life. They couldn't look her in the eyes. They all thought I was dead, or about to be.

It seemed like a long time before they could give me drugs. First they had to do all the initial care, and they don't want to do that with any drugs in you. Finally, after hours and hours, they gave me morphine and I drifted off. For the next two weeks, I was in something like a drug-induced coma.

Morphine does the job. You don't feel the pain. But I wouldn't recommend it to anybody. While I was taking the morphine those two weeks, I created a whole world inside my head. It was part reality and part hallucination. Some parts were terribly frightening. At one point I was certain this one nurse was trying to kill me. It was horrible, absolutely horrible. Like I say, it killed the physical pain. But what was happening in my head wasn't pleasant at all.

It turned out my entire body was burned. But the serious, third-degree burns were from my knees to my buttocks. Also, both my wrists were burned all the way around. From the top of my head to my eyebrows had to be grafted. A section of my neck had to be grafted. I lost pieces of both my ears. I lost part of my nose. They had to rebuild my eyelids. That's just a fast run-down of the burns on the outside. Plus, there was some damage to my throat and lungs. That was actually the main concern—the respiratory part. How much steam I inhaled.

Psychologically, it was very difficult. For twenty years, you are in the position of helping other people. Suddenly, you are the victim. Now you have to rely on everyone else, and that took quite some time for me to adjust to. The toughest part was the burden I put on my family. I remember crying in the hospital, just thinking about what I had done to them. I didn't want them to worry, and I knew they were. I kept trying to communicate to my wife, "Don't worry. I'll be all right. It doesn't look good, but I'll be all right." It was a hard thing to get through. I couldn't help myself, let alone anyone else.

It took me a long time to even look in the mirror. And up until the first time I did, I never realized the extent of my injuries. I mean, I knew they'd done operations on my eyes. I knew they'd grafted my forehead and the top of my head. I knew all that, but somehow I still thought I looked exactly the same. It was my mind, obviously, protecting me in some way. When I finally looked in the mirror, it was very shocking to see the change.

You know what got me through? The support I got.

I got letters from people I'd gone to grammar school with. I got letters from people I'd never met. Firefighters from all over the country were sending me their fire department T-shirts, or these gorgeous baskets of fruit. In the neighborhood we live, they actually organized to show their concern. They delivered a meal to my house every day. Outstanding, delicious meal, but my wife finally said, "Please, only make it a few times a week. There is just so much food!"

If there was even one inch of snow on the ground, the local volunteer firemen would come and shovel my driveway. The support I got was amazing. Unbelievable. Especially from my family. Every day at the hospital, my wife and four daughters were there for me. Every time they came in, they had smiles on their faces.

I even asked my wife, "What did you tell the kids? They were always so upbeat, joking around. It's just what I needed."

My wife said, "I never said a word to them. They figured it out themselves."

I ended up at the burn center for twelve weeks. During this time, I had eight operations. The final one they did was a skin graft on my head. I received that skin from a fireman on Long Island who had died. Either his family or himself, before he died, chose to donate his skin for other burn victims. That made me feel good. While this man was alive, he tried to protect people from fire. Even after he was gone, he was still helping others.

In some way, I also felt that things had come full circle. I was a donor myself in 1990. About six years before that, my daughter Mary came down with a rare form of kidney disease. She was treated by drugs through 1990. But over the years, the disease progressed to the point where Mary would have two choices: go on dialysis or have a kidney transplant. Knowing how hard it is to live a normal life on dialysis, both my wife and I were happy to donate a kidney. So we went in and got checked out and both of us matched. But when the time came up in 1990, I told my wife I wanted it to be me. All I could think about was how much I wanted to do this.

So I went in and did it, and there's no describing the feeling. This was the little girl you cradled in your arms. You held her and tried to protect her. Now she is grown up, and you have a chance to improve her life.

So that's why I felt things had come full circle. I did my share as a donor, for my daughter, and now this dead fireman was helping me.

I'll never forget the day I left the hospital. The president never got better treatment than I did. They had news media outside. A couple of fire trucks. A good crowd of people. There were bagpipes and speeches. Then the fire department presented a plaque to myself and a fireman friend of mine, a guy who had helped me tremendously during my stay. So he also got recognition and I thought that was great.

I assumed that was the end of it. The next thing I know, there's a white stretch limousine waiting to take us home. With a full police escort leading us, they closed down the FDR Drive, closed down the tunnel, closed down the parkways, and we just sped along. When we got one block from where we live, we passed the nursery school where two of my daughters had gone. All these little kids were standing outside. They had one of these banners that said, "Welcome Back."

When I saw that—all these little preschoolers out there—I really got emotional.

I said, "Gee whiz, they're making this into like I'm a hero or something."

The kids took me by surprise. They really made me feel special. Everyone did that day, and it made me realize something. What all those people were doing was celebrating life.

Because everyone knew I could very well have died. But I didn't die. I was on my way home, ready to go on.

That was the celebration, the exuberance, the excitement. We are all still here. We can go on.

It's always there in the back of your mind: Something tragic could happen. But you always think it will happen to someone you don't know. It's not gonna happen to you, or to a close friend.

Well, then it happened to Marty. When he got burnt by that steam, it was very troubling to me. Marty only lives about six houses down from us. He's godfather to one of my kids. He's just one of those strong silent types. His nickname used to be "the monk." Those rare times when he speaks, Marty has that knack that all good captains do. He cuts to the chase without pissing anyone off.

I saw him that first night in the burn center. He was just fading out of consciousness when I got there. He scribbled a few notes on a piece of paper. He didn't look too bad. But then we stayed the whole night in the hospital. In the morning I drove out to pick up one of his daughters at college. By the time we got back to the hospital, it was two that afternoon. His head was twice the size of a basketball. I say this with no exaggeration.

When I first walked into his room, I saw three beds. One was a fireman from another incident, one was an injured worker from Con Edison, and Marty was in the other bed. I walked over to the wrong bed.

The nurse said to me, "You here for the captain?"

I said, "Yeah."

She said, "Well, that's him over there."

That messed me up. Here's a friend of mine I've known for so many years. I could not even recognize him.

One night I was driving Marty's wife home. I had a few cocktails in me.

I was even telling her, "I got real mixed emotions here. Since I was four years old I wanted to be a fireman. Now this job I love so much did this to him."

It wasn't a very rational reaction. We all know the calculated risks we take. But I felt embittered. When everything goes along great, everybody is "rah rah rah" at the firehouse and the parties. We're all full of macho bullshit and bravado. But when one of your buddies gets hurt, it sobers you very fast.

In time, I got over my bitterness. I realized it wasn't the job I was mad at. This job is everything I dreamed of when I was a kid. What was really making me mad was the pain that Marty was in. I wanted it to stop, and I was just looking for somewhere I could vent.

THE SCARIEST THINGS THEY FACE

Any big steam leak like that is always frightening. So are live power lines. But my biggest fear is getting trapped in a fire. I fall through a floor, into a fire. I can't escape and I *know* I can't escape. Those last few moments of terror—that scenario bothers me a lot.

I've been to many funerals. Firefighters I knew and firefighters I didn't. What scares me the most is leaving my family behind.

I'm not a big fan of electricity. One time on a structure fire, I had a rookie with me. It was a large industrial building that was burning. We were assigned to the rear division. We were going to cut a chain fence with a rotary saw, break down this corrugated-metal wall, and attack the fire from that side. So my rookie is holding the saw and he wants to cut something. He doesn't care what it is. But he's *going* to cut something.

So we get the order. "Okay, now cut the fence." Our rookie starts walking forward and I say, "Wait. Let's see what we're doing first. Let's look at the fence. I want to make sure you know exactly how to cut a Cyclone chain-link fence. There's a specific way to do it."

He says, "Okay."

So I walk to the fence to show him how it's done. Well, what's the first thing you do when you walk up to a chain-link fence? You rest your hands on it and you look through it. It's instinct, right? Well, about half a block away, the fire was burning so hot it burned through some power lines. The lines came down on this fence, charging it with about forty-four hundred volts. The moment I touched it, I did a Michael Jackson moon walk and fell right on my ass.

I wasn't hurt from a trauma standpoint, but it had dried out all the fluid in my kidneys and in my gallbladder. Everything in there was boiled. They stuck with me two large IVs full of saline water, and I still didn't have to pee.

Well, none of us likes propane much.

When you get a shooting, you are told not to go in until the police arrive. But sometimes you pull up first and you see somebody down. What do you do? Sit in the rig?

No, you go in. Later on, you realize you were standing next to the shooter. Or you were standing next to the stabber. I fear those calls more than I fear fires. At least fire is a scientific phenomenon. I can predict that a little bit. What I have trouble with is all the crazies.

My great fear is getting caught in a booby trap. These drug dealers don't want people inside their locations. Not cops, not firefighters, not other rival dealers. They want the place secure.

So they'll take a two-by-four and hammer some nails through it with the spike ends up. They'll leave it in front of the door for you to step on. Sometimes they'll remove a couple stairs, so a cop might fall and get hurt. They've gone so far as to put linoleum over a big hole in the floor. In a smoky room, that's something you might not notice. And if you are above the fire, you can end up falling right into it.

I remember this story back in the late seventies. They were taking gasoline and putting it in rubber balloons. They were thumbtacking the balloons to the ceiling. When a fire began, the rubber would melt. The gasoline would splash down and intensify the fire. And this would sometimes happen *after* our people were in there.

The Los Angeles riots. We had no control at all. We had no protection. We had *zero* training for something like this.

We asked for bulletproof vests but our staff said no. They said they would give us a false sense of security. I could not believe that line of reasoning. Did they think we'd go up to a looter and tell them, "Stop looting that store"? That was just flat-out stupid.

Things were all turned around during the riots. It was safer *inside* the fire than it was outside. We would be inside the fire building, and we could hear all the gunfire back outside.

On one fire, we saw people drive a truck right through a storefront window, start carrying out refrigerators and couches. I was standing outside on that one, in a command position. I saw these two guys walking along. I could see it in their eyes. They wanted to mess with me.

But I can't do anything, because I'm in command of these guys who are fighting the fire inside. So these two assholes walk up to me, real casually, and they pull out guns.

One guy says to me, "Maybe we ought to kill you."

I'm standing there holding a radio. Completely at their mercy.

The guy says, "Hey, this is your lucky day."

They just walked off, but they could have easily killed me.

My biggest fear is doing a search above the fire. The fire is on the second floor, and you're in there looking for people on the third. You're on a truck company, so that means you have no water. And the fire is burning right up to where you are.

Being up on a roof. Since I've been on the job, I can name seven guys we've lost on roofs. Going up on the roof is not real glamorous, either. You don't make a rescue up on a roof. You don't get any medal. To be honest with you, I don't like going to the roof. I'd rather be inside the burning building.

SECOND-GUESSING THEMSELVES

We had a job in a school. The school was closed. Most of the fire was in the auditorium. There was a tremendous amount of fire. The smoke was dirty and rotten, like that Styrofoam type of smoke that looks like black garbage. It was a battle, just a horrendous battle. Very hard to make headway.

Finally, we just kept banging and pushing and made some progress. The next thing you know, we had knocked it down pretty well. But then we heard this excited yelling on our handie-talkies. It was obvious something was wrong. So we went outside. Everybody was yelling about a missing fireman. They couldn't find this guy on a truck. And his company was beside themselves.

When a firefighter is missing, it's easy to lose your head and just run amok. But you can't. You gotta get a grip on it. Certain things have to happen. You have to have a roll call. That's where each individual officer of a company gets his men together and does a head count. Once they determine who's missing, they start asking questions. They have to be the right questions.

"Where was he working? What was he doing? Who was the last person to see him?"

Everyone else has got to listen, intently, to what is being said. Because guys can say things and get it a bit turned around, and this is the time when *everything* must come together. This is the ultimate of ultimates. Now you're going in to rescue one of your own.

We put everything aside, and we went back in to find this guy. The smoke conditions were still horrendous in there. This stuff was just laying at ground level, settling in these buildings. On top of that, we're talking about a school, a big area to search, with classrooms, libraries, auditoriums and a gymnasium.

While I was searching one hallway, I could hear guys still yelling on their handie-talkies. It was obvious now; this guy was definitely missing. Because he had a handie-talkie, too. And he wasn't answering.

You know what I did? I missed the door to the room he was in. I missed the door to the library. I couldn't see my hand in front of my face, and I passed right by the damn thing. I kept trying other rooms. Meanwhile, time is passing and this guy is still not answering. But now the smoke is starting to lift a little bit. And I see this door. This library door.

To myself, I said, *Oh, God, I hope not.*

Two guys from his company, young kids, came by and saw this door the same time I did. I went for the door. They went for the door. Went in the door, made a right turn, and here he was. Right there. They started screaming, just screaming. I grabbed the guy, dragged him to the door. Dragged him out into the hall. I started mouth to mouth on him, but he died.

What do you do? You talk to the guys. They tell you it's one of those things. You even know it yourself. You go to so many fires, it's impossible, under zero visibility, to hit it right every time. I gave it everything I had. It wasn't like I saw the door and I was afraid to go in. The hell with that. I just missed it. That's it—I missed it. But still, yes, I was very annoyed with myself. I was pissed. I was bent out of shape. Yeah, you talk to the guys. But I still missed the damn thing.

This was about ten, eleven years ago maybe. I still think about it. Once a year, on Memorial Day, when all the deceased firemen are thought of, I think about it for sure. But you can't let it eat at you. You just got to keep going, so you can do your job. It happens. It happens. It happens with kids. Oh, God, I can't tell you. You go to a job and people are screaming, "There's kids in there, there's kids in there." So you go in, and you kill yourself to find them. I mean that literally. Firemen have been killed because they heard, "Kids are in there." You know this when you go in, and you go in anyway. You go past your limit, because you've got to get that child. You've got to. There's no two ways about it.

And you miss them.

Sometimes, in the ghetto, babies will be sleeping in

drawers. It's one of the places you always want to look. Because if the family has no money for a crib, they'll just open a drawer and put the child in there. And you will miss an infant. You will miss a child. And then when you find the child later, it's like, *Jesus, how the hell? I should have looked . . . I should have looked.*

Do you learn to block it out, so you can try and go home after work, and have a normal life with your wife and kids? Sure you do. Do you forget it? No, you don't. Do the macho guys cry? You better believe it. You supposed to cry in front of the guys? No way. It's impossible. You're not supposed to do that. You're too macho for that.

But you think about them. Always. The people you can't save. You think about them. And you never forget.

Fighting a fire is like a football game. We are like a team. We have books like football teams have playbooks. Our books are full of tactics and procedures. Truck company operations in tenements. Truck operations in fireproof buildings. Truck operations in taxpayers, which are one- and two-story commercial buildings. Engine company operations in private dwellings. And so on. Those are our game plans, and when we pull up to a fire we all know our positions. But once the action starts, no two fires are ever exactly the same. Everything happens fast, and you have to make quick decisions. I mean split-second decisions. Sometimes, later on, when the fire is out and there's time to contemplate, you naturally wonder if those decisions were right.

One night on the truck we had a tenement fire. I was the roof man. My job was to hustle up to the roof, open a hole in it with my pike pole and ax, and relieve the top floor of smoke. That's a very important job in a tenement fire. When most people die in these fires, it isn't from getting burned. They die from smoke inhalation. So you can have fire on the first or second floor, and the people on five and six can be just as endangered. Because once the smoke reaches the top of the building's interior, it mushrooms back down and starts seeping into the apartments.

In a tenement fire, there are usually three routes up to the roof. One is an adjoining building, if it is attached to the fire building. Two is an aerial ladder. Three's the rear fire escape. For me the fire escape is the lousiest option. It not only takes the longest time to get up there, but if fire starts blowing out the rear of the building, and the roof man is coming up the fire escape, he can be walking right into an inferno.

On this fire I went into the adjoining building. But once I got inside, that building ignited, too. Some flames had jumped onto it from the windows next door.

So as I'm going up the stairwell of this second building, there is an elderly woman on the third floor. She's crying, and it's hard to understand her. Then I understand. She's saying her husband is trapped in the rear bedroom of their apartment. Their front door is closed, but there's black, yellowish smoke pushing under their door into the hallway. We call this "pushing under pressure."

So, she wants me to go get her husband. She's crying and practically begging. But that is not my job. So I make a split-second decision on my own. I say okay, I yes her, but I instantly continue up to the roof. Under no circumstances should you deviate from your job. There are people depending on you to open the roof next door.

On my way upstairs I notified the chief. I told him we had two burning buildings now, and I told him what the woman just told me. Then I radioed the roof man from another truck company. I said, "40 Truck roof to 30

Truck roof. In exposure 2, there's supposed to be a guy trapped in a rear bedroom on the third floor."

Once I got on top of the original fire building, I found this small shed. It was on top of the stairwell inside the building. When residents took those stairs to the top floor, they could also keep on going up to the roof. When I opened the shed door, three people fell out. All three had taken some smoke, but all three survived.

I'm an officer now. I'm a lieutenant. And I still tell that story to all the guys on our truck. I want them to perform their own assignments. I want them to see how critical it is. But I do have to admit that this was a hard decision. Not in terms of our tactics and procedures. In that respect, I knew I did the right thing. Morally, it was hard. Because here I was pretty sure that the woman was telling the truth. More than likely, her husband was in that apartment.

By the way, he wound up getting rescued. The roof man I called from 30 Truck rescued him.

Unfortunately, the man died later on from his injuries.

I still felt I made the right call, though. If I had not gone up there, those three people in that shed would have died for sure. They were lucky to be alive as it was.

And that's just how it happens sometimes at a major fire. Nobody will ever say it, but it's like being inside a submarine. You close the door on six people to save ninety-six.

Everyone's got one that sticks in their mind. *Everybody* does.

We had a fire a long, long time ago. I was still a fireman, not yet a captain. It was the Pallozi fire. He was a city supervisor in San Francisco. He had a large three-story home in a well-to-do neighborhood. I was on the rescue squad at the time, so we arrived there on about the second alarm. The building by then was roaring.

There were four children, I think, trapped on the upper floors. We went in the front door, into the front room, and up the stairs to the upper floors. The top three or four stairs were already burned away. So we would have had to leap to make the next floor.

I never made that leap.

Realistically, I knew if I jumped I wouldn't survive. Even if I cleared the steps and made it up to the hallway, I knew all the stairs would be gone within two or three minutes.

People said to me afterwards, "Shake it off. The kids were dead when we got there."

I knew it was true. The place was an inferno. But it still haunts me.

I give my best on every call I go on. I really do. I give 100 percent. So I don't feel bad about any of my actions. But I have felt guilty on certain calls. Not because I didn't do my job, but because of the thoughts I had while I was on the call.

Let's say you've been going on runs all day long. You're hungry. You're starving. You need some recovery time from your tour so far. Finally, dinner is hitting the table—and you get another run.

So you go to another call. Once you are there, someone is facing the biggest crisis of their life. But since this is something you see every day, numerous times, you're thinking about eating dinner. I mean, how cold is that? Someone has been shot or hit by a car, and you're thinking about food.

I once had two people die right in front of me. They died while I was climbing a ladder to get them.

We get a fire about four in the morning. When we pull

up, the police are telling me there's a woman in an air shaft. She's on the third floor.

So I go and get this thirty-eight-foot ladder, and these three cops are helping me with it. All our other guys are busy with other tasks.

We raise the ladder, but it's a real weird raise. The ladder is straight up and down against the building. I start climbing up and it starts falling backwards.

The cops are screaming, "Get down, get down! It's falling!"

So I run back down. I try to maneuver this ladder again, up to the third floor. Meanwhile, I'm scared that this woman will jump on me. That's common, and you can get killed. I mean, if someone jumps on your head from the third floor.

Just as I get the ladder positioned again, I tell her I'm coming to get her.

I say, "Ma'am, I'll be there in a minute."

That same moment I look up and see her nephew. He is in another window now.

I say to him, "I'm coming. I'm coming. Just hold on a minute."

I start climbing the ladder—and the whole second floor lights up. Fire everywhere. It is like an explosion.

To accelerate like that, it must have been arson. It is just rolling from stem to stern inside. Now I can't do anything for them.

To make matters worse, the fire kept going another ninety minutes before we could get inside there. I knew where we'd find that woman, and that's where she was. Right there next to the window, totally charred. The roof caved in on her and everything. It was obscene.

I don't like to think about it. But to be honest with you, I always think about it. I always think, *What if? That first time I put up the ladder, what if I stood it up on the hood of a car?*

I didn't want to do that—put it on a car hood—but at least the ladder would not have been straight up and down. And maybe I could've shot up there real fast.

Then, of course, there were a lot of guys who told me, "Hey, if you were up there putting her on the ladder, you would have got killed when the place lit up. You would have been dead."

Probably right, but it's still a really hard thing. I told them I would be there.

If you're the first company in and you lose someone— a person is killed—there is definitely a sense that you didn't do your best. That kind of fire will be critiqued in your firehouse for months. Not every day, but it will be brought up, and it will be beaten to death. You will turn it over in your mind, and turn it over in your mind, until you've resolved it down to the zillionth detail. Only then, when you can say, "There was nothing more we possibly could have done," will your mind give you any rest.

Traditionally, the first ladder company in takes the fire floor. The second ladder company takes the floor above. One time, a few years back, we had a fire in a two-story brownstone. We were second due in, so we had the second floor. Just before we got in, the rescue squad had also gone up there.

It was smoky. We couldn't see. And we had been told there were people trapped. A guy from the rescue squad was in front of me. He forced the door and I went in right behind him. He went to the back of the kitchen and broke a window. I came in standing up, and I banged into the kitchen table. Then, since I knew the rescue guy was already searching the kitchen, I went into another room and searched around there. Still couldn't find anyone.

A few minutes later the fire was out. The smoke began to lift. But the chief was still outside, saying, "A mother is saying her kid's up there. Give the place another good search."

By then the second floor was relatively smoke-free, and we had about ten guys giving this apartment a toss. We still didn't see anything. Then another firefighter was coming up the stairs. As he looked into the apartment, he was eye level with the kitchen floor. He saw this three-year-old kid beneath the kitchen table. He grabbed him, got him outside, and the kid died. I felt like shit. I had banged into that kitchen table. I mean, when I hit that table, I might have even been standing on that kid's foot.

In this particular case, the child was probably dead before the first companies got there. I know that sounds cruel, but this place was pumping big-time. There was just so much fire.

Still, when they found that kid, it was a grim, grim discovery for me. Because I went into that kitchen standing up. That's not the proper way to conduct a search. You have to get down on your hands and knees. Now sometimes we have no *choice* but to go in that low. It just gets so damn hot. But when it isn't that hot, you almost feel like an asshole crawling around down there. There are other firemen stepping over *you,* to get further into the apartment. But that doesn't matter. You *still* gotta get down on your hands and knees. If victims are overcome, they could be lying unconscious on the floor.

Now that I'm an officer, I still use that call as a subject during drills. I tell my troops, "Hey, screw what the other companies are doing. Screw what the other guys are doing. If you want to search and find people, get down on your hands and knees. You don't want to make the same mistake I did."

LEADERSHIP AND THE CHAIN OF COMMAND

The best officers are those who admit they're human. One time I had a chief who always admitted mistakes. I loved him for that. Everyone did. But usually, no. People in command will not admit they were wrong.

I've been around both, and I think cops and firemen look at their bosses differently. Right now I'm a captain, which means I'm still considered one of the troops. I still go in on the hose line. I still crawl around with the guys and make searches. I still eat and sleep and live at the firehouse with them. Whereas in the police department, the bosses are on a little higher plateau. You don't see a police lieutenant or captain rolling around with some asshole on the street.

A good leader to me is someone who is honest. Somebody who's already done what they're asking you to do. Someone who's not a pretender to knowledge they don't have.

I've been a lieutenant for thirteen years. I've never considered myself my men's superior. We work together. And I tell them all the same thing when they join our crew: "My job is to get you home to your wives in the same shape you came in this morning. We're not supermen. We're gonna win and we're gonna lose. We're gonna retreat if we have to. None of us here have suicidal tendencies."

We had this one guy at Engine 3 who was a madman. He's a good guy. I love the guy. But when you got to a fire, he was an absolute madman.

He was a captain, extremely aggressive. He wanted all his guys to do the same stuff he did. But he was being a little bit unrealistic. Because it was almost like this guy had a death wish.

One time he had a probie. They're both on the fire escape and he says, "Get in there!"

He kicks this probie into the window. The probie disappears. Evidently, he found a stairway and he was fine. But this was his first day in the fire department. And he thought he was going to die.

We had another call at a high-rise hotel. We got a room on fire on floor eleven; flames coming out the window. They had sent in the engine first, then they called in our rescue squad. So we go up and this captain is in the doorway. He's got the line and the fire is really rolling. But he doesn't have a mask, and it's so hot in there, he isn't even able to enter the hotel room.

So I say, "Hey, Joe, give us the line."

He says, "Fuck you."

I say, "Okay, but I'm going in. There might be somebody in there."

He says, "No, you're not!"

He wouldn't let me go in! So I grabbed hold of his back and shoved him down. He fell to the floor, and I got the line, and I put out the fire myself. All this time I could hear him yelling at me.

The funny thing is, they promoted him to battalion chief, and this guy who was a madman as a captain, turned out to be the best battalion chief going. He was very concerned about people getting hurt!

I don't know how that happened. Maybe it was the change in the way he perceived himself. Once you're a battalion chief, you're out of the line of fire. As a captain or lieutenant, you're still one of the boys.

Our firefighters are pros. They know what's required of them at a fire. There's no need for me, their captain, to give them constant direction. So I'm not the guy they tend to have problems with. What sometimes frustrates them is when they feel the guys above me, the really big bosses, have lost all touch with what goes on in the street.

Here in New York, the biggest thing that annoyed us was our helmets. We used to have the same helmets that San Francisco had. The leather New Yorker. It was a very good helmet. Nothing deficient about it. But for some reason they decided, "We have to change this."

So, now, our new helmet has a chin strap. Nobody likes to wear it, so nobody does. And the guys upstairs are real hot on it now. Actually, most chiefs are pretty good about it. But every once in a while, you get some stick in the mud. He'll come to a big fire and order some lesser chief, "Tell those guys over there to buckle their chin straps."

We're like, "Hey, get a life."

I mean, we understand that New York is an OSHA state, so our department must comply with their regulations. But it's one thing to comply. It's another thing to be making eighty-five, ninety thousand dollars a year, and you're walking around telling guys to buckle their chin straps.

Some people take to leadership naturally. Others get promoted and go off the deep end. I've seen it happen. New officers get to a fire and they lose it. For instance, they'll throw a ladder where you don't need one.

They'll tell you, "Hey. You three guys go and throw the thirty-five-foot ladder."

Tie up three guys? For what? You're never gonna use it.

We got one guy in our firehouse. He was a terrific fireman as a private. He's an officer now, and he's like a blooming idiot at a fire. "Do this, do that, do this, do that"—and you're not accomplishing anything. You're not doing anything that will put out the fire. You're just following orders.

When I was young, I disobeyed an order on one of my rescues.

It was a cold, miserable October day. We got a call that someone was in Lake Michigan.

The girl was four. She'd been standing on the pier with her twelve-year-old cousin. They had a black lab with them. The lab jumped up on the girl, just playing with her.

He knocked her into the water at the end of the pier. The twelve-year-old ran out to Lake Shore Drive. He flagged someone down and we got the call. We got there and looked at the end of the pier. We didn't see anyone.

All of a sudden, we saw something pop up. It was a little blue coat. Inside it was the girl and she was unconscious. My lieutenant took a pike pole and tried hooking her with it. At the very same time, as soon as I saw her, I dropped my pants and took off my shoes.

The lieutenant said to me, "Don't go in without a rope."

But we didn't have a rope with us. So I was thinking, *Fuck it. I'm not waiting.*

The water was cold and choppy, but I didn't care. I used to be a lifeguard. And I swam at this place when I was a kid. That's where we hung out.

So I dove in.

I swam out toward her and she went down again. I saw her little blue coat under water. I grabbed her, swam her back, and handed her up to the paramedics who were there now. And this guy was fucking pissed.

He said, "You disobeyed an order."

I said, "Well, I'm sorry. But I used to be a lifeguard. It was a thing I was comfortable with doing."

So the chief comes by. He says to the lieutenant, "Write him up for an award."

He says, "I'll write him up. But I'm going to write him up for disobeying a direct order. I told him not to go in the water."

The killer of this thing was, he kept me out doing inspections the next two hours. It was freezing out, too. Cold, October, rainy. When we finally get back to quarters, a policewoman comes in and says, "The little girl lived. She's alive."

And you know what this guy, this pig, had put down in the journal? He had written that the little girl was DOA.

They transfered her downstate, to the University of Illinois. I went and saw her and she had brain damage. She was also blind and in a wheelchair. She was pretty badly messed up, but her mother and her grandma were still very happy to have her.

When she got out, I would go and see her at her house. I kept tabs on her, and she was the only person I ever did that with. She was a beautiful little girl. She was only four. I just couldn't get her out of my mind, you know?

If a captain gives an order and someone doesn't agree, most younger guys won't speak up. They're thinking, *This guy has been around. He knows better than I do.*

But sometimes you have guys who've been on for fifteen years, and they're still at the rank of fireman. Sure, he's a lower rank, but he's been on a thousand fires, and he knows the captain is wrong. That's the guy who might tell the captain, "Bullshit. I ain't doing it."

Technically, you're not supposed to do it. The fireman could get in trouble. But usually if a fifteen- or twenty-year fireman does not want to follow an order, he's got a good reason. The better captains know it and hear what he has to say.

In wildland firefighting, you are completely dependent upon your supervisor—a.k.a. your foreman or your superintendent. When you're on the fire line, you don't have all the information they do. You don't have direct communication with the Incident Command Post. So your life is essentially in your supervisor's hands. So are the twenty lives of your entire crew.

Before I joined the Los Angeles Fire Department, I worked in the Forest Service. I saw a few bad situations. Most recently was 1994, the same summer as the fire in Colorado. That's when fourteen firefighters died at South Canyon.

About four days after that fire, we flew to another fire in Colorado. One of the things we heard about South Canyon was that they didn't have the proper weather reports. So when this low pressure system suddenly moved in, they weren't informed of it and things got out of control.

So here we go into a fire in Colorado—not too far from South Canyon—and we don't have a weather report, either. That had never happened to us before. In five years of working with the same people, we'd never had any problems like this whatsoever. But now no weather report? And after what had just happened in South Canyon?

It really bothered me and I questioned my supervisor. He's the one who talks to the planning people. If he doesn't feel comfortable with an assignment, he has the right to turn it down. And if he didn't have a weather report, he should have turned it down.

When I questioned my supervisor, it wasn't taken too well. So I had to trust in his judgment, but I didn't like it. I wasn't the only one, either. One of our firemen quit when we returned from that fire. This was his fifth season, but he felt unsafe. He felt our superintendent had lost his edge.

I had another memorable fire, probably the hardest fire I've ever been on. All these snags were burning off and falling down. A snag is a dead tree that is still standing. When one of them burns off at the ground level, it can fall without a sound, and it can kill you. These particular snags were pretty large. Maybe two hundred feet tall and several feet wide. Three or four guys couldn't get their arms around them. We were also working on a steep incline, and when snags break off they slide and take other trees with them. It was a perfect scenario for people to get hit.

So me and my partner both expressed our feelings. He had thirteen years on the job, all of it wildland. I had five years of wildland. But when we told our supervisor that we were concerned, he said, "When it's your time to die, it's your time to die."

That's all he said. Those were his exact words.

My partner will not be returning to that crew. He's transferring to another one. As I said, I'm now with the Los Angeles Fire Department. This was always my goal.

I didn't come here because of those incidents. But talking about them does bring back some uneasy memories.

FIGHTING WILDLAND FIRES

In the course of my career I've worked on them both—wildland fires and also structural fires. There are broad similarities, but also dramatic differences. Both jobs are real stressful. In both jobs you must deal with tremendous heat. The biggest difference I see is in the length or duration of incidents. With a structural fire, you are normally there a couple of hours. Those hours are very intense, but then you're done until the next call. In a wildland fire, you might spend three weeks on a single incident. You're out there day after day, and it's not unusual to work fourteen hours a day. So I think wildland fires are more of a test of endurance.

Also, when you roll up on a structure fire, what you basically have is a burning box. There may be human life involved, or there may not. But either way, that incident will not get bigger than that burning box. But in a wildland fire, the sky is the limit. If it gets away from you, it can burn for weeks.

In wildland firefighting it's open land, so we don't have to worry about ventilation. We don't have to worry about depleting our air tanks, because we don't wear them.

What we're most concerned about is wind conditions. In trying to control a wildland fire, wind is probably the most important factor. Wind can cause fire to move at tremendous speeds. It's also knocking out the humidity. When you get low humidity and high winds, an entire mountainside can explode into flame.

The wind at a fire works like a little blowtorch, almost like a blower on your heater. It shoots the hot air a certain direction, and the hot air preheats everything it touches. The wind will also propel any burning embers, needles, or branches. We call them firebrands, and they can start smaller fires, which are called spots. If the wind intensifies spots before you can put them out, now you might have fires burning on several sides of you.

It's the wind that makes wildfires so hard to predict.

Oh, Lord, no. It isn't just fire that kills and maims our people. Many of our people die in aircraft accidents. The machinery they use gets pushed to the limits. It's being used every day and for long hours. The pilots are real good about keeping the maintenance up, but fatigue sets in on them, and on their equipment. Maybe when they're making their water drops, they aren't as sharp as they normally are. Maybe they fly a little too low into a canyon. When they try and lift back out, the aircraft is tired, too, and something terrible happens.

Believe it or not, falling snags may be the biggest hazard of all. They can be lethal, especially at night. That's one of the reasons we did not work night shifts in Yellowstone. Usually on a big fire, weather conditions and topography allowing, you'll work twenty-four hours a day, because night is the best time to catch a wildfire. As soon as the humidity comes up, the fire lies down.

We couldn't do that in Yellowstone. There were too many large dead trees that mountain pine beetles had killed. The snags would burn off and fall with no sound, and of course at night they're even worse. You could be looking right at them and still never see them. They're kind of the silent killers on the fire line.

Yellowstone was very frustrating for us. We had, I think, some of the best wildland fire suppressionists in the United States there. The amount of expertise and effort was astounding. And we still couldn't make any headway. We had day after day of single-digit humidity and double-digit winds, and you just can't catch a big fire in that situation. The columns of smoke in Yellowstone were tremendous. They were bigger when we left than when we got there.

We're not too used to that in the Forest Service. We're used to success. But that's the frustration sometimes on major wildland fires. You have all these creative minds combining their efforts. And you wind up being reduced to hoping for weather changes.

Some timber fires are made by man. That runs the gamut from arson, to the sparks coming off the chain saws of the woodcutters in the woods, to the campfires that get away from people out there camping in the forest. But by and large, the majority of forest fires are started by Mother Nature. Specifically, by lightning. Lightning generally tries to seek the higher points, like up on a mountain ridge, but I've also seen strikes in deep canyons and at the bottoms of meadows. There's just no way to say, "We're gonna get pounded here, we won't get pounded here." Lightning hits everywhere. It does what it wants.

Once a timber fire gains momentum, it is an awesome sight. They kick up huge flames, maybe two hundred feet. They take gigantic trees and just rip them out of the ground, or snap them in half. Everyone has their pet name for what timber fires sound like. An airplane taking off. A freight train rolling in. Timber fires put out some pretty tremendous noise.

But they aren't the spookiest fires. I think brush fires are. Brush burns faster than timber, generally. And when brush fires get running and burning intensely, you can easily get trapped. They cover so much ground and do it so fast.

Sometimes you have no choice but to turn and run. It's happened to all of us. We all have turned and run for our safety zones. That's just a fact of life in wildland.

A safety zone is simply that: a safe refuge where we can ride out the problem. It may get a little bit smoky and a little bit hot, but at least we can survive. It's a place where we can stand back, watch the fire roll by and take pretty pictures.

It's kind of like checking your mirrors when you get into a car. It's a very basic thing that can save your life. And a safety zone can be one of several things. It might be a road, or an area that's been bulldozed of all vegetation. It might mean going back into the burn, the blackened earth that is next to you, where the fire has already burned and there is no more fuel. But even in the black, appearances can be somewhat deceptive. Solid black is the best safety zone there is. There is no potential for fire rebirth. But sometimes you don't have that solid black. While the under-vegetation might all have burned, the vegetation above it has merely been preheated. So that upper layer is actually waiting to burn. That's why you have to be careful about the black. Even that requires risk assessment.

If a fire starts chasing you, the last thing you want to do is use your fire shelter. That's when the shit is the worst. The fire shelter is the absolute last resort.

I've only deployed my tent one time in nine years. We were fighting a wildland fire in Malibu. Our whole strike team—five engines—had to deploy them. We were getting overrun.

We were assigned structure protection of this cul-de-sac area. At first the fire was still a fair distance away, but we had our lines pulled out and were ready to go. Well, the wind abruptly changed. And now here comes the fire real fast. Then, as we found out later, the fire licked around and cut off our exit.

We're trapped. I mean, this is it, do or die, let's get it done or see ya. There's gonna be twenty-five dead guys over here.

But you're pumped up and pissed off and you're saying, No way, you ain't taking me today, fuck you, no way. I haven't seen a fire yet where I haven't kicked its ass, and this isn't going to turn into the first one.

At the same time, you're scared. It's gut-check time, nervous time, you can't drive a needle up your ass with a hammer. Because you all just heard it come over the radio: "All units deploy your tents. We are cut off."

So we took out the shake-and-bake tents and got inside them. They're made of aluminum foil and fiberglass. They're supposed to withstand heat up to sixteen hundred degrees. We call them shake and bake because it looks like something you'd wrap a potato in before you stuck it in the oven.

It's a real strange situation. You can't see, you can't breathe because of the smoke and heat, and just getting into your tent is a challenge because you have all your shit on. Then you're lying inside there. You can hear the fire coming at you—it sounds like a train—and the thermal effects of the fire are shaking the tent, and you're thinking to yourself, *If this works, great. If not, I'm gonna be dead right here inside it.*

It's not like these tents are fail-proof. The manufacturer might have made it with a few pinholes. Those pinholes will roast you. They'll roast you like a chicken.

We were deployed in our tents for maybe five minutes, but I swear it seemed much longer. It was so fucking hot in there that guys were screaming and yelling.

In retrospect, we could have done different things. There was no forward lookout for our strike team. So we didn't see the head of the fire until it had cut us off. But hey, it's Mother Nature. If the wind changes, it changes. You're kind of at its mercy. And if you're working in a place like Southern California, where there's been eight years of drought and everything's ready to burn, sometimes you find yourself in insane situations. Other guys in other states can't *believe* what goes on here. I went to Chicago once with my wife. We went to visit the firemen. "Hey, guys, what's happening? I'm a fireman in Southern California."

They thought I was fucking nuts. Because we have no control in some of these wildland fires. Worst-case scenario with a building fire, everybody backs up and the building burns down. It is not the same with a wildland fire. It just keeps getting bigger and moving faster, and if you get trapped you just cannot outrun it. A lot of times, remember, you're trying to run up a mountain that's full of brush, and the grade is probably 12 to 15 percent. A situation like that, you ain't going anywhere but straight to hell.

I'm usually a smokejumper in West Yellowstone, Montana, but I was working out of Missoula when the South Canyon fire started. I was twenty-eight years old. It was my seventh season. By then I'd made over 150 jumps.

Smokejumpers are a small group, nationally. There's only about 450 of us. We take a lot of pride in what we do. We get to the fires by air, and usually we're the ones who do the initial attack.

Before we went to South Canyon, our crew was in Santa Fe for about a week. I believe the South Canyon fire started on July second, but they didn't do much about it until July fifth. That's the day we arrived—one day before the blowup. About eight of us flew from New Mexico in one planeload.

They thought the fire began from a lightning strike. It was near Glenwood Springs, located on a steep ridge and very close to the ridge line. It was probably twenty-five acres, pretty good size for a jumper crew to get on. As I said, we are normally initial attack. We catch them when they're smaller to keep them from ever growing.

That first night we dropped out of the plane on the east side. We walked down to the fire edge and dug a fire line, but the slope was steep with a lot of rolling rocks, so we pulled back out of there just around midnight. Then we headed back toward the ridge line at breaking light. We improved our line and widened it, and we were fairly happy with how things looked. Unless it got driven by wind, it didn't look like the fire would run that hard.

Later that morning, we also started building a second line, downhill. About four that afternoon, I was standing at the bottom of that line with two other firefighters: Sarah Doring and my wife's brother, Don Mackey. We were just doing a little B.S. and trying to catch our breath. Then Don asked Sarah and me to go back up the hill and make sure the other line was still clean. So we started walking back up. That's just about when it started going bad.

From where I stood, behind a little knoll, the wind was still pretty calm. I did not feel a perceptible change in winds. But down below us, I could see the fire was really wind-driven there. All of a sudden, the fire jumped across the canyon bottom. Then it started up the slope, and I could see hardhats above it. They were coming up the hill, all the folks that were hoofing it out of there.

I was standing above them with Brad Haugh, another firefighter. We could see the main fire come up behind them, but that fire still did not look too serious. The fire that now looked spooky was just to their west. It was just a little spot fire, but it was growing fast. So I instantly notified them on my radio.

I said, "You guys got a spot fire below you. You get the hell out of there now."

As they started getting closer, about fifty yards, Brad and I started screaming for them to go faster. But even then, it still did not seem life-threatening to me. I guess you play cat and mouse a long enough time, you never think you'll get eaten.

When the closest person was maybe thirty yards away, I asked Brad to pull out the camera in my pack. My wife's brother, Don, always loved pictures. I knew this would make a hell of a shot for him. But when I looked into the camera, all I could see was bright orange.

It happened real fast. The spot fire kept advancing, and suddenly people were getting close to me. I spun around on my knees and started facing uphill, but I can still remember to this day: I didn't want to get out of there too fast. Because the guys behind me would think that I was a pansy.

I guess my sixth sense took over right about then. It got hot, extremely hot, and I knew I needed to get the hell out of there. I went over the top of the ridge as hard as I could, then went running down the slope on the other side. I took another look back, and flames were curling over the top of the ridge. They were shooting straight out over me like a roof. Then everything was quiet except for the fire.

I ran into Brad Haugh again on the backside. We talked about what could happen from that point on, and I kept thinking that side of the canyon would blow. With all that flame going over the top of us, I figured it would throw spot fires down below. Then I thought those fires would snort right back up the canyon. I was pretty sure it would happen and I was getting scared. I started thinking a lot about my wife and kids.

On our way down the hill, we kept running into folks who were coming out of the trees. There were already ambulances waiting down at the highway, and I got into one with another burned firefighter. Even though the flames had never touched my skin, I had secondary burns on my elbows, shoulders and neck. That was just from the hot gases that rolled up the hill. At the moment I got burned, I'd have to guess it was over four hundred degrees. I have a pack with some nylon webbing on it, and it is supposed to withstand four hundred degrees. When I looked at my pack, the nylon was all crinkled up.

That afternoon was tough. I had never been in a situation like this. I had been in fires where you had to pull out, go hang out in the rock slide while everything burned around you. But I'd never been on a fire where I thought people were dead, and I had a good idea that was the case. Except for Sarah Doring and Sonny Archuleta, I figured the rest of the jumpers had all been killed. The hardest thing was, I couldn't call my wife. I thought her brother was killed. But I didn't know for sure.

Later that afternoon, some folks came out and took me to the Red Lion hotel. There were a bunch of people there from the Hot Shot crew. Then some of our own people began showing up; some smokejumpers. It was so damn sad. Everybody was walking around in a daze.

We found out fourteen firefighters died. Nine were Hot Shot crew members from Prineville, Oregon. Two were helitack from Grand Junction, Colorado. And three were smokejumpers.

Two were from McCall, Idaho, and the one from Missoula, Montana, was my wife's brother, Don. Once they told us that, I finally called my wife. She asked me to call her mom and dad. She said she couldn't do it.

There was a funeral held for Don later that week. First, they wanted to keep the bodies up on the hill for documentation. After the accident investigation team was through, they flew home all the bodies. We had Don's service here in Hamilton, Montana. This is Don's hometown and a lot of folks showed up. I guess I can't really explain how I felt that day. Don was my brother-in-law and a real good friend of mine. When a good friend dies, it hits you deep. It's almost like a part of you dying, too.

Yes, there were mistakes made there. Hell yes, there were. If no mistakes had been made, then nobody would have been killed. But I really don't care to expound on those mistakes. With fourteen people dead, this was one of the worst events in our history. They're going to pull it apart, twist it and turn it until it's inside out—and these people don't need any more finger-pointing. No matter how well they're trained, firefighters and their supervisors are only human. And when humans are facing an entity like nature, I guess sometimes nature is bound to win.

One thing I heard mentioned a lot in the critiques was the "can-do" attitude of our firefighters there. I heard it talked about like it was a negative thing. Well, maybe our firefighting was too aggressive. I'm not saying it wasn't. But it is our job to catch fires. Every fire we go on can potentially hurt someone. If you want us to just sit back and watch them burn, then hell, why even hire us? Because we're not going to catch too many fires.

As for what happened up there in South Canyon, maybe our can-do attitude was the offshoot of somebody's can't-do attitude. That fire was already there a couple days, and they hadn't done anything to it. They could have caught the damn thing when it was just a spot fire.

When I first got home from there, my wife asked me not to jump anymore. She didn't want me fighting any more fire. We had only been married seven weeks, and she had just lost her brother.

At first, I didn't want to jump anyway. I had a lot of things running through my mind. I didn't know why I was spared when other people weren't. Maybe it was just luck. Maybe it was Don's sixth sense. He told me to go check that fire line up ahead. I wish I did know, but I don't. I don't have any good answers.

Now, I'm honestly not sure. I still might jump again. My wife is starting to see that it is part of my life. I mean, it's one of those jobs that gets in your blood. Where else do you get to fly around in an airplane, fairly low to the surface, seeing some of the most rugged country we have left? Then you jump out of a plane and fight some fire. The pay's not great, but you're out there trying to save a little chunk of nature. That may not matter a lot to many folks. But it matters to us.

Still, it's hard to say what I'm gonna do. I'm still oscillating between fighting fire or not. When your best friend gets killed, doing the same job you do, it's damn emotional. So I guess I just don't know yet. I can't say yes and I can't say no.

4
DEALING WITH DARKNESS

The awareness of dying for something great and noble strips death of its absurd character, not only for those who die, but those who survive.
—Ignace Lepp, French priest

Death hangs over thee. While thou still live, while thou may, do good.
—Marcus Aurelius Antoninus,
Roman philosopher

Fires, stabbings, shootings, domestic violence, terrorist acts, car wrecks, airplane crashes, hurricanes, earthquakes.

For most of us, these are unnerving items in the morning paper. Firefighters deal with them in person, and they often confront them first, even before the police, when grim sights and smells are still fresh. In the aftermath of these tragedies and traumas, they may experience anger, depression, anxiety, withdrawal, flashbacks, insomnia, nightmares, alcoholism, divorce. In one form or another, their lives are shaken. It is an occupational hazard. The price of doing good.

For many years, and as recently as the early 1980s, both the public and firefighters promulgated an image: Firefighters are pros. They are warriors. They can handle things the rest of us can't.

That image may be entirely realistic. But firefighters also have softer dimensions. Firefighters can *feel*. As man-made and natural disasters keep piling up in this country, the public and firefighters now recognize that.

How can it *not* get hard sometimes? They witness despicable acts, then go home to try and lead normal lives. One firefighter, after carrying out a dead child from the Oklahoma City bombing in the morning, could not even look at his two-year-old daughter that night. He told his wife to please take her from the room. Once his daughter left he allowed himself to weep.

After encountering darkness—especially when perpetrated on children—some firefighters turn to religion. Even if they can't remotely understand it, they trust and accept God's plan. Others start asking if such a being exists. Those who admitted this seemed deeply angry at times. They also seemed deeply compassionate. If they stopped questioning atrocities, possibly they would also stop feeling outrage.

"They may be acid-tongued when they're with each other," says one lieutenant, "but firefighters are very caring people. Not only do they help the victim, they have the presence of mind to talk with the children or parents. They take care of their worries, too. I think some of that comes from all the tragedy we see. Seeing it *makes* you more caring. But a lot of it is inbred. They come into the job with this marvelous sense of humanity."

Like doctors, police officers, and combat soldiers, firefighters use dark humor to distance themselves from horrors. Wisecracks and jokes, however twisted, can help ease them through the rough spots. One firefighter with six months on the job was called to a hanging. The woman had left a suicide message on her boyfriend's answering machine. The boyfriend came home and heard it and called her apartment. After getting no answer he dialed 911. When firefighters busted in her door, she was dangling from a rope secured to her upstairs loft.

"She was real young," the firefighter recalls. "Maybe twenty-seven or twenty-eight. My captain knew I only had six months on. So he asked me if I was okay. I told him, 'Well, I'm hanging in there, Cap.' "

Later that night at the firehouse, his thoughts kept creeping back to that afternoon. Evidently so did the thoughts of the other firemen. They all started discussing the suicide call. They wondered how someone so young could lose all hope.

When one of their own is killed in the line of duty, they pull even closer and closer together, and then attend the funerals in crushing numbers. In Seattle in 1995, when four firefighters died in an arson fire, ten thousand firefighters helped bury them. They came from fire departments across the United States, to show their respect and affirm their solidarity. Such is this tightknit culture.

Perhaps because they grapple with so much death, firefighters seem to know what is real in life. Not fame, not possessions, not even money, but friendship, family, love, and doing good. These are the cornerstones that help them deal with darkness.

Death is reality. You have to learn to deal with it.

The grossness and the horror, that is reality too. The challenge is not to take it home with you.

We use coarse language at times, but not because we're

coarse people. We use it as a way to protect our psyches. **Sometimes we call dead bodies "crispy critters."** It makes it seem less real, like it isn't a human being.

If they're not living and they're not breathing, it's almost like they're an object and not a person. I just can't relate to them anymore.

With burn victims, rigor mortis sets in almost instantly. So most victims of fires don't look like human beings. They look like mannequins. That is what allows you to desensitize yourself.

Sometimes you'll work on someone who resembles you in age.
Like you try and resuscitate a thirty-seven-year-old man who's had a heart attack. Your efforts are unsuccessful. Before you leave, you take a real strong look. You think, *Goddamn, I'm glad that wasn't me.*

Whatever happens to grownups doesn't faze us. It's just a piece of meat laying there. That's all it is.
But kids are always traumatic. It hits you and stays with you. You might get to sleep that night, but if you do, you'll wake up in a cold sweat. We all got our own kids, you know.

The first time you pull a dead child out of a fire, there's a photograph in your mind. That image stays there the rest of your life.

**If it's an eighty-year-old man who is having a heart
attack, that person had eighty years to enjoy this
world and its pleasures.** But when you go into someone's home and there's a five-year-old girl who's had
juvenile asthma all her life, and this final asthma attack is
taking her life, and you're giving your medications and
she's not responding, and the parents are seeing their
child being lost, it's impossible not to react. Those are the
saddest calls. Tremendously sad. The children are sacred.

I just turned forty last month. I've been a member of
the Oklahoma City Fire Department for the past eleven
years. But I'm not from here originally. I'm actually from
Chottaw, a small town about twenty miles east of
Oklahoma City. But it didn't matter what part of the state
you were from. Everyone felt the same way. This just
doesn't happen in Oklahoma.

The bombing occurred on Wednesday, April 19, 1995.
I was working that morning on Engine 31, but we were
away from the station when the bomb actually went off.
We had gone out to buy groceries for the day. It was my
day to cook.

We had just gotten back on the rig when we felt the
explosion. We felt it so strongly, we thought it was
maybe within a half mile. In reality, it was seven miles
away. As we found out later on, some people felt the
blast who were twenty-five miles away.

The alarm came in just as we got back to our station.
There had been some kind of explosion downtown, and
they needed more companies there. So we probably got
to the scene fifteen minutes after the blast.

As we approached the federal building, we had no
idea it was a bomb. So the first thing we all thought of
was a gas explosion. We figured there'd been a gas leak,

either under the ground or in the building, and it had somehow ignited. But then as we got closer, we all realized that this was no gas explosion. Even a few blocks away, there was simply too much structural damage. And the closer in we got, the more windows were blown out and sides of buildings destroyed.

The federal building is on Fifth Street, between Harvey and Robinson. We had to park about three blocks north and walk the rest of the way. Well, as soon as we turned the corner at Fifth and Harvey, I just stopped for a moment and looked down the street. And that picture will always be with me—the pure devastation. It looked like a war zone. Cars were smoking and burning. You couldn't even tell there'd ever been a street there; this street was completely covered in concrete, glass, and metal. Some of the people were dead. Others were screaming and hollering and bleeding and injured. It literally looked like hell. If hell can be described.

As we we started working our way toward the federal building, we began treating the injured. We followed the simple rule that's known as triage: Treat the most seriously wounded first. So if they were able to walk—if they were walking wounded—we just kind of let them go by us.

Those first few moments there, we mostly put people on backboards and carried them half a block to our triage areas. But at one point I was right in front of the building. I was down on one knee, quite a ways up into the debris, tending to a lady whose arm was almost severed. She was still alive, and I remember looking at her and thinking, *I hope a lot of help arrives here soon. We're gonna need a lot of help. Because I can just imagine what's inside that building.*

At that very moment I looked down the street, through all this drifting smoke and total wreckage. And I recall seeing these nurses come running toward us. They had their blue smock jackets on. They had just come from a nearby hospital, the moment they heard what happened. And as they ran toward us, their blue smocks were waving in the wind. It reminded me of angels. I don't know why, but it did.

I thought, *The angels are coming. The angels are coming to help us.*

The next few minutes we spent just sifting through the debris, trying to work our way into the front of the building. At this point things were still very chaotic. You had cops going through the rubble, military people, state troopers, businessmen in suits—there were hundreds of people there and everyone wanted to help. But then everyone got the order to pull out. Apparently there were reports of another bomb in the building.

Personally, I wasn't too thrilled about that. Though our crew at the time wasn't working to free anyone, we did feel we were close to finding some trapped survivors. To be pulled away from that left some real bad feelings with us. We're just not used to that.

We were outside the building for less than ten minutes, and it was during this time that some order was established. For one thing, no more civilians were allowed back inside the building. The only ones who went back in were rescue workers, and that was mainly firemen. Because we had protective gear on.

This is also when they started assigning us to teams. We were on rescue team three. Our assignment was to enter the east end of the building, then go one floor down into the basement.

They told us before we left, "If people are dead, then leave them. Concentrate your search on people who are alive."

This particular part of the building had not pancaked,

the way it had right in front of the bomb-blast area. So we could actually maneuver a little down there. I was just in awe as I looked around. There were chunks of human bodies everywhere. One man you could tell had been sitting at his desk. He had no face left and his shirt was gone, but his pants and shoes were still on. He must have been one of those who took a direct hit.

There was another woman down there who was in our way. And that was something else that they had talked about. They said, "If dead bodies are in the way, it's okay to move them." So we went to move this woman, because she was right in the way of one of our few pathways. We wanted to use that pathway to bring in tools.

When we lifted her up, I remember looking at her face. She was a blond-haired lady, probably in her fifties. I remember thinking that she must have fallen. She must have been up on a higher floor, and it was the fall that killed her. Because unlike that man whose face was gone, this woman had no signs of damage. I got a very clear look at her face, and she just looked asleep.

Shortly after we moved her, I heard a cry for help.

This young woman was probably in her twenties. She had some cuts and bruises on her head, but mainly her legs were pinned and trapped by debris. She was under steel beams and ceiling tiles, so we kept sending out for stronger tools. But just about the time we could pull her loose, the second bomb scare came in. I remember hearing it over my officer's radio. They had "found a second device," I think is the way they put it. And they ordered us out again.

This time, our crew decided we weren't leaving. There were eight of us there and every person agreed. Because we were just so close to getting her free.

So I said to the young lady, "Look, we're not gonna leave you. We're gonna get you outta here before we leave."

And we did. Within five minutes of the evacuation order, we went ahead and freed her, put her on a backboard, took her out of the building and handed her off to some medical people waiting. Then they brought in a dog to sniff this apparent device. It wasn't a bomb, so back we all went in.

That's when we got involved with Dana Bradley. She was the woman whose leg got amputated, because that was the only way to get her out.

We were not the first ones to come upon her. Another crew, Truck 31, had found her down in the basement. Dana was lying in maybe a foot of water. One of her legs was pinned by a four-foot-wide concrete beam. The rest of her was pinned by various debris. The first time I saw this area she was stuck in—how small it was and compacted—I remember thinking, *How are we gonna get this lady out?* In fact, I'm still amazed that she survived. Down in that cold, wet place with her health going bad on her fast, this lady must have felt she was in her tomb.

When we finally cleared enough stuff to even get close to her, we tried to free her leg but it was still trapped. We even tried power tools, but I don't think they make power tools strong enough to lift that concrete beam. This was one of the beams that had been supporting this building.

So we told our supervisors, "There's no way we can get this beam off her."

That's when the doctors came in. So in order to give them some room, our crew had to back out a little bit, but one of my friends, Jeff Steel, stayed close to her. Jeff works out of our station, and he was riding that day on Truck 31.

I remember when they made the decision. I could hear Dr. Sullivan telling Dana, "Dana, we have two choices. We can amputate this leg and free you from this debris, or you're gonna die."

She told Doc Sullivan, "You do what you have to do to get me out of here."

You're not going to believe this, but I swear to God it's true: he did this amputation with one hand. This space was so tight, it was all that he could reach in.

I can remember the screams. I'll never forget the screams. The media didn't tell anyone about this, but it took the doc three times before he finally got her leg amputated. To listen to this poor lady scream for that long, and *not* be able to help her, it just sent chills up your back.

About 10:30 that first night, we were literally ordered to go back to the firehouse. But right before we left, we got debriefed by CISD—our Critical Incident Stress Debriefing team. I still remember what one CISD member told us.

He said, "When you leave here and go to the station, get away from it. When you go home tomorrow morning, get away from it too."

I thought, *If we leave here, isn't that what we're doing? If we leave the scene, we're gonna be getting away from it.*

I didn't understand what he really was trying to say.

Until I got home that next morning.

We got off shift around 7:00 A.M. First thing I did at home was turn the TV on. It hadn't been on five minutes when I saw this girl. She looked like she was eighteen, nineteen years old. She was holding up an eight-by-ten picture of her mother. She was asking, "Has anyone seen my mother?"

It just hit me like a ton of bricks. This was the blond-haired lady down in the basement. The lady who was dead, and who just looked asleep, and who we had moved because she was in our way.

My first instinct was, I want to call this girl. I want to

get a hold of her and tell her, "Your mom is dead." If it
was my mom, I'd want to know.

But then I thought, *No. This girl still clings to some
hope that someone will find her mom. The bad news will
come through soon. I'm not gonna be the one to take
away her hope.*

In the long run, after talking about it with other people
and the debriefing team, I felt like I'd done the right
thing. And now that time has passed, I still don't think I
would tell that girl. But it was a tough decision. It really
haunted and bothered me for a while.

After what happened that morning, it began sinking in:
that's what they tried to tell us the night before. It wasn't
enough to get away from the scene. You had to get away
from the media coverage.

After that first day off, I wound up working the bomb
site nine more days. But after that first day, we never
found anyone else who was alive. I think that's what
made our recovery process so hard. We're so used to saving lives and keeping people from dying. And we never
had that feeling again throughout the whole rescue. We'd
go in there each shift thinking, *Tonight's the night we're
gonna find somebody. We're gonna free 'em and dig 'em
out and save their life.* And then it didn't happen. And it
was just killing us.

There was a lot of anger among us, too. One day I
found a child's shoe with the foot still in it. This child
was probably three or four years old. I remember holding
it in my hand and thinking, *Who could do this? And why?*

And I don't think the question of why will ever be
answered. Whoever this child was, I don't think you
could ever give their parents a reason that's gonna satisfy
them as to why this happened. And when you see something like that, a child's foot, it's really hard to describe
how angry you get. I mean, it just runs through you.

Some firefighters, obviously, are having more trouble with this event than others. As for myself, I haven't had any nightmares. But of course I've had problems. I lie awake a lot of nights and think. And there are some images I will never get out of my head. That child's shoe. The face of the woman whose daughter was looking for her. The total annihilation when I first turned the corner at Fifth and Harvey. Those things will always be with me inside my head.

But I think what helped me cope was all our debriefings. During the entire search and rescue, Southwestern Bell donated their building to us. So we'd all go into a real nice meeting room, sometimes for up to an hour. They would take us in groups of ten, or sometimes twenty-five; whatever the size of the group that just came in from digging. They wanted you to address it right away, before it could even start to fester inside you.

I gotta say, it really helped. To sit in a room with other firefighters, and see they were feeling the same frustration you were, that's just not the same as a one-on-one with a counselor. If they did that to me, I'd probably clam up. I'd say, "I'm doing fine. I'll be okay." But with other firefighters, you really express yourself. And that has played a great part in the healing process here.

The other big thing that helped was the endless support. I can't stress enough how much that mattered to us. The people in this community—the businesses and the volunteers—all wanted to be involved in some way. They knew they couldn't go down there and dig for survivors, but they wanted to show their support. So if we ran low on gloves, the gloves wouldn't come in a box. They'd come to us in truckloads. That was the attitude the entire community took. I'm still in awe of these people here. I really am. They were grieving and angry, but they just all pulled together. They wanted to show these people who did this wicked crime, You can hurt us, but you can't keep us down. We are going to keep on helping each other. We are gonna survive this.

Here is something that probably touched me the most. I worked the night shift a lot. Sometimes they'd give us a choice, and I just preferred working nights. So I would go down to the scene at 10:00 P.M., and work until early the next morning. Around 2:00 A.M. each shift, we'd break and go for lunch.

The first time that we did this was on a Friday, which was about the third day after the bombing. I remember thinking, *Well, where are we gonna eat at two in the morning?* So as we were taking our gear off I asked someone.

They said, "You can go down by headquarters. Or there's a parking garage at Fourth and Harvey. There's some food in there."

So we went to this parking garage at Fourth and Harvey.

There's about six of us from our crew, and no one else is in there except these volunteers. It's two in the morning and these ladies are cheerful. They're smiling, the food is hot, and they're there for one purpose only, and that is to get us fed before we go back in and dig.

So I remember sitting there, eating this hot meal, and there was a lady there who was pushing a broom. When she came near our table I said, "Where you from?"

She said, "Dallas, Texas."

I said, "You came all the way up here from Dallas, Texas, to sweep the floor?"

She said, "I came up here to do anything to help. I'm sweeping floors tonight 'cause that's where they need me."

You just don't know what that done to my heart. You just don't know what kind of energy that gives you. And we thrived on that. Whether people were pushing a broom or cooking a pizza, or serving somebody hot coffee at three in the morning, or sending us thousands and thousands of letters from throughout this country, telling us that we were in their prayers, we took those people with us when we went inside that building. That's what kept us going. Every time we went in, those people were by our sides.

SHOWING THEIR EMOTION

Last Christmas I had a bad feeling. It wasn't anything extraordinary. It was probably just me being glum about having to work that day.

But that morning I told my wife, "Pray that nothing bad happens today. Because I don't want to deal with it on Christmas."

I was working on a very busy engine. The bells went off around 10:45 A.M. It was for a shooting at an apartment. We put our body armor on—they're like bulletproof vests—but we weren't terribly excited about the call. In this particular area, shootings are not uncommon.

We got there and the cops were waving us in, kind of frantically. One cop told us, "All the way in the back bedroom."

I was working as a firefighter/paramedic, alternating between fire and medical calls. On this, a medical call, I was what we call the patient man. It was my responsibility to do a rapid patient assessment. Well, I'm going down this hallway to the back bedroom, and I can see blood all over the place. It was everywhere—the walls, the ceilings, the doors. I could also hear the TV in the back bedroom. It had Christmas music on.

As soon as I went in, I saw three bodies. We didn't know if they were salvageable or not, so I started my assessment. On the bed was a mother. She was clutching her infant in her arms. It looked like the mother was shot in the chest. She had no vital signs, no cardiac rhythm at all. She was not salvageable.

I looked at the baby. The baby was disemboweled.

I don't know how that happened. This was called a shooting, but it didn't look like a gunshot wound. There was probably a knife somewhere.

Next to the bed on the floor was a guy and a gun. As we later came to find out, he went into a jealous rage. This guy killed his girlfriend. Killed his baby. Then killed himself.

It was really hard. My wife and I had just had a baby. And to see that little baby and her mother ... you just keep envisioning your own family lying there. It's just so hard not to.

As I hunched over the mother, I could feel it coming on. It was like a surge. My nose was starting to run and I could feel my eyes begin tearing up. But I was able to maintain control inside the room. Then, as soon as I left, it hit me like a ton of bricks. I just purged myself. I cried. I went to the back of the engine and let it all out. A good five minutes, just purging myself of that event. And it felt good. It felt really good. And I didn't feel embarrassed or ashamed. It just reminded me that I was human. Because I had been on so many other calls, where an average person would have a strong reaction. And I did not have that strong reaction. So I was almost thankful when I cried that Christmas. I knew I still had feelings.

It's such a strange job we have. There is such a wide parameter of feelings. Before I left that apartment I was thinking to myself, *This is the most vile, disgusting job in the world. No amount of money in this world could adequately compensate me for what I am seeing right now.* That's how I felt at that time. I resented the job. Because once you see something, you can't just pull it out of your mind. You're forced to deal with it, and there are some things in life that no one should really ever have to see. It wasn't the first time I felt this way, either. I've been on other calls when I told myself: *I would rather shovel shit, and do it with a smile, then see what I am seeing here right now.*

But then I left that apartment and cleansed myself. I cried. And it was only eleven in the morning, so we still had a full day ahead of us, and so we went on more calls and we made a difference. We got to places where people were still alive, and we helped them stay alive. By the time I was going home the next morning, I felt very, very thankful for my job. It was the best damn job in the world, and I would do it for nothing.

Nine times out of ten, you don't cry until you have dealt with the situation. After you have treated them, after you have transported them to the hospital, and now you are on your way back to the station, that's usually when it comes out. And it may come out real hard.

We pulled up on this wreck and the car was on its side. It was pretty severe. There were a lot of neighborhood people standing out there. There was already an ambulance from the fire department.

In the middle of the street, there's a young man being worked on. They're doing CPR, but the paramedics can't save him. One of them walks by me when it's over. He throws his rubber gloves into the street. He starts cussing and he's really disappointed.

I go over to him. Because we have got the public watching us. We have to maintain our composure. It's right for us, it's right for the public, it's right for the families of the victims.

I said, "Are you okay?"

He said, "I just don't like to lose them."

I said, "That's the nature of this job. You're going to have to try to cope with that. Or look for a different profession."

You have to get rid of the ownership. You saw it. It touched you. It's tragic. But you don't own it. It isn't yours.

For example, I had a call one night. Some sonofabitch went into this apartment house, poured five gallons of gasoline in the lobby, and torched it. The fire went up the stairs.

So we went in and knocked down the fire. We kicked in this bedroom door, and it was so hot we ended up on the floor. Here was two little kids. They'd been crawling on the floor, trying to get to the door of the room to get out. And they died. They couldn't get out, you know?

You never forget seeing something like that. You don't even try. But you have to give up the ownership. If you took everything to heart—that's terrible, that's tragic—then you become part of the crowd. You're no longer part of the people who fix it.

A lot of people think firemen are macho. Some firemen try and create that image themselves. We don't cry, we don't talk, we don't have feelings. But that isn't true. We just do our crying in private.

It might be the death of a child that sets us off. It

might be a firefighter we just saw killed at the scene. Or it might be something personal—someone's divorce, or their children are sick. Firemen have problems just like anyone else.

So it can pretty much happen anywhere; just not in front of the public. Firemen might be out fishing with other firemen, or sitting behind the station. They start talking, and they break down, and that's totally okay with other firefighters. Because the compassion we show other people, we show ourselves.

We had a shooting one night in Prince George's County. It's not far from where I grew up in southeast D.C. Six young black guys were shot. They were sitting on a porch, cutting each other's hair. They were ready to go back to school the very next day. Someone ran up on the porch and started shooting at them.

One of the guys was shot in the head two times. His brain was lying beside him, so he was dead. The other five guys were shot in their backs, legs, stomachs, chests. The one particular guy who I worked on, we found in the house. He must have run inside to try and escape.

We had to roll him over, check for entrance and exit wounds. We found both wounds, bandaged and dressed them. We applied a C-spine collar and put him on a backboard. We loaded him in the back of the ambulance, and transported him to D.C. General Hospital. This kid was seventeen. He was crying and scared, and I was in the back taking care of him. He asked me if he was going to die. I didn't know, and I wasn't going to lie.

I told him, "All I can say is we're giving you the very best care."

I provided oxygen for him. I monitored his vital signs. I also kept talking to him, just trying to keep him calm. I prayed for him at one point. He saw my eyes close and heard me mumble something.

He said when I finished, "Were you just praying for me?"

I said, "Yes, I was."

He said, "Thank you for praying for me. Thank you for your help."

I said, "Anytime. I hope you make it."

It turns out he did make it. He's back in school now and he's doing all right. But I didn't know that at the time, and I cried that night when I got off work. I didn't cry long, but I cried. I was just tired of seeing all my black brothers get shot. I hate the idea that my race is killing each other off.

It's one of the driving forces behind what I do: I want to be a role model for young black kids. I want them to know there's other ways to make it. They don't have to sell drugs or join gangs. Hell no, they don't. There are positive ways of getting the things they want. I know that's true. I've done it myself. But a lot of these kids don't believe there's a better way. So sometimes I still cry. Sometimes on our way to another call, I'll pray not to see the death of another young black man.

The call came in about 7:00 A.M. Mud slide, with possible victims trapped. For almost a week, it had rained like cats and dogs in the city of Ventura. Mountains were saturated. The river was overflowing. All these trailer homes were washing away. At the same time, there was a condominium complex up on a hillside. The top of the hillside came loose, and all this mud came rushing down the hill. The mud uprooted a tree, then the tree and the mud crashed right through this bedroom window. A husband and wife were sleeping in there. It buried them in about seven feet of mud. In some parts of the room, there was mud all the way from the ceiling to the floor.

We get on-scene and it's total chaos. The rain has not let up. All the neighbors are soaking wet and frantic. Everyone's talking at once, but we're finally told what's really going on. The woman inside is only twenty years old. It's her birthday that day. She is nine months pregnant.

Picture yourself in this situation. You gotta listen to this pounding rain the whole time—on your helmet, on the roof, it's coming right through the window into this bedroom. You're knee-deep in mud in there. There's a tree in there with you and it's right in the goddamn way. You're digging for a woman you know is pregnant. Deep down, you think she's dead. But for all you know there could be a pocket of air, and in this job we tend to be optimistic. So we're not gonna give up. Not until we find out if these people are still alive.

I grabbed a chain saw and instinctively started cutting up the tree, so we can take it out. I'm being extremely aggressive, because we gotta make this thing work. But I'm starting to have these flashes while I'm cutting: *Where are the husband and wife? What if I go too deep and the chain saw cuts them?*

Moving this mud is brutal, exhausting work. It's wet, it's heavy—thirty minutes into it I feel spent. An hour into it, we're still not anywhere near them. Hour and a half, we finally get to the couple. The wall behind their bed has fallen on them. We pick it out piece by piece with these heavy pliers. Once we remove the wall, we pull their headboard off them. It's almost surrealistic: There's a man with his young wife cuddled next to him, and she's due any day. They look totally peaceful. It is such a loving scene. Just a classic example of a young family. And here they are buried in mud.

I went back to the station after the scene. They had a

stress incident debriefing for us. You're starting to see this now all over the country. After something really traumatic, the fire department brings in specially trained personnel, and everybody talks about how they're feeling. "What are you feeling? Why are you feeling this way?"

It's interesting. Once you start seeing you're not alone—everyone else is having these feelings too—it really helps you deal with it. In the old days, a lot of guys would just keep it all inside. It would accumulate in there, and that's when guys would snap. This way is much better. You're confronting your own feelings. You're being a lot more honest with yourself.

When I went home that night, I thought I was fine with what happened. I was still upset, but I felt we did everything we could to save them. All that night, the rain never let up. It just kept pounding. When I finally went to sleep, I woke up at three in the morning, totally freaked. I had had a nightmare. The mud came down the hill and I was buried alive. I was just freaked. Just blown away. I couldn't believe that could happen to those young people.

THE PSYCHOLOGICAL TOLL

This job may not always affect you in obvious ways. You're not necessarily going to kick the dog. It may affect you in the middle of the night, when you wake up breathing hard and sweating. Or else you dream about calls. You do it a lot. But you always dream about people who were alive, people who you worked on that didn't make it. That's the one common thread. If you get there and the person is dead, that's no big deal. It's the living people. Those you cannot save. That's what gets in your head.

The only recurring dream I've had is when we went out on strike in 1980. I was out for twenty-three days with the union, and there must have been some guilt about not being out on the streets and serving the public. Anyway, during the strike, there was no advanced life support. The only paramedics were trained in basic life. That was if you could get an ambulance at all.

So the dream is this guy is having a heart attack. He's in a steakhouse right near our firehouse. I don't know who he is. I've never seen him before. In come the paramedics working the strike. I don't know them either.

I say, "You gotta get an IV into this guy. And get him on some oxygen right now."

They say, "We're basic."

The patient looks at me. He turns white, like he's going to die. I wake up and I'm like, *Holy shit!*

We got a call around two in the morning. We go to this house and the kid's maybe twenty-two. He's there with two friends. There are no parents there. These kids are renting a house.

They had been sitting in one of the bedrooms. One kid was kind of a gun nut. He was showing off for his friends, just playing macho, and he put the gun to his head. There was one bullet in there and the gun went off. Maybe it was strictly accidental. But I think the kid was playing Russian Roulette.

The police were already there, so the front door was open when we arrived. We went right back to the bedroom. There was blood and skull and brain matter on the wall. The kid was sitting back in his reclining chair, making these real guttural heaves, maybe six times a minute. That means the only part of the brain he's functioning on is the stem—the medulla. So even though he's still

breathing, practically speaking the kid is already dead.
But we had to try and revive him anyway. So we did CPR
and it was an awful thing. We're doing the best we can,
but he's gasping and heaving and brain matter's hanging
out.

Later that night, every time I fell asleep, I started
dreaming about this kid. I would doze off, and then I
would be there again. Right in the middle of all that
mess.

After a while I started having flashbacks. I mean during the daytime. I got real uncomfortable with that, so I
wanted some critical incident debriefing. But I never said
anything to anyone. I should have, but I didn't. It was
peer pressure, I guess. If I got debriefed or got therapy, I
felt I would not be accepted by the guys. They think
being debriefed is real wimpy, especially the old-timers.
It's fear-based, in my opinion. They don't want anyone to
think they're grossed out by what they see.

It's that macho thing.

**When I came on, they didn't have the counseling they
do now.** Somebody wanted to get something off their
chest, they just talked to another fireman. Now, after
every thing you do, you can talk to a shrink if you want.
Because nowadays, with these new sensitive guys coming
up, these nineties yuppies, they figure they gotta go see a
professional.

One time I saw a kid burn. They sent me to a psych. I
told him I thought he was full of shit.

Because he said to me, "Hey, I know how you feel."

That instantly turned me off. I told him, "I don't think so."

Then I asked if he was ever in the service. Did he ever

do active duty in wartime? No. College guy all his life. So what have you seen? How do you know?

When I went back to the station, the guys were curious.

"Hey, how is the head doctor?"

I told them the questions he asked me.

They said, "Well, that guy is full of shit."

It really irritated us, that someone would be that presumptuous, to claim to know how we feel. He doesn't fucking know.

Everybody's a tough guy when they're at work. Nothing bothers anybody there. You can't sit down and go, "How do you feel about that?"

They'll be like, "What are you talking about? I don't give a shit."

But I've got this friend who's not a firemen. He sells vacuum cleaners. I will usually talk to him because he's neutral ground.

In my opinion, a lot of us come from dysfunctional families. So even when we were children, we were already taking the role of the rescuers.

In my case, my dad was an alcoholic. My mother was codependent. So I turned into the rescuer for us. After I got my driver's license, I was always being told, "Go get your dad. He's in Klamath Falls, Oregon." Or, "Go get your dad, he's in a bar in Berkeley." So when it came time for me to pick a profession, what was I gonna be? I was either gonna be a firefighter, a cop, a nurse, or an ER doctor.

I picked the fire service. And then I came into this stressful occupation—I started seeing this stuff year after year—and I would reach for the booze or I'd reach for the drugs.

They didn't do any drug testing in this department, so I was already using before I came on. But I started doing much more after I joined. I really screwed things up. I mean royally. I got a divorce. I started going to bars where there were a lot of drugs. I wound up shooting heroin and speed. All kinds of fucked-up stuff.

You know, I'm shaking a little bit just talking about some of this. I remember a fire in 1982, maybe 1981. We found a whole family dead. We found the father sitting up, with a beer in his hand. He died of smoke inhalation. The mother died of smoke inhalation, too.

We also found a baby on the couch. That's where the fire started, and the baby was just consumed. At first we didn't know if it was a pet, or what it was. We started looking closer—ears, nose, eyes—and we said, "This is a fuckin' baby, you know?"

That was horrible in itself, but then we saw one of those poignant things we see. Although the mother died of smoke inhalation, her hands were badly burned. That was the only part of her that was burned. She obviously tried to beat the flames off her baby.

After the fire I went back to the firehouse. By then it was almost four in the morning. I was on a truck company, so we had our axes and shovels and saws to clean up. I was the youngest one at that station, and I had never seen anything like this. The other guys had, but no one was talking about it. It was just real quiet.

So I said, "Gee, I would really like to talk about what just happened. I don't feel very good about that fire."

Someone said, "Hey, kid. Just clean your tools and go to bed."

So we did just that. We cleaned our tools and went to bed.

Where I work now, it isn't like that. The guys I work with here are like a family, and we have this little pact.

We're gonna sacrifice our face to save our ass. If we see something traumatic, we're gonna talk about it.

But that fire really bothered me at the time. And those were the type of events that would trigger my drinking and using. I think it probably escalated from there, until I was a full-blown drug addict and alcoholic.

I started with cocaine. Then I switched to methamphetamines, and I was injecting them. I was doing heroin near the end. I never got a heroin habit, but all in all, when I was at my worst, I spent about three hundred dollars a day on drugs. It didn't take long for my money to run out.

It got real nasty toward the end. By 1987, I was only working half-time. I was taking all these sick days and faking disabilities. When I did go into work, sometimes I was still high from the night before. One time I had been up for three or four days, partying the whole time. I went back to work and after we'd gone to bed, we had a fire in the middle of the night. My equilibrium was off. I would be walking around this burning house, and I would almost fall over. I was mortified, but I was powerless, man. I was using this stuff against my own will. A few times during work, I even snorted coke in the firehouse.

I hit my bottom in August of 1988, right around August sixth. That's when I just quit going to work. Normally, whenever I had time off, I'd stop using two or three days before I went back to work. But this last time it happened, I was supposed to return to work and I couldn't stop shooting speed. I had needle marks all over my right arm. I hadn't slept in days.

I kept saying, "You gotta clean up. You gotta stop, you gotta stop."

But then when the day came for me to return to work, I was too wired to even call the firehouse. I'd been up so long, I couldn't have found my ass with seven hands. So I didn't go to work that day. I didn't call. I just went

AWOL. Then I went AWOL for six more shifts. That was my rock bottom.

Somebody came to my door one afternoon. He was an acting battalion chief. He had these papers with him. I had been terminated from city employment.

I called the department later on. They said, in a nutshell, "We'll tell you what we'll do. We'll give you an opportunity to get your job back. But only if you go for long-term treatment."

So that's what I did. I got clean September 2nd of 1988. It's seven years later now and I've been clean ever since. Now I help other guys who might be developing problems. They know I've already been there and come back. So they'll talk to me and I'll help any way I can.

I wasn't there, but I've heard stories about the Hyatt hotel in Kansas. The catwalk collapsed. A lot of people were crushed. There was blood all over the lobby. People were pinned beneath all this concrete, so the firefighters there were doing amputations. They simply couldn't move these huge blocks of concrete. It was the only way to get some people out.

One year later, on the anniversary, one of the firemen went out and bought something like twenty-seven chain saws. One by one, he threw all twenty-seven into the river. That was the number of people that had to be amputated. Obviously, it was still affecting him one year later.

What has changed me the most is not seeing death. What has opened my eyes is working in the ghetto. These people have nothing. When I was growing up, I never even knew that lives like this existed.

For an example, I have a friend who just bought a beautiful huge home. And he was complaining. He said he should have got a four-car garage.

I said, "Why don't you come down on Monroe Street and live in one of those houses for a week?"

That's how this job changes you. Things don't bother you so much away from work. Because you know how it could be.

I don't know if seeing death has *changed* me. But I am a lot more comfortable with it. It's probably true of a lot of firefighters. We look in all those dead faces, and yeah, it's terrible for the living, but the dead don't seem to be doing any complaining.

For me, accepting death made it easier to take risks. I can honestly say, and I say this with the conviction of a saint, I do not fear death. I really don't. I'm not going to wantonly walk in front of a truck, but I don't let it cloud my judgments anymore. Sometimes, I used to let it. I used to be afraid of jumping in these canals, with all those gators in there and all that other shit. I mean, there's nothing gloomier than searching for a body in a dirty, murky, goddamn lake or canal. But I don't fear it anymore. I don't worry about it. I swim around down there as happy as a clam.

It does change you, seeing death. It makes you accept it better than most people do. That's why I hate it when people say, "Well, you've just gotten callous."

I don't think we're callous. I think we're spiritual.

Since this is not officially on the record, I don't believe in God. Maybe that comes from the job. You see so much misery and suffering, it's hard to sustain a belief. Let me put it this way. If there is such a thing as God, he's got to be pretty damned cruel.

I lost a boy myself back in 1980. He had leukemia. He was only seven. And every time on the job when I saw a little kid, I would question this. Why? Why little kids? Especially when you'd find that someone else was negligent. Boy, you talk about rages. I would say to myself, *Just let me get my hands on the person who was responsible for this. Just let me get him in a room with a Louisville Slugger for about fifteen minutes.*

Did I hate God because of that? No. Hate's not the word I'm looking for. It's just confusing, that's all. Because I never found any answers to my questions. I don't know if there are any.

When I came onto the job, I never had much spirituality. I was like, Shit, half the people die and that's how it goes. I mean, what if we got to a scene and a person was in cardiac arrest? Me and my partner shocked him, intubated him, gave him drugs, and the next thing he's pulling the tube out and he's alive. Now, did we do that, or is there a Higher Power, somehow saying, It isn't this guy's time?

I used to think it was us.

But then the same thing would happen, except the guy would die. Well, then, did we do something wrong? No, we did everything right. We arrived in a timely fashion. Everything went smooth. This guy was even ten years younger than the other guy who made it. Except this guy never comes back.

That's why I started believing we don't run the show down here. You really can't take credit for the big win, and you can't kick yourself in the head for the guy who doesn't wake up, or the child that doesn't respond after being struck by a car. You can do the best you can, and that's what we do every day, but you can't get too grandiose. You have to believe there's a Higher Power out there.

I guess the turning point for me was when a good friend of mine died in a car accident. His name was Marty. He was with his fiancée when he died.

We went to work the next day and the first run was a wino. He had woken up drunk for the umpteenth time. But this time, the wino was having a seizure. I was looking at him, thinking, *Why are you still alive and Marty's dead?*

I started putting the boot to him, yelling, "Get up, you scumbag!"

That was it. I came to right there and said, "What am I doing? Who the hell am I to kick this guy in the head? Because he's a poor bum, alcoholic, or whatever? I'm not God. I can't do nothing for Marty, and beating this guy up won't help Marty either."

I realized then that I needed another outlet for all these emotions I had. Because up until that point, I was drinking a lot. I wouldn't even wait until it was nighttime. I would drink in the morning when I got off work. And I don't know if this job caused it, or just contributed to it. But I do know it gave me a great excuse.

There was no single event that told me I had to get straight. It had to do with my marriage, but it was cumulative. You can't keep running and running, and burying all your feelings in all this booze. That's what I did for my first ten years on the job, and then my tenth anniversary came up. I had been looking forward to this big party. One month before it, I found myself in my first meeting. The day of my tenth anniversary on the fire department, I'm smoking a cigar and eating a bowl of ice cream. No booze for me that day or any day since.

I've been going to AA for the last ten years. Recovery is the best thing that's ever happened to me. You know, you really can't train anyone to have spirituality. They've all got to find it inside themselves. I found it from drinking too much, and I was lucky to find it. It has kept me sane in this insane job. It's made me understand that I don't run the show and I'm not God. I don't have the weight of the world on my shoulders anymore.

You get these tremendous head-on collisions. Death is instantaneous. You can't help, so you just stand there looking.

What that does is make you cherish life. Maybe that person was just like you. He was going to see the doctor, or going to the dentist, or he had plans with his wife to go Christmas shopping. All of that is stopped. He's just not going to do that anymore. And that is one of the things that this job has really brought home. How life is truly a gift. It may sound trite, but it should be used the best way you can use it. Every single day.

THE VALUE OF HUMOR

Our humor is adolescent. Frequently, it's dark. If other people heard us, they'd call us crazy or harsh. But we use black humor to cover the sins we see.

Once in a while, unfortunately, it happens at an incident.

Guys are making gallows jokes and the public hears it.
Usually, then, the city gets a call: "How come those guys
are standing around in front, joking and laughing, when I
just lost my house?"

It doesn't mean we don't care. It's just a psychological
safety net. If you never did it, you'd be a blithering idiot.
Blithering idiots can't keep doing the job.

**We had an incident where this woman news reporter
kept getting in our way.** She wanted to get an interview
from a fireman. Well, he was still busy doing an extrication. It was a terrible three-car wreck and there were dead
bodies all over. But she just kept sticking herself and her
cameraman right in there.

She finally went to the captain and complained. The
captain said, "Look, we got a busy scene here. How
would you like to help out and give us a hand?"

She said, "Yeah, sure, I guess I could."

So he gave her the severed hand of one victim. The
reporter fainted on the spot. So now we got a new victim.

It would seem very morbid to an outsider. But it's all
relative. A buddy of mine is an arson investigator. That's
one of my goals, to be an investigator. One day we were
hanging out and he said, "Hey, I gotta go down to the
coroner's office and give an autopsy as part of this fire.
You wanna go?"

At first I thought, *How sick!*

But then I thought, *I've been in anatomy class and
I've seen cadavers, but I've never actually watched one
being worked on. If I really want to get into investigation,
I'll have to do this at some point anyway. So I might as
well get it out of my system now.*

I went and I watched, and the coroners were doing this autopsy. You wanna talk about a dark sense of humor? These guys made firefighters look like choirboys. But there again, it's perspective. That's what they gotta do to keep themselves sane.

Not all the humor is black. A lot of it is just one-liners and zingers. Most of it comes at odd times, like six in the morning when your shift is almost over, but you're out fighting a fire and it is thirteen below. Your mustache is frozen, your turnout clothes are ice, you're frozen to the bone. And yet you have to work, because it's your job. It isn't so bad when you're near the fire; the fire is warm. But once you put out the fire, and you're outside cleaning up, and now your adren-aline stops, that's when you really freeze and get miserable. And that's when you hear a lot of puns and zingers. I guess the joking we do fills up the space.

A lot of humor comes from the goofy calls we go on. Just last night, we went on a call for a twenty-seven-year-old male. We get there and the guy says, "No can poo poo."

He's an immigrant from another country. He called us because he couldn't take a shit.

What do you tell a guy like that? "What do you expect us to do for you, stick the hose line up your ass and flush you out?"

It's really very strange. People do not understand what we can and can't do.

We get those all the time. People that can't pee, people that can't poop, people with hemorrhoids. How many stories you want like that? I got a thousand.

Every morning when our shift began, we used to say, "Can we get the Five S's today?" One was a seizure, which was almost a cinch to get. One was a stabbing, also almost a cinch. One was a shortness of breath. That *was* a cinch. A shooting was the fourth one, but that was more difficult. The choice of weapon where we worked then was knives.

Then there was "Shit your pants." We were actually called to bars where guys had soiled themselves, and the bartender wanted us to get them out. That was the hardest one. That was the one that would keep us from getting Five S's.

People phone up for the tiniest little things. One time we got a call at four in the morning. You know what the lady's complaint was? Her teeth were tight.

One person's hair hurt. That was the call.

People call out the fire department for headaches. They think we carry aspirin, so this way they don't have to go to the store.

People just want a ride to the hospital. They'll call 911 on a Sunday night. We'll show up and their bags are already packed. They're supposed to check into the hospital Monday morning. Rather than bother a neighbor or pay for a taxi, they call us. It's comical, but it's not. There's a tremendous abuse in this country of 911.

One woman wanted us to prepare her taxes. Of course, that's not what she told the dispatcher. She said she was suffering from anxiety. What really happened was, she was trying to fill out the tax form by herself. She didn't know how, so she called the fire department.

The silliest call was for cardiac arrest. We went there on the truck, plus an engine showed up, plus the paramedics. That's seven or eight guys all showing up for this call. So we go inside and the guy is on the bed. We ask the lady what happened.

She says, "I came in from watching television. He was just laying there."

The first thing we do is walk over to him.

"Sir, sir, are you okay?"

"What, what?! What's going on?"

He was asleep.

People do all kinds of weird, stupid things. We always get these guys who think they can accomplish something, and then they screw up big-time. Like they say they're going to clean their motorcycle parts. So how do these guys clean their motorcycle parts? Like idiots, they clean them in gasoline.

Then they say, "Well, I'll do it outside. It's well ventilated there. So what the hell?"

The guy's feeling real smart about this thing. Right up

until he realizes that the gasoline fumes are heavier than air, and they roll downhill right toward his water heater. Boom, flash fire, he gets his ass burnt a little bit and the fire goes out. You go out there and you almost want to ask, "What the hell were you thinking about here, pal?"

Kids will get into *everything*. We had one little boy who was five years old, from a middle-income household. He's home with the baby-sitter. He's playing with matches. He lights a fire in the living room.

The baby-sitter, much to her credit, puts out the fire and calls 911. We show up and this kid is now scared shitless. Because any fire like that, we also call in arson. Then they come out and do counseling with the kid.

Arson says, "How did it start?"

Five years old. He never batted an eye. He said, "There was a match on the carpet. I slipped on it. It started a fire."

For a kid that young to come up with that shit so fast? I thought, We got a future president here.

Kids do all kinds of strange things. We had one mother tell her son, "Go in and wake up your father."

So he went in and woke up dad with a hammer. It was only a play hammer, but he whacked him right in the grape.

Mom panics and calls us. The kid is bawling his head off. Mom is pissed at him. Dad is bleeding and *very* pissed. To dad or mom or the kid, it isn't funny. But to us, that's funny shit.

We got a call about one in the morning. A man had a foreign object stuck in his rectum. When we arrive at his trailer park, there is this twenty-four-year-old woman sitting in bed and giggling. Sitting down at the edge of the bed is this twenty-year-old guy. He is motionless, like he's scared to move.

We interviewed him to find out what happened. We came to find out that his girlfriend had been using a vibrator, and she lost it up his rectum. That was pretty amusing in itself, but then we were trying to get this guy on the stretcher—he couldn't sit up because of the pressure—and his girlfriend was laughing hysterically at him. She couldn't stop. Neither could we. We didn't even try and keep straight faces. All the engine company guys were laughing right with her.

They took an X ray of him at the hospital. You could still see the thing buzzing around.

Day before Thanksgiving. These two Mexican guys bought themselves a live turkey. This bird is huge. They're driving back home and they have it in the backseat. Somehow or other, the bird goes berserk. It jumps up in the front seat, and it's flapping its wings and gouging them, and they're trying to tackle it, and the driver loses control of the car and slams into a telephone pole. Just crunches the telephone pole. Kills the bird. The bird goes out the windshield—the bird is dead. Meanwhile, both these guys got broken legs, internal injuries and shit, so we work on them. We pull 'em out, splint their legs, get 'em all fixed up and ship 'em off. Once they were gone, I grabbed the bird, threw it on the engine and took it back to the station. We ate him the next day for Thanksgiving dinner. Yeah, he was a big son of a bitch!

We had one guy who lived in an old frame house. It was a foot or two off the ground, on blocks or pilings or whatever the hell they put them on. This guy was trying to get under his house, to get something down there, and he got stuck.

When we pull up, his rear end is sticking out from under the house. And he had—I swear I'm not making this up—this German shepherd dog on top of him. The dog is humping him. He's screaming bloody murder, just yelling at the dog at the top of his lungs.

We stood there and looked for a second. Then my captain says, "I wonder if that dog bites."

I said, "He don't look in the mood to bite right now."

WHEN FIREFIGHTERS DIE

The job is very high highs and very low lows. The lowest of all is one of our own getting killed.

One guy got killed and we all came back to the firehouse. We had been playing cards. His hand and his cigarettes were still sitting there.

It jerks you back to earth. You think, *Maybe I better get my life in order, and my spiritual life in order. Make sure I'm on the good side, because the return date on my forehead might also be stamped soon.*

I was never working when someone died. But last summer, a guy I used to work with had a roof fall on him. He didn't die, but he's paralyzed. I feel for him and I think about him. One time he saved a little kid from drowning, and he can't even swim. That's a true story. He was jogging one day when he was off-duty. A lady on a dock dropped her infant in the water. The baby went right down in the murky water. This guy ran up and dove in, went down about fifteen feet and pulled this baby out. He's scared of water, can't swim, but he saves this baby. I thought that was a beautiful thing. And that's what I focus on when someone gets killed or badly hurt. I think of all the people they helped while they were still on the job.

We lost seven men in my company once. Twelve men died in that fire, but seven of them were from my company. It was a ten-story building collapse on Twenty-third Street.

This is it, in short: The building at that time abutted up against the building on Twenty-second Street. So, in the basement of the building on Twenty-third, the owners had gone down and broken the wall that connected the two buildings. They dug it out and made a big storage area for both buildings. But in doing so, they reduced the live load of the first floor from 120 pounds per square foot to forty pounds per square foot. In short, this floor can hold much less if a serious fire starts.

Here is how I know this. We had an architect teaching us fire science. He got up in front of the class and he said, "I used to make millions of dollars as an architect. I'm teaching now because I feel so bad about what happened on Twenty-third Street."

We went berserk! So then he tells us he wasn't responsible for it. He just feels bad because it happened. Still, I couldn't believe this guy had the balls to say this in front of firemen.

When the fire started, the brothers were on the first floor. All twelve of them, just standing around in the lobby. The floor collapsed. And they fell right into the basement, to their death. They were all burnt up.

Twelve guys altogether, and seven from my company, Ladder 7. This was a real jovial crew, always kidding around, doing little sadistic jokes to one another. But there was an honest-to-goodness silence after that. They were shocked. For months and months, a lot of guys couldn't get over it. Some guys never got over it. They were very close. Some guys had worked together for twenty years.

I was brand new, with just about a year on. That was a dose of reality to me. But even after it happened, I still knew I'd never die in a fire. I knew this in my heart. I felt I was slick enough to get in and out of anything. On the other hand, maybe it was just a matter of what do you call that?

Denial.

Everyone says kids are the worst thing you'll ever deal with. But as bad as that is, there is nothing else like losing one of your brothers. It's very hard to explain unless it has happened to you. That's why, when tragedy strikes, we all draw even closer into ourselves. No matter what people say, no matter how nice they are, they don't understand what it does to you over the years. It's the toughest thing in the world to keep seeing brothers dying.

By far my worst experience was the explosion. December 27, 1983. A report came in of a leak in a propane tank. It was a four-story brick factory building. Up on the fourth floor, they were moving a propane tank with a forklift. They dropped it off the forklift, the neck broke off, and five hundred gallons of propane vaporized. Since propane is heavier than air, it started going down into the building. Worse, all the windows in this building were cinder-blocked up.

The workers left the building and called the fire department. Ladder 5 arrived, and the place blew up. It killed five members of Ladder 5. They were on location thirty-seven seconds. They never even made it inside the building. They had just gotten off the rig, and the chief was giving some orders.

He was telling them, "Okay, here's what we're gonna do. We gotta ventilate this place and get it opened up."

With that, it just blew. There were no warning signs. There was no way that anyone could suspect.

Besides the five dead members of Ladder 5, nine members of various companies got hurt severely. Two civilians died, and probably another hundred were seriously injured.

I still remember pulling up to that scene. The first thing myself and another firefighter did was kneel down and say an Our Father. It was probably not the most appropriate time, but we were overwhelmed. If you told firemen from all over this scenario—propane leak, old building, what do you think would happen if it exploded?—no one would guess it would look like this. It was truly eerie. This building had been tremendous; now it was rubble. You literally couldn't recognize what it had been. And there was no sound at all as we pulled up. It was just very quiet and now the place was on fire.

We found one Ladder 5 guy real quick. He was relatively intact, so he looked savable. We did CPR on him. But he was dead. Dead as a doornail. The other guys were all terribly destroyed. Complete devastation to their bodies.

I was still relatively new. Needless to say, it was a very long night. And that night was also my wedding anniversary, and the reports coming on TV were really brutal. First they said twenty-five firemen were dead, including the whole third battalion, which I worked in. My wife was terrified. She started making calls to the department, but no one really had information yet, and people all over the city were calling in. So then she called a few emergency rooms. One of the places she called was Buffalo General, where she works as an ER nurse. There was another nurse there who already knew me.

She told my wife, "Yeah, I heard. We have one guy

down here who is just about Mike's size and he has a mustache. He's badly mangled. And he's dead. I think you should come down and see him."

My wife was beside herself. She went down there, and it was another guy who'd gotten killed. He didn't really look like me, but he did have the same size and features. Meanwhile, at the explosion site, all the telephone lines and power lines were down. The explosion had happened about 8:30 at night. By four in the morning I still couldn't get to a phone. Finally, around five, we got back to our firehouse. I called my wife and told her I was alive, but it was a real, real, real long night for her too.

This was back in 1983, when stress counseling was still a pretty new thing. Mostly, we just talked amongst ourselves. We still talk about it today. Last year was the tenth anniversary. There were probably six to eight companies who went by the site. One of our chaplains came there and said Mass for us.

It's funny how it works. Right after it first happens, you're caught in a whirlwind. There are reports being done, funerals being arranged. Things are happening fast and you don't have much time to think. Afterwards, you have a ton of time to think. You're on watch at three in the morning on December 27, and it's *all* you can think about. Those are the loneliest moments. When you're all by yourself in the firehouse and all the ghosts come back.

When someone dies at a scene—in the line of duty—it almost always means a mistake was made.

Oh, no. Absolutely not. I can't think of *anyone* here that died making a mistake.

When I first came in, a guy went out a first-floor

window. It wasn't even six feet high, but his foot got hung up on something in the window. It turned him head down and his helmet caught on something. His helmet came off before he struck the ground. So his air-pack cylinder hit the back of his head, and this forced the front of his head into the concrete. Bingo. He was dead. Coming out of a window less than six feet high. But I don't see that as making a mistake. It was just one of those inexplicable things.

I don't think mistakes are always made, but I do think there are *reasons*. They can be very small, like a kink in the line. Or maybe three or four kinks, which happens a lot with the inch-and-three-quarter lines. Say I'm on the engine. The truckies break the door in the tenement. I walk in the door and I call for water. I have a fire that's brewing, and now with that door open, I also have a tremendous influx of air. So now the fire has what it's hungry for. It has oxygen, which means it can really take off. So I need water now. I'm *expecting* it now.

But if there's a kink in the line, I've got to wait another thirty seconds, just for some guy to run around and unfuck the line. The line could be stuck on a banister, or wrapped around a car. Whatever it is, that's all it takes for a backdraft to occur: those first crucial seconds the fire gets oxygen, and I don't have any water.

When people get hurt or killed, that's all it really comes down to many times. A few seconds here and there. A few tiny things. Then those few seconds and tiny things add up to disaster.

It isn't the equipment. The equipment we have now is better in every way. And we're still getting killed. So, no, it's not the equipment. We *have* the equipment. But sometimes we don't use it, and that's the tragic part.

I just got back from Pittsburgh, where we buried three firefighters. It was a typical bread-and-butter house fire, and so none of them activated their PASS alarms. That's our Personal Alert Safety System, a device we have attached to every air pack. Whenever you go inside an atmosphere where there's smoke, you should turn these on every time. Because if you are motionless for thirty seconds, an alarm goes off. It goes off loudly, too. It's louder than a smoke detector. So it helps other firefighters locate you.

In this particular fire, they didn't have theirs turned on. And when they were found by their fellow firefighters, they had no burns. They suffocated because they ran out of air. If they had their PASS devices on, I'm not saying for sure they would have been found in time. But I think I can say for sure their chances would have been better.

These are the kind of tragedies where you just shake your head. Because it's not the first time. We've heard these stories before. We had the equipment but didn't use it.

We just lost four firefighters here in Seattle. A few days later, we had a counseling session for firefighter families. During this session, a firefighter said he was really saddened by the fact that we were all looking for a reason why they died. He felt we were trying to finger someone for the blame, and he thought that was wrong. He said nothing *had* gone wrong. Everybody did what they were trained to do, and given the same scenario, same situation, they'd do it all the same again. He ended up by saying that it was an act of God.

I agreed with part of what he said. When we lose one of our own, we do tend to look for a flaw. We do it because we need to. If there was a flaw, we can go back to work tomorrow knowing we can correct it. We don't have to face that ominous thought: *We can do everything right and we can still die in a fire.* I don't know if that's good or bad psychology, but it does let us go on.

What I guess I don't believe is that this was an act of God. I'm fairly religious. I don't attend church regularly now, but I did for some time, and I have a pretty fundamentalist Baptist upbringing. And I still don't believe it. The only act of God is that He gave us salvation and wants us all to live eternally through grace. The rest of it is science. The rest of it is natural laws and physics. When bad things happen to us, or to our patients, it is because of those natural laws and physics. I just don't believe that God put that ice on a patch of roadway so that somebody can get killed. It is just there. It is just the timing of events. And then firefighters come along and try and reverse those events. But it isn't God we're confronting. We are trying to overcome those natural laws and physics.

We lost nine guys in 1972. An old hotel under renovation collapsed. I was off that day. I wasn't there. But I talked to guys who were and they said it was, like, fate. After the fire was basically knocked down, the chief came into the building. He went up to Engine 3 and Engine 32. They were side by side, and he told Engine 3 to go get cold drinks or coffee. So Engine 3 went outside and 32 stayed in there. There was this rumble, and there goes the nine guys from 32.

All the guys from 3 were saying later, "Why did the chief pick them? Why wasn't it us?"

As a wildland supervisor, I must believe there are

logical reasons for things. I am leading people into dangerous situations, then leading them out again. If I start believing we're not in control of events, that might not be healthy for me or for my crew.

I fought fires for thirteen years. I was a smokejumper for eleven of those years. In 1976, I moved into investigating fatality wildland fires. Since 1988, I think I've gone to every one in person. I would say that would be about ten to fourteen.

There was a time when I always believed a mistake had been made. As I get older and I suppose more spiritual, I'm not sure anymore. In other cultures, death is accepted as a very natural process. Here in the U.S., we have a tendency to hide death and be embarrassed by it. So whenever we lose a firefighter here, we almost always say, "Hey, that person screwed up."

What we are saying, in part, is we don't believe that this could be something spiritual. Therefore, we will attach our own label to it. We will call it a mistake, because we are dealing with death, and death is something we don't understand.

Whenever I go to fire-line fatalities now, I look at them on two levels. We go to the site and do a thorough analysis. Everything is gone through with tremendous care and attention. And then there's another level, when you're out on the site and you're saying to yourself, *Maybe there was something that pulled these people together. Maybe this was their time to leave, and because they were firefighters, this was the way they decided to check out.*

I do believe in fate. I do believe in the hand of God. Some things are too mysterious to explain.

We had a very close call once in downtown Houston. About 8:45 in the morning on a Sunday, it came in as an ammonia leak at Borden's Ice Cream. I was on Ladder 7. On our way there, we could smell the ammonia from four blocks away. It was so bad we put our air packs on.

It was a three-story building, about a block by a block. The ammonia was flowing out of there pretty good. But this particular kind of ammonia—anhydrous ammonia, or refrigerated ammonia—was supposedly the type that never exploded. It simply could not explode. That's what we'd always been told.

The security guard met us out on the street. He said he knew where the valve was to shut off the ammonia. We put an air pack on him, but the guard had never worn an air pack before. Just as we were about to enter the building, he started to panic and he ran out. He ran back up the street to where we had started from. So we stopped what we were doing and walked back to where he was. We showed him how to breathe with the air pack on, and he told us he was okay. We started back, and it just blew up. Bricks flying everywhere, glass shattering for blocks. It was stone silence except for that, because we were just in shock. This was the ammonia that couldn't explode.

We never saw the security guard again. Once that building blew, he took off running. In fact, somebody said he still had our air pack on. But it was the guard who really saved our lives. If he hadn't felt uneasy and backed out, we would have been in the basement tightening up the valve. It would have killed nine of us. Eight fire-fighters plus the guard.

I still pass by that building all the time. Every time I do, I make the sign of the cross.

5

IT ISN'T A JOB, IT'S A LIFESTYLE

A firefighter, an ex-marine, was sitting in church when a woman passed out. As he ran to her aid, no one else moved to help except one other man. They stopped after church to talk and learned they were both firefighters.

Good firefighters are never quite off duty. They are also rarely surprised by the randomness of life. So each time they go to work, the only thing they expect is trouble in some new form.

It's really a very strange job, where stretches of boredom take turns with manic bursts of activity. When alarms go off in the fire station, firefighters may be drilling or training, inspecting their equipment, diagnosing how to fight various fires, cleaning toilets and mopping floors, just sitting down to dinner, or fast asleep.

It doesn't matter. They're on their fire engines within moments, racing into what might be life-or-death circumstances. So each time they leave their firehouse, they know they might not return. This is a weight they carry, an uncertainty at their core. Their families carry it, too.

"Before I go to work," says one firefighter, "my wife and I have a little ritual every morning. I kiss her on the forehead and tuck her back into bed. Then I never say good-bye. I always say see you later. Meaning, nothing major is going to happen. I'll be back tomorrow."

There are more subtle strains on family life. Just the schedules they work can be disruptive. In most urban fire departments, shifts start at 8:00 A.M. and run for twenty-four hours. The rule is one day on and two days off, but when the city is willing, many firefighters work overtime shifts. As for federal firefighters like smoke-jumpers and Hot Shots, hopping from blaze to blaze and state to state, many are gone for virtually whole summers. So much for the rhythms of home and family.

In addition to working overtime, many firefighters have what they call "side jobs." Working on their days off as carpenters or in construction, they can pick up a quick $150. Some design and sell T-shirts with fire emblems. Others double as fire photographers, listening to their scanners at home and in their cars, then rushing to fires with cameras when they hear something exciting. And in what may or may not qualify as a "side job," San Francisco has two dentists on its department.

With so many firefighters raising families, the extra income can ease financial pressures. Today a starting fire-fighter's base salary is $29,000 a year. After ten years, if they remain firefighters and don't promote, which many top firefighters prefer to do, they earn a base of $38,000. Considering their high rate of cancer, lung disease, heart attacks, and line-of-duty deaths—and that these sacrifices are made as they safeguard us—the money isn't great.

What is fabulous, they all say, are the friendships built with other firefighters. Unlike people in more conventional jobs, firefighters share all their meals, their sleeping quarters, their showers. The close proximity fosters close relationships, often as intimate as those with their families.

Today a small group of women are trying to crash

that peer group. It's been complicated, however, and arduous. Of the roughly 260,000 career firefighters nationwide, women only constitute about 3 percent. In this nearly all-male domain, some women say they still encounter harassment, prejudice, and adolescent mind games. But if their workplace is still not close to ideal, most women say it's improved since 1976, when the first American woman became a full-time paid firefighter.

"When I got hired on, a lot of the guys had nothing to say to me," says one woman firefighter. "If they talked to me at all, they tended to be rude. When we went outside to drill, they watched everything I did so they could pick it apart. But they didn't really know me. They just figured, She's a woman. No way she can do this job. Let's pressure her and maybe she'll quit.

"As they *got* to know me, I think they realized I wasn't that different from them. I wanted to be good at every aspect of the job. I got great satisfaction from helping other people. I couldn't wait to get to work in the morning. I wasn't gonna kiss management's butt.

"All that helped, I think. But what helped the most was showing them I could do it. Once they saw me pull hose and go inside burning buildings, they honestly made me feel like I belonged. They actually treated me like one of the boys."

This isn't a job. It isn't even a career. It's who and what you are. When I get off shift, I don't stop being a firefighter. If I see something on the way home, I'm gonna stop.

I was at Brighams Ice Cream store at a shopping mall one day. I was with my two daughters. While we're standing there waiting for them to make our ice cream, this big commercial blender they had started sparking and burning. The waitresses started screaming. None of the people there really knew what to do.

So I just walked behind the counter, unplugged this blender, carried it outside and put it down, and let it burn out there where it could do no harm. But I was in civilian clothes, so the people in the store were saying, "Who is this guy?"

So I said to the manager, "By the way, I'm a firefighter."

He said, "Oh, yeah, sure! Thanks a lot!"

Then my teenage daughter says to him, "You might want to keep the door open for a little while and turn on your ventilation system. It will air out all the smoke."

I said, "Firefighter's daughter. What can I say?"

Honestly? This job is harder on wives and kids than it is on us.

That goes double when a major disaster strikes. For example, we were at home when Hurricane Andrew hit. It totally destroyed everything we own. Our house was intact, miraculously, but everything else was gone. Our car, our truck, our boat—everything was destroyed.

Then as soon as the wind let up, I had to kiss my wife good-bye at seven in the morning. I went to the fire station and I was gone for five days. My wife and my children were living without phones. They were living without electricity. They were living in an armed camp, because there was so much looting after the hurricane, almost all the residents near us were loading their guns. For those five days while all this was happening, they also lived without their father and husband. Because the public needed me.

I live in Homestead, about thirty miles south of the center of Miami. We didn't get hit quite as hard as Cutler Ridge; that took the worst of the storm. But we did take a real good direct hit. Fortunately, Hurricane Andrew was a very fast storm. It was here for maybe four hours. If it had stalled over us for, say, nine or ten hours, which I guess is fairly common, I think every building in Homestead would have been destroyed. I have talked to some of the old-timers, people who were here for hurricanes Donna and Betsy. They said those were nothing compared to this. The old-timers couldn't believe its power and fury.

That afternoon, before it got here, my dogs wouldn't go outside to go to the bathroom. They would stand at the door and whimper, but I couldn't drag them outside. My father was in the South Seas in the Second World War. He'd been through a couple hurricanes, or typhoons as they call them there. He always told me to keep an eye on the animals.

Later that afternoon, I went outside in our front yard. We had a sixty-foot Norfolk pine standing out there. I thought about cutting the top down, so if it fell over it wouldn't hit the house. I looked up in our tree and it looked like a scene from Alfred Hitchcock's *The Birds*. There were hundreds and hundreds of them, sitting right next to each other. It was real eerie.

At three-thirty in the morning, my wife got me up and said it was getting windier. I'd say the Norfolk pine lasted about ten more minutes. I could see it whipping back and forth. I mean, it was touching the ground on both sides. Luckily, it broke and snapped and flew away from the house. If it had come toward the house, it would have come right in.

I was hearing explosions outside the house. A bottle-brush tree had slammed down on the roof of my truck. It hit so hard, it smashed out all the windows. It was also about this time that we lost power.

At just before five in the morning, it got real calm. From what I understand, this was the eye of the hurricane.

If you go outside during the eye, you need to be real careful, because it can come back real quick from the other side. We had the eye here in Homestead for maybe thirty minutes, so I went outside to see what had happened. Trees were uprooted. Power lines were lying in the street.

The eye had passed over by 5:30 A.M. Then the other half of the storm hit. If we thought the first half was bad, the second half was much worse. The roaring sound was just incredible. It was coming in gusts, and each time a big one blew in, the whole house would shake for twenty or thirty seconds. Toward the south of the house, we have an aluminum window in the kitchen. The wind was blowing so hard there, I could actually see the window frame bowing in and out. So we took out a mattress. I stuffed it in the window in case the glass broke.

Then we heard something break on the east side of the house. The wind had ripped off our hurricane shutter.

It also broke the glass, so the wind came in the house. It blew down the hallway and slammed the bedroom door shut. We had carpeting in this hallway, nailed down at the threshold of this bedroom. The wind picked the carpet up three feet in the air. It was just flapping all the length of the hallway.

The first part of the storm, I had been walking around the house trying to see what it looked like. The second part, we were in the bathroom. It was my wife and I and our friend Wayne. Wayne is a Coral Gables firefighter. He was staying with us after surgery on his knee.

We were huddled in there for probably an hour. In the toilet bowl, we could see the water rise up and down a few inches. Then it would go way down, just like you'd flushed it. But we *didn't* flush it. It was the atmospheric pressure from the storm.

Outside, we could hear the wind banging into the roof. If we lost the roof, I honestly didn't see how we could live through this. I had been scared before, but not terrified like this. Without trying to sound too dramatic, I was actually facing my own mortality. With the sound and the wind, I thought, *We are going to die if the roof comes off this house. We will be sucked right out.*

By 7:00 A.M. it was calming down. I was supposed to start work then. I am a paramedic right here at the Homestead Fire Station. But before I went in, I got some plywood and nailed it over the windows. I boarded things up as much as I could, and then I went outside. The wind was still gusting at maybe sixty miles per hour, but that was nothing compared to what it was. At some points this thing went over two hundred miles per hour.

Outside our house, it was just getting light. Telephone poles were cut in half, held up only by wires. What trees were still standing upright had lost all their leaves. Cars were rolled over. It looked like the pictures you see of Hiroshima after we dropped the bomb on it. Over in Cutler Ridge, I later found out, a school bus got blown on top of a house. Out in the countryside here, it blew a horse into a tree. The horse was stuck up there about ten feet off the ground.

We had no power or water or telephone service. But I wound up going to work at 10:30 A.M. My wife was pretty upset. She didn't want to be left alone. Thank God she had Wayne, but Wayne just had his surgery two days before. His leg was in a cast. He really couldn't do much at that time.

I understood why my wife was upset. And I didn't want to leave her. But here in the fire department, we take an oath to protect the community. And we also have rules: if you can physically make it to work, you go to work.

It was as simple as that. So I put it off as long as I

could, and did whatever I could around the house, and I got in three hours late.

I guess it could have been worse. I mean, if I had been working when Hurricane Andrew hit. If my wife was dead, if she was injured, if the house wasn't standing, I wouldn't know. Not knowing—but still having to work—that would have been the worst. At least this way, I knew she was safe and sound.

You really don't worry that much about yourself. Your main concern is your family. You always make sure your life insurance is paid.

My wife is the sister of a volunteer fireman who I knew real well. She's been around the fire department for a long time. I think it still scares her, but she doesn't say anything. She knows I'm gonna do this no matter what.

Still, I don't want her to worry. So the first thing I do when I get home, I call my wife at work. I know if I forget, she assumes I got decapitated in a fire. So I have to call right away and give her my whereabouts.

Before I leave for work, sometimes I'll tell my wife I'm only driving that night. Driving, to me, is the least dangerous job. So I tell her that just to keep her from worrying. Even though it's a lie.

My wife probably wishes I'd tell her more. There are times I'm sitting at home, and I'll get a flashback of something bad. It's real quick. It's there and it's gone. But my wife will notice it. She'll wait for me to talk, and then I won't. That's just my nature. My family doesn't need to know all the bad things I do.

We had a fatal one time. This common-law husband set a fire in the hallway, and the mother and two kids died. The mother was by the door, by the fire escape. The little ones were in bed. After the fire, the son of a bitch got on a plane and went back to Haiti. As far as I know, he has never come back.

I came home the next day and my wife went to work. I was baby-sitting our kids. And I would have given them anything! You want ice cream for breakfast? Fine! You want to jump on the couch? Whatever you want!

I overcompensated, but that's what happens. We see all this bullshit happen to children. It just makes us love our own kids even more.

I was working Christmas Eve. I had four kids and the family never liked it, but it went with the job. I told my wife this even before we got married.

I said, "I want to be a fireman. That means birthdays, anniversaries, holidays I might miss. It's going to happen. So we have to get used to it and work around it."

This particular Christmas Eve started out quiet. Gas leaks and stuff, just the routine. About 4:30 in the morning, we got a call. It was 117th Street in Harlem, between Morningside and Manhattan Avenue. We pulled up and there was black smoke rolling out the third floor window.

So the guys went in the front door.

Meanwhile, I climbed up the aerial ladder and went in through the front window. You couldn't see anything through all the smoke, and as I went in I knocked the Christmas tree over. I could feel some boxes and some presents. I thought, *Ain't this a bitch. Santa was here.*

But the good thing about it was, Jerry Anken was the forcible entry man. Jerry made the search of the apartment.

He pulled an eleven-year-old kid out of the back bedroom. The kid wasn't breathing, no pulse, but they dragged him out in the hallway and gave him mouth to mouth. And they brought him back. He started breathing again.

When I got home that morning, I was still high. But I was late, and my wife and kids were upset. We had this rule on Christmas: until dad got home from work, the kids couldn't come downstairs to see the tree. And normally I would be there when they woke up, because one of the other guys would come in early for me.

This time I didn't get home until 10:45 A.M. Everyone was mad, so I started telling my wife and kids the story.

As I'm telling the story, I'm getting all teary-eyed.

I said to my wife and kids, "If I knew this would happen every year, I'd work every Christmas Eve the rest of my time on the job."

I probably sound like a nut, but it was awesome seeing that kid start breathing again.

My wife is a wonderful, wonderful person. I've been burned and I've had broken bones, and she's put up with all my whining and complaining. She's the true hero, not me. Because dying is a tough thing, but much worse than dying to me is the thought of being woken at three in the morning, with someone at your door to tell you, "Your husband is dead."

That's got to be some terrible thing to live with. But she lives with it anyway, because she knows I've wanted this job since I was a little kid.

When the phone rings at night and I'm at work, I'm sure that's what she thinks of.

Yeah, it's a bitch. It's a horrible situation to be a wife and look on the news and know that somebody is missing at a fire and your husband is on shift and you don't know that he's okay. That's a terrible burden, and we don't like to talk about it much. We don't like to talk about the stresses of shift work, or the holidays and birthdays and weekends we miss. Every one of us knows how tough it is on our families, but instead of talking about it, we suppress it. Not only to other people, but also to ourselves.

You know why? It's the selfish part of us. We suppress it because we still love being firemen. We don't want to give that up, so that's why we don't discuss the sacrifices. Because once we start to address it, we begin thinking, *Well, fuck. What a selfish son of a bitch.*

We had a structure fire in a two-story, single-family dwelling. This fire had a real big head start. It had been burning in the attic a long time before the people reported it.

So we go up on this roof, which is an A frame. As I sit down on the top of the ridge, I start putting my Nomex hood on. I want my face protected, so I can work close to this fire with my axe.

Suddenly, the fire burns through the roof. We have two ladders up there, but they're on one side of the fire and I'm on the other. As I'm sitting there looking for another escape route, the fire shoots up between my legs. I know I'm in trouble. I better do something quick.

So I look off to my left, and I see just a little patch of blue sky. Still on my butt, I am going to try and scoot over that way. But as I start scooting over, I feel myself falling. A couple of rafters have burnt and the roof has collapsed. I am falling through the roof into the attic.

I probably fall about six to eight feet. I have roof above me and ceiling below me. I'm in the middle of this fire-engulfed attic. All I can see is red. I think, *I am a goner. I can't believe this is happening to me.*

Because nothing ever happens to me, you know?

Then I flash on my family. I start thinking, *Hey, I gotta survive. I'm not gonna sit here and just give up. If I'm going to die, I'm gonna be* doing *something when I die.*

So I stand back up, and I just start walking. I'm fanning my hands, like you see in the movies when guys are on fire. I'm trying to keep my cool, knowing that when guys panic that's when they get hurt. So I'm walking in there, and there's fire on three sides. So I walk to the only side where there is no fire. I realize I'm walking out toward the street.

I just keep walking out of the fire and smoke, and one of the other guys sees me. He lets out a yell and everyone pulls up a ladder. It's a twenty-foot ladder and I'm twenty-four feet up. So I figure I'll just jump down and grab out my hand. But when I jump and get my hand on the top rung, my lower body comes swinging back up. I do a somersault in the air and come straight down. There is a rookie standing there who breaks my fall. I actually pile-drive him into the ground.

That was the biggest scare I've ever had. I ended up at the burn center for three days, with second- and deep-second-degree burns. I got burned around my eyebrows and my eyes, my nose and both my cheeks, and my bottom lip and chin. I was really concerned about how my wife would find out. She was pregnant with our second son, and I was afraid of her panicking. I was scared for her health and for the baby's.

But the fire department was really good about it. I told them my concern, and they notified her by phone. They told my wife I was injured, but it was no big deal. They said they were sending someone to pick her up, but only so she could come see me. She was suspicious of course, but they did a real nice job of not making her alarmed. Without the phone call first, I know she would have died if she saw the red car pull up. That's every wife's worst dread.

Even before this happened, my wife and I had a good marriage. We were really happy with each other. But afterwards, it was the best it had ever been. We were like kids again. We would be driving somewhere and holding hands in the car.

After I got burned, my wife was at the hospital every day. Her boss gave her almost four weeks off. So every time I'd wake up, she'd be sitting there. I never saw her cry. She was very strong. I don't know how she did it, because I was pretty ugly-looking then. Without exaggeration, you couldn't recognize me.

The low point was probably the first skin graft on my lip. Under my nose and above my lip, the skin had burnt so bad it drew my lip upward. So first the doctor dropped my lip back to normal height. Then he laid a piece of cadaver skin across there. He left that there for a couple days. Then he covered it with my own skin, from my stomach.

In this interim period, before he covered up the cadaver skin, I went into the bathroom and took off my bandages. It was the ugliest thing I've ever seen in my life. I swear to God it was. I looked at myself and I thought, *This doctor fucked me. He screwed me over. I'm going to look like this the rest of my life.*

It was just a temporary skin graft. After a while, it looked much better. I mean, I still look in the mirror and say, "God, you are an ugly son of a bitch." But I can deal with that. I may not look as pretty as I did before, but I still have my family. And that's a lot.

Because of the economy, most fire guys with young kids now have a wife that's working. They are known at the station as Mr. Mom. They come home from work and the roles are reversed.

I know that's how it works with me and my wife. She works during the day, so I cook dinner every Monday through Friday. It's not really fair for your spouse to work all day while you sit on your ass eating Bon Bons and watching Oprah, and then you say to her when she walks in, "Honey, I want some dinner."

So I cook and then I clean up. And that's the other good thing for firefighter's spouses: most firefighters are clean. Because you can't get away with being a pig at the station. If you leave something out, whether it's a bowl of spaghetti, your shoes, your socks, your candy bar wrapper, you'll find it in your bedding. If you leave your sheets unmade when you go off shift, you'll still find the sheets when you come back in. Only they will be in the freezer, frozen solid, stuffed in a coffee can they filled with water. It's just a small reminder. Hey, we're not your maid. Pick your shit up.

Part of the problem for families is overtime. The more overtime you work, the more money you bring home. But when you work overtime, you are working another twenty-four hours! There are people who work five days in a row, which I think is absolutely outrageous. Not only can no one work at their optimum that long, you don't see your family for one whole week.

Overtime stresses families in other ways. The money becomes addictive. When you start working four overtime days a month, or six days a month, that's a couple of thousand extra dollars, easy. That looks pretty good on your take-home pay. So you start changing your lifestyle. You start to upgrade things and live beyond your means, and rely on the overtime to keep it all going. But what if you get injured, or that overtime dries up? You are going to find yourself in a world of hurt. So is your family, because everything you do is affecting them. It happens a lot, believe me. Probably a lot more than people ever discuss.

Unless they are firefighters, people do not quite understand what we do. Even my own mom didn't understand.

I was on the job two years when we had a Thanksgiving dinner at the station. So I invited my parents and my brother. We cooked a big turkey, got chairs from a local church and set it all up. As I'm talking to my mom, the alarm bell goes off. Then over the loudspeaker, the dispatcher comes on and tells us where we're going. Well, as soon as it starts to ring and he starts to talk, I get up and walk out. My mom turns to my brother.

She says, "God, how rude. Just to get up and walk away in the middle of a conversation!"

Now my mother knows. That's my occupation. You have to change hats in an instant.

In 1978, a guy I worked with got killed. Good friend of mine. Some kids were playing with matches and started a fire. My friend stepped on a gutter and fell off the roof. Landed on his head and that was it. He died the next day.

I was crying at home for two or three days. My wife never saw me like this; I knew it blew her mind. I tried explaining to her, the camaraderie and stuff. But I don't think she understood it. Not completely.

Last year this guy I grew up with died of a heart

attack. He died at home, at night, but it was termed a line-of-duty death, because he'd been at the firehouse that day. They'd worked a fire that afternoon, and afterwards he felt shitty.

My wife went to the funeral. It was the first one she attended. Both my friend and I belonged to the Gaelic Brigade, and the whole brigade was there with pipes and drums.

My wife told me after the funeral, "I never realized how close you guys were until I saw what happened there today."

CAMARADERIE

Our bond is real. If anything, it tends to get understated. But you really get to see it after a major fire. When everything went well, no one got killed or hurt, there is almost a party atmosphere at the station.

Conversely, there is an attitude of defeat when someone dies or gets injured. Every man is staring into his coffee cup, wondering what he did wrong that caused this to occur. That's what holds the bond. Everyone takes the credit and everyone feels the pain.

There's nothing that feels so good as going inside a fire with several other firemen. It's black. It's hot. You're breathing real heavy. You're ducking down low and opening up your hose line. Once the water hits the fire, you feel the steam around your ears and wrists and neck. But then you hear the saws on top cutting holes, opening up that roof, and a minute later it starts to cool off a bit. You keep spraying water. A couple more minutes pass and things are almost returning back to normal. Later on you come out and you look at each other. Everyone is filthy. All your helmets are messy. It looks like you just got back from an explosion.

It's a tremendous feeling. Wow, man, we did it. We kicked some ass. We had a good time. Let's do it again!

I have two close circles of friends: those who are fire-fighters and those who aren't. It gives me a good balance, because there are other ways to look at the world than how firemen look at it.

When I go to a movie and I sit down, the first thing I look at is where the exits are, and whether they are lit, and how I can get to them. I don't even look at the door I came in, because I know six hundred people will try to get out that door. That's just the way we're taught: it's always good to have another way out.

My nonfirefighter friends don't look at things that way. I'll sit down at dinner and they'll see me looking around. I only do it for a second, but they'll say, "What are you looking at?"

My wife will say, "Well, he's looking around to find another exit."

They'll say, "Jesus Christ. Can't we have one fucking dinner without you worrying about Armageddon?"

I'll say, "I'm not worried about Armageddon. If fire happens, I just want to know where to go."

When I was a probie, I remember going to firefighter parties and seeing guys my father's age act a certain way. I was flabbergasted.

I said, "My God, my father would never do this."

But then again, my father wasn't a fireman. These

guys, myself included, need an escape valve. So they
drink a few beers and talk loud and everyone has a good
time. When I socialize with my neighbors, or my wife's
friends, it's always much different. Everything's much
more staid. A couple times, I've said something I knew
would go over fine in the firehouse. And these people
give you this look, like, *Are you for real? Where are you
coming from with a statement like that?*

You're standing there thinking, *Well, I guess that just
went over like a lead balloon.*

You just can't talk shop to people who aren't firemen.
The things we see are too unbelievable. At a barbecue
with neighbors, if you were to tell this story of what you
saw last night, they'd think, *This guy's the biggest bull-
shitter I've ever met.*

So you don't even bother. But if you were talking to
another fireman, he'd understand implicitly what you
meant.

Nothing is sacred in the firehouse. You rag on each
other brutally. I work in a house with seven guys, and
four of them are fairly religious. So it keeps our humor
pretty clean. But don't get me wrong. We give each other
crap nonstop. I mean, it's flying all day.

We're like a family with lots of brothers and sisters.
There is a pecking order, and you all fit into your little
realm. But no matter where you stand on the totem pole,
you can't have thin skin. They'll eat you alive.

We call our kitchen the Kevlar room. You need a damn
bulletproof vest just to sit in there and eat.

Are you serious? The comments *never* stop. It sounds like a bunch of old ladies. That was the saying, in fact, back when our department had only two women on it.

"We have two women firefighters in Buffalo, and 860 old ladies."

Firefighters have these dual personalities. One minute they might be in the fire station, ripping somebody's character apart. But in the next minute, they're willing to save your wife and children. They will die for you, and they don't even know you or your family.

Totally schizophrenic.

There's a lot of ethnic humor around the firehouse. I'm Jewish and I still hear it: "Why ain't you in the banking business, huh?"

But everybody gets ribbed. I'm the first guy to use the word *dago* or *mick*. Then someone else comes back, "Hey, did you hear that? The Jew's calling you a dago."

But actually, it's calmed down quite a bit. Back in the seventies, we had a group of World War II veterans. Well, they were bigoted fellows. They were Irish or Polish, and you'd be sitting there, and they would make a remark about the Jews. It wasn't directed at you, so you didn't want to jump up and defend it right away. But sometimes you had to tell them to lighten up. You had to draw the line, and they had to know they could not jump over it.

You know something, though? When my father died, they all came to his funeral and put the yarmulke on. When it came down to that, they were there for you.

We had twenty-one guys eating every night at our

station, and this one guy did most of the cooking. It was his firm belief that every meal should be kept as cheap as possible. So he'd buy six packages of macaroni and cheese. Then he'd buy frozen meat to go with that. He would do everything he could to keep it under two dollars a man. And guys argued with him constantly about this.

"We'd rather pay the extra money," we'd say.

This guy wouldn't budge. Pot roast and macaroni, chicken and macaroni, pot roast and macaroni. We were sick and tired of it.

So one night he brings in half a chicken a man. When I walk in the kitchen, I see him filleting these chicken cutlets. He also has macaroni for a side dish. So now I'm a little pissed off. But you have to realize that I'm a lieutenant, so I'm supposed to have more decorum than most guys. So I just stand there, staring at these chickens.

We cook the meal. Put it on the table. The engine and truck get a run while we're eating the meal. So, they go out. Meanwhile, we're on the rescue and we aren't dispatched. So just as those guys leave, just as we're putting tin foil on their plates, I get totally pissed. I'm just so pent-up and frustrated, I guess. Anyway, I take down my pants and rub my balls in his food.

To make a long story short, they come back from the run. And the six of us in the rescue now bust out laughing. I mean, we are on the floor. But nobody ever told. This was one of those deep dark secrets that never got out for years.

The next day or so my wife was was doing the laundry.

She said, "You've done a lot of strange things in your life, but can you explain the macaroni and cheese in your underwear?"

So I told her the story. She knows my history. She knows I'm a little bit of a comedian. But this was too much. She was beside herself.

She said, "How could you lower yourself to do this?"
I said, "I don't know. I just did it."

Humor in the firehouse is constant. It's just a constant humorous picking on somebody's tastes and quirks. All you have to say is, "I don't like chicken." You'll never eat anything else the rest of your life.

We had this one guy early in my career. He was a very officious German-American person. A huge man, an excellent firefighter, but a know-it-all. He was an expert on anything he did.

So when he bought his Volkswagen—even before he bought it—all he did was talk about this thing. It was made by the Germans, and it got tremendous mileage and all this stuff. Well, it didn't have a gas gauge. It had this little do-daddy instead. When it got down to a gallon and a half, it gave him a signal to get some gas.

After he got the car, all he talked about was how great his mileage was. We listened to him for a while. Then we would all add two bits to the price of dinner, buy a few gallons of gas, and put it in his car without telling him. He thought he was getting, like, eighty-three miles to the gallon.

He'd come in and say, "Hey, I haven't filled the Volkswagen in a month. You know how many miles a gallon I'm getting?"

He would tell us and we'd say, "You're full of shit. You're just bullshitting us."

The guys would just rag on him, but he didn't care. He had this fantastic car. Finally, he wrote to Volkswagen company and told them what a marvelous car this was, and that he was getting eighty-three miles to the gallon. Volkswagen must have thought he was full of shit.

We let it go on for about six months. Then when he

came to work, we started taking gas out of his car. Now he was getting, like, eight miles to the gallon. He was running out of gas every two days.

A lot of the horseplay revolves around ice cream, because ice cream is such a big part of our tradition. If you go into any fire station from coast to coast, and you walk in with cream, you da man. They know you know what you're doing.

Yeah, ice cream is huge. First day on the job, it means you buy everyone ice cream. It's your birthday, your anniversary on the job, you screw up during a drill? Better come back from the grocery store with ice cream.

It's really just a way for guys to get dessert, and it does promote camaraderie, but I've never liked the tradition. Some of the guys can carry it to excess. They end up getting fat.

I've seen it all with guys protecting their cream. Let's say one shift gets to be known as ice cream hogs. Like maybe our A shift bought cream because someone screwed up. We don't finish it all, so there's some left over. The B shift comes in the next day and polishes it off. Well, that will piss us off, because we want the rest of the cream our next shift back. So you doctor up the cream. You set them up.

I've seen every kind of insanity. I've seen guys shave Ex-Lax into chocolate chip. We had this other ice cream hog who just kept powering into everyone else's stash. So they put a condom in there. They melted the sides of the container, so the whole block of cream would just slip out. When it was nice and soft, they stuck a condom in the middle, then put it back in the freezer. It melted back together to form another lump. Firemen can be ingenious.

Only it backfired on them. The day they tried to nail

him, it just so happened their chief was coming over. The chief took a big scoop and lo and behold; there was the condom. He wanted to know who did it and no one was saying of course. They told him they thought it came from the store that way.

People seem to think the city pays for our meals. When we're shopping in the store, they walk up and say, "What are we buying you today?"

"Pardon me?"

"Don't we pay for your meals?"

No. Everybody pitches in five bucks. That's our budget per day, and whoever is shopping had better stay in that budget. The meal better be good, and there better be a lot. So every day, we have to shop. That's why a lot of people say, "Geez, I see the firemen at my store every time I go."

Well, yeah. It's not like your house, where you can buy a bunch of stuff and freeze it. There's no room at the firehouse. Plus, we have twenty-four guys working out of that place. You can't have twenty-four guys with one loaf of bread a week and a half gallon of milk. You gotta keep hitting the store.

The five bucks we pay each day is just for dinner. Then you pay an additonal three bucks a month for the station fund. That goes toward the salsa and mayonnaise and relish and mustard and peanut butter and jelly. Then there's an additional fund for those who drink coffee. That's $2.50 a month and that buys all the coffee, Cremora, Equal, and sugar.

On every shift, there's a guy in charge of each of these different funds. Because if you make money on dinner, you keep that in a kitty. Because when Christmas or Thanksgiving come around, you all want your families to

come and eat with you. So that excess money goes
toward a really nice holiday dinner. We'll get a turkey,
some ham. Maybe some Marie Callendar pies, that kind
of thing.

We had a guy at Station 16 named John Byars. He
was a big, fat, ugly guy. His favorite saying was "If I'm
lying, I'm dying."

We used to call him Fry-Daddy. Everything he
cooked, he fried, and he always had grease all over the
front of his shirt. It was incredible. Every time he cooked
we had to repaint the kitchen.

That's how it is in the firehouse. There's always a lot
of different personalities, and all these ethnicities. It
makes firehouse life very interesting, too. For example,
we got a guy we call the Camel Jockey. His name is
Socrates Isenberg, of all names. But the guy is
Nicaraguan or something. And after he goes fishing and
catches some snapper, or yellowtail, he brings it into the
station for us to eat. Except that he don't gut them, he
don't scale them, nothing. He throws them in a pan and
throws them in the oven. The thing comes out and its
eyes are looking at you.

We are like, "Jesus Christ, man, don't you even gut the
damn thing?"

One time, we had what we called "The Great Station
16 Conch Day." Down here in Dade County, we have
what we call conch. It's a type of snail that grows out
here on the reef. One day, the word came down from the
state: pretty soon they'd be no more harvesting conch,
because they were becoming rare. So all of us got
together, and we took out our boats and got our limit of
conch.

We brought it all in and made our assembly line. We

have to clean these conch. What this involves is knocking a hole in the top of the shell, then jerking the snail out of the shell. This thing looks like a gigantic booger, okay? I mean, they are really disgusting-looking, right?

So my job was to cut the beaks and feet and dicks and everything else off the thing that wasn't eatable. And Socrates was standing right behind me, picking all this stuff up and eating it raw.

I said, "Man, what's the matter with you?"

He said, "What are you talking about? That's the best part of the conch."

That's just a little story about the ethnicity that goes on here. What we throw away is the stuff some guys like to eat. But I will say this about Socrates. He was a real hard worker, and he had a real good sense of humor for a Latin individual. He just had some weird eating habits.

There's a tradition in our department. Whenever you're moving on to another station, they'll pull a prank on you. Usually, they do it on your last shift.

On my last shift, we had an emergency medical drill. It was on how to do patient care at the scene of a traffic accident. There were about eighteen people there, our nine guys and another nine guys who were drilling with us. They asked me to be the patient, and they were really smooth.

They said, "Hey, Jim, why don't you go ahead and lie down on the floor, and Fireman So-and-So will do a patient assessment."

I was one of the younger guys. So I said, "Okay, sure!"

So I lay down on the ground and he looked at me.

He said, "Well, you've probably got a neck and back injury, so I'm gonna need a C-collar."

That is basically a plastic neck brace. But that's not what they brought in. They brought in a backboard, the kind we use for people we think have back injuries. That's when it clicked: they're gonna tie me up.

I tried getting up real fast and everyone jumped on me. So now they're holding me down, putting this backboard beneath me, and tying me to the board. After I'm tied up I can't escape, so then they take me out to the back of the station. They tie me up to the hose tower. They start hosing me down with the fire hose. One guy is taking pictures the whole time.

I guess our cook that day was in on it, too. He had bought some extra eggs at the store, and then, when I was all wet, he came out and poured eggs on my head. Now everyone's laughing and pointing and making snide comments, and I'm still tied to the tower. Then someone else comes out and dumps flour over my head. Now my face is all white.

After they hose me down some more, they let me go get cleaned up. I take off all my clothes and get in the shower. After I'm cleaned up, I get all dried off and go to comb my hair. I look in the mirror. My hair looks like dough. It's from all the eggs and flour and water. So I have to go back in there two or three times, to finally get all that dough shit out of my hair.

No, I wasn't pissed. Why should I get pissed? If they did it to someone else, I woulda been in there too.

A lot of it is frustration. If you get stuck with an extra shift, you're spending forty-eight straight hours with the same people. None of you have any privacy. You're all wearing a uniform all day. Sometimes you feel stifled.

It's not like being at home. You can't just crank your music. You can't just go to the fridge and grab something to eat. You can't decide not to make your bed that day. Imagine making your bed for twenty years. Tugging around your gear for twenty years. Not having your own bathroom for twenty years.

It makes you nuts. And that leads to people getting on each other's cases.

We have a fire captain here who just went off the job with a heart attack. He had a quadruple bypass surgery, and he's making a fantastic recovery. He wants to come back to work. He's already done all his treadmills and his stress test. He passed them easily. He's better than he was before the heart attack.

But the doctor said he can't come back to work. He basically told him, "You can climb Mt. Everest. You can run marathons. You can do anything in the world you want to do, but one. You can't sit around a firehouse waiting for the alarm bells to go off."

It tells you a lot about the stressors we have.

Getting woken up in the middle of the night—nothing's more stressful than that. Nowadays, in Houston, it isn't that bad. The lights just kick on, then it goes beep, beep, beep, beep for about five seconds. It's really pretty gentle compared to the old days. With those clanging bells just knocking them out of bed, you'd hear stories about these guys found dead in their bunk. They had heart attacks from the shock of getting woken like that.

If I go on a mundane call at one or two in the morning, I can go back to the station and be sleeping again in thirty minutes. But if I go on a call that really tests me, I can lie there wide awake the rest of the shift. After something *really* tough, I get a funny metallic taste in my mouth. I don't know if it's adrenaline or not, but I know I can't sleep. I think it happens to other people, too. Because, very often, I will not have any trouble finding company to talk to.

How well you sleep depends on where you're stationed.
For a few years, I worked on one of the top forty busiest companies in the nation. The shift was twenty-four hours. You worked all morning and afternoon. Then you ate dinner, went on some more calls, and went to bed at eleven. In the course of the night, you woke up five or six times. When you got off shift in the morning, you'd barely slept.

Even at a slow station, you're fucked if you're a light sleeper. You're sleeping in a dorm with eight other guys, so you can bet one of them snores and does it loudly. That's a real problem if you're a light sleeper. And then there's all that farting and goofing around, especially when there's rookies.

Sleeping at the firehouse is a bitch.

FEMALE FIREFIGHTERS

Those are the number one and two questions from all my girlfriends: "Where do you sleep? Do you sleep right next to the guys?"
I'm not kidding. They're really fascinated by the sleeping stuff. They'll make statements, too. Some of them say, "God, it must really be hard for you, being around all those guys all the time."

I say, "Yeah, it is."

But a lot of them say, "God. You are so so lucky."

I say, "Yeah, right."

Actually, each firehouse is different when it comes to

sleeping arrangements. When I first started out in one fire department, we just had one big dorm with a bunch of beds. But at least we had dividers between the beds. Since that time, I've also slept in a station without dividers. In that firehouse, you were pretty much talking zero privacy. Because a lot of guys would change right there by their beds. It didn't bother me, but the thought went through my head: *How would they react if I did that? I would never hear the end of it.*

The bathroom can be a nightmare in itself. At the station I'm at now, they recently had a woman's bathroom built. This is like heaven. A whole new bathroom and no one to bother me.

But previously, I would share their bathroom with them. The shower, the toilets, the sink—I mean everything. We'd all be lined up in the morning, brushing our teeth, looking nasty.

The biggest drag was trying to take a shower. I worked at one station where there were thirteen of us, and everybody wanted to get their shower. I tried everything. First I tried getting up at six in the morning to shower.

But then I said, "Screw this. I don't want to get up at six if I can sleep in until seven."

So then I'd get up at seven. But there would be two or three guys already inside the stall, singing and talking and taking their shower. So I'd have to wait. Because we had this sliding sign that said WOMEN/MEN, and they'd have the men's sign on. So I'd wait and wait and wait, while all these *other* guys just kept walking into the shower.

I finally had enough. So I go to work one morning and grab a chair. I put it in front of the door while there are guys in the shower.

I sit in front of the door and say, "Nobody's coming through!"

They're going, "Oh, c'mon, I'll just take a minute!"

I said, "No way. Sorry. You have to wait."

They started complaining.

I said, "Sorry! No!"

Soon as those first few guys in the shower came out, snap, I was right inside. That's what I had to do if I wanted to shower. But I always kept things light. Because I am a realist. And I am in a profession that's mostly men. The only way to fit in is to show them you can't be rattled.

No. I wasn't accepted right away. Our fire department had about eighty people. When I joined, there were only two other women. But they both worked the other shift. That made me the only woman on mine. So I was fresh bait, you know?

We had this one kinda country guy, very traditional. He didn't think women should be in the fire department. Period. He was also going through a divorce, and he was bringing all this stress to work. I guess being the only woman there, I was easy to take it out on.

As soon as I started working, he told me I was really disrupting his life.

I asked him what he meant.

He said, "Now I have to wear boxer shorts to bed!"

I said, "Oh, darn. That's really a bummer. Then again, I have to wear underclothes and a pair of shorts to bed. So I guess we're even, aren't we?"

That's how he started out; this trivial stuff that was mostly just annoying. Then, as time went on, I think his goal was to make me quit. He would talk behind my back. He would talk about me when I was standing there. He was an engineer, and every time we'd have a particular drill, he would single me out.

He'd say, "Go retrieve the ladder and carry it over. Then go ladder this building."

As I would be doing this, he would be making jokes at my expense. Whether you're male or female, the drills we do are physically demanding. I didn't need that extra crap.

One time I said something to him. He went right to our captain. The captain told me later, "I heard what you said today. You really have to be careful how you talk to these guys. You're gonna hurt their feelings."

I said, "Hurt their feelings? They oughta stop and put themselves in my shoes!"

Most guys never do, though. Whether they're in the fire department or not, they want you to bend to them.

I never had a problem with any of them. Not even one. I was accepted. I was one of the guys. We were all one unit. It was great.

Oh, God, yeah. Sexual things at work go on all the time. Just the other day, I got slapped on the butt by an assistant chief. That's way out of line, but I'm thinking, *What do I say to this guy?*

Because it puts me in a very awkward situation. If I ever get back on his shift, he could squish me down on the ground and make my life hell. So I just ignored it. I don't know what I'll do if it happens again.

It's probably not that different from any other job. I work with gentlemen and I work with dogs. Last week I came in, and one of the dogs had folded up something and put it in my mail slot. I pull it out, and it's this poster of a half-naked woman. Nobody else was around, so I didn't say anything. But it bothered me. I thought it was rude. Later that day the chief walked in. He's a new chief on our shift, so a lot of things are changing. I mean little things, like mail slots.

So he says to our crew, "If you don't all know this by

now, you all have your own mail slots. Periodically you should check them. There may be something important in there."

I said to myself, *Ta-da! Here is my chance!*

So I reached down for this thing and I held it up to the room.

I said, "What, Chief? Mail like this?"

I think I shocked him. His mouth dropped open.

I said, "This apparently *doesn't* belong in my mail slot. And I hope it disappears. And I hope I don't find anything else like that."

The chief called me in when the meeting broke up.

He said, "If anything like that happens again, I want you to go to your captain or supervisor."

I said it seemed like something *he* should know. I said it seemed like the right opportunity to tell him.

He repeated himself. I should tell my captain or supervisor. He was basically saying, "Don't come to me with this stuff." He was using the chain of command as an excuse, but that's what he was saying.

There's plenty of great guys, too. If there wasn't a lot of great guys, there wouldn't be *any* women in the department. A few of my closest friends are male firefighters. We go out sailing, or drinking beer, and I know they're my friends. There's no romantic interest, so it's a lot of fun. I can talk to them. I can be myself.

I think the best part for me—what helps me survive—is how this job makes me feel. Everywhere I go, the public is very supportive. Unbelievably supportive. Especially other women. At the grocery store I shop at before I come into work, other women see me dashing around. I'm in my uniform and they say, "Going to work?"

"Yeah."

"Go get 'em today. You gotta do it for us women."

Or they say, "It's great to see women firefighters. We're real proud of you."

The job is hard, but it is very rewarding. I go to sleep at night feeling good about what I do.

THE PHYSICAL PRICE THEY PAY

Mentally, I think it keeps you young. You see these young people coming in, learning the job and getting better at it, it takes you back to your own youth. In a way it's like seeing your own children grow up.

But physically, this job will make you old. When most firefighters join the department, they're more fit than their peers in the general public. By the time they retire, many of them are less fit. The job has taken its physical toll on them.

I can be in a dead sleep, and in four minutes I am performing at maximum effort. The heart isn't meant to do that. It's meant to gradually increase, maintain a certain level and then come down. That's why fire guys retire and five years later they're dead. The wear and tear on the heart.

At the Interstate Bank fire in downtown Los Angeles, we had thirty-pound hose packs on. We had thirty-five pounds of air tank on our backs. Along with our turnout pants and turnout coats, we were easily carrying a hundred pounds over our body weight. And then, at the Interstate, the fire was up on the sixteenth floor. So you're carrying a hundred pounds above your weight up sixteen floors. *Then* you start fighting the fire.

For me, the toughest physical part is doing roof work.
Opening up a roof, you got to punish yourself. Because you don't have a mask on up there. You cannot work on a roof while wearing a mask. The mask is too cumbersome and the visibility's poor. If you're gonna use a saw, you gotta see what you're cutting.

Once you cut the hole—about four by four—you have to pull up the top of the roof. That is usually made of tar and gravel. After you pull that up, you punch through the ceiling down below. As you are doing this, you are sticking your face right over the fire. You're gonna take a beating, but you just gotta keep going, until you accomplish the ventilation you need. There are firemen underneath you, trying to enter a room or make a burning stairway. There might be civilians. You must draw that heat and fire away from them.

The other thing about roof work is, nobody's up there watching you. No one is saying, "Good job." You're by yourself. So it's kind of a self-flagellation thing. If you feel the heat coming out and hitting your face, you know you're getting it done.

I've been hurt a lot, but everyone has. I've been very lucky, though. I never had that real serious injury. Mostly what I get is cuts and burns.

Sometimes an ember will go down your coat. I had one a couple months ago. You know it's down there, but you're all dressed up like a mummy and you can't get to it. So the only thing you can do is push it into your body. It's not real comfortable. It's kind of like putting a cigarette out on your tongue. But otherwise, as it keeps working its way down, an ember will keep burning everything it touches. You're better off taking the burn right there on your chest.

Our people are always getting these strange little injuries. We had one guy get hurt by falling into a bathtub. The odd part of it was, the bathtub was outside the house. So this house was burning up, the guy was pulling a line, and he fell in this tub on the side of the house.

He wound up having surgery on his knee. He was off the job for several months.

You can see smoke. You can usually see the fire. It's the unseen thing that reaches out and gets you. When someone gets hurt that way, we call it Fucking Magic.

In 1988, I went off the job for a year because I got hurt. I lost my eye. I have one eye now.

It was the last way on earth I ever thought I'd get hurt. My wife too. She always figured me getting burned or falling off a roof, the typical ways that firemen get hurt. This was just a freak thing. It really sucked.

We were at a bona fide working fire, and I pulled up in front of the fire building. Normally I don't drive, but I drove that day because the regular driver was off. When I saw we had a fire, I was gung ho. I wanted to get right in there.

I was stepping off the rig and it was just split-second timing. One of the guys was pulling off the pike pole. It has a point on the end for pulling ceiling down. The point went through my eye. It didn't knock me out, but I went down to the ground and I just stayed there. I knew I was hurt bad.

At the hospital, I wanted to call my wife. I didn't want anyone else calling her, because it was one in the morning by this time. When she picked up the phone, I wanted her to hear my voice.

So the chief dialed the phone and handed it to me.

I said, "Hi, Elaine."

She said, "Hi, Jim, what's wrong?"

I said, "I had a little accident. I got something in my eye."

It turned into the lousiest night of my life. I was having emergency surgery in the morning, so I couldn't drink or eat and they wouldn't give me medication. I just laid there in shock and pain. And it was just as bad for my wife and my dad. They were hurting, too.

That next whole year was difficult for us. I wound up having six surgeries. But they ended up taking my eye out anyway. Then I had to decide whether or not I wanted back on the job. At first, I was all over the place. One minute, I wanted back. Then I would be ready to pull the plug, just take my disability and move on. For a while I thought of becoming a teacher, because I was finishing up my bachelor's degree. Like I said, I was torn.

When I finally decided I wanted to come back, my wife wasn't real wild about my decision. But she still stood behind me 100 percent. She could tell I was miserable. When you love something that much, then you get hurt and it's taken away from you—it's a devastating thing.

So I told the fire department I wanted to stay on. One day soon I got a call from the chief.

He said, "Jim, you gotta come down and talk."

So I went down and he said, "I don't think you can come back."

I said, "Chief, I know two guys with one eye who are on the job right now."

They hadn't lost them on duty the way that I had. One guy lost his to cancer. The other guy got hit in the eye with a bottle in a barroom fight. But both these guys were still working.

The chief said, "Oh, really? I didn't realize that."

So I did it. I came back. And then I got promoted to lieutenant. Not because I lost my eye; I was already on the list.

After I made lieutenant, I became a training officer. I wasn't in the field. I was teaching new recruits at the academy, working eight hours a day like a normal person. I didn't like it. Even though I made great friends at training school, I missed being on a rig.

So next I went out to work on a squad at the airport. I was back on a rig, but it was kind of dull. There weren't any fires. You were there in case a plane crashed. You wound up looking at airplanes all day.

I was really bummed, so I put in a transfer and got this place I'm at now. I'm been here over a year, and I feel like I'm back in the fire department again. I'm on a truck. So I still gotta be careful about my eye. But I'm real happy again. I got great guys in the firehouse with me. I look forward to going to work. That's another reason I didn't want to leave. My best friends in the world are on this job.

When firefighters get killed in the line of duty, everyone talks about it. As well they should. But when they die later on from occupational illness, you really don't hear too much. Yet it happens all the time, because every single time you take in smoke, it never goes away. Your body just absorbs it. At minimum, if you're fortunate, it will only destroy your nose's inner lining. You'll wake up every morning with congestion. But at its most corrosive, smoke is related to cancer and heart disease.

Even if it doesn't bother you at the fire, you can't help but ingest some smoke. You know how you know? At three o'clock the next afternoon, you're sitting around and you smell like a ham.

While you're fighting the fire, it gives you a runny nose. The smoke goes into your nose and irritates the mucous membranes in there. So, your nose starts running. It's like your body is saying, "I don't want this smoke to go any further. So we'll stop it right here in the nose."

That's why most firefighters have mustaches. When your nose runs inside a fire, having a mustache keeps it out of your mouth.

My first seven years in the fire department, I was a professional Santa Claus at Macy's in San Francisco. One year we had a big fire at a hotel. The next day I went into Macy's. This little kid comes up and starts sniffing around.

He said, "Santa, you smell smoky."

I said, "Well, it's all those chimneys you go down. That's what you get."

One thing about being a fireman: you're always inhaling tons of shit you shouldn't be. Over the years, in my case, I guess it took its toll.

In October of 1991, we were having a pretty quiet night. Then we went on a run about five in the morning. It was one of those fires where everything was going wrong from the get-go. To make a long story short, the chief was pulling all the hairs from his head. So then he orders us, the rescue squad, into the fire building.

He says, "Get in there. Make sure they're putting water on this thing."

I made it inside the apartment door, took a little smoke, and that's where they found me. I was in respiratory arrest. I had stopped breathing. My entire system completely shut down.

So they dragged me out to the street and got me breathing again. I woke up in the hospital six hours later, with this tube down my throat and my arms tied down. Apparently, I had been fighting them the whole way, trying to keep them from putting the tube down my throat.

Their diagnosis is what they call a hyperactive airway, which is a form of asthma. And they tell me I can't go to fires no more.

Right now, I really don't know what I'm gonna do. I'm hanging on. I've got a light-duty job. I'm still a member of the fire department. But I was one of them guys: I was gonna stay until I had thirty years on the job. Now it will be cut short, and it's a tough thing. It's everything I always wanted to do. And it's ending a little too soon.

I joined the Fort Lauderdale Fire Department in 1966. Three years later, we had the Everglades Fertilizer Factory fire.

We were off duty that morning. But I was driving down the highway with a buddy, another firefighter, and we looked out to the west.

He said, "Holy Cow! Something is really burning!"

So we drove toward it.

When we pulled up at the scene, the black acid smoke was just rolling up in the sky. The entire factory was totally involved. The roof had caved in. There were a lot of explosions. It was spectacular to see. Even though it's deadly and destructive, sometimes fire's a very pretty thing.

We jumped out and ran to a lieutenant. We asked if we could help.

He said, "Yeah. We need somebody to drag the hose, and we need somebody to go up in the basket."

This fire ended up burning for three days. The smoke coming from this place was just amazing. We had some trucks that weren't even by the fire. When they got hit by the smoke and soot, it looked like someone threw acid on the paint. The paint was all pitted out, like it had been sandblasted.

I remember a couple of guys saying, "My God. We were breathing that stuff." It was a little scary. But we didn't think, down the road, we'd be dying from it.

Sometimes at that fire we had our masks on. Other times we didn't. This was 1969, almost thirty years ago. Our masks weren't nearly as good as the ones today. The masks today have inner seals, so it makes for a much tighter fit. The old ones didn't have the inner seals, so the mask would get clogged with soot and and we'd have to pull them off. At the Everglades fire we'd wear them and take them off, wear them and take them off. Each time we took them off, we'd take some pretty good gulps of the acid smoke.

Firefighters were different back then, too. I was young, just three years on, but the old-timers used to call themselves "leather lungs." They'd be in a fire breathing that stuff, and they'd look back at you struggling with your mask. They'd say, "What are you doing, kid? How can you fight a fire when you're messing around with a mask?"

So a lot of times we'd just pull it off. If I had known then what I know now, they could have called me anything they wanted. I would have kept that mask on.

We didn't know *anything* then about toxic smoke. There was no EPA yet. That would not be formed for more than another year. So no one was keeping track yet of dangerous substances. On our inspection sheets, there was nothing said about ammonium nitrates, sulfates, DDT, things like that. When you went to a fire, the buildings didn't have placards to warn you what was inside. If a place was burning, we'd kick in the door and go in and put it out. No questions asked, including what kind of chemicals were inside. That's how we were. We never worried about our health. We just thought, *The good Lord's looking out for me. He's not gonna let anything happen to me. Because I'm doing something good.*

Over the years, after the Everglades Fertilizer fire, a bunch of us from this department began getting cancer. It was weird, because other fire departments didn't have that many cancer cases. The police department didn't have that many cancer cases. We started checking around with the phone company and the power company. *Nobody* had the cancer rate that our fire department did.

So one of our officers, Steve McInerny, started doing some research. This was probably around 1985. Steve looked through old logbooks. He tracked people down. He started seeing a pattern. All the guys with cancer had been to that Everglades fire.

So we started watching. And, sure enough, more and more came down with cancer. We would then go ask them, "Were you at the Everglades fire?"

"Yeah, I was."

That is when it started getting scary.

As of today, I think thirty-one of the one hundred firemen present there have cancer. Nineteen of us have died. These are guys you spent your life with. When they had trouble at home, you heard about it. You saw their children growing up. When they started getting sick, you didn't want to believe it. These were tough guys. To see this silent monster take hold of them . . .

I was fifty years old when I found I had it. I felt a

lump in my neck and my doctor performed a biopsy. I couldn't believe it when he said it was malignant.

I mean, I spent a lot of time with the guys who got sick. For twenty-two years, I ran the committee that took care of sick and hurt firefighters. As our guys came down with cancer, I saw to all the needs of the families. So it was always there in the back of my mind. But then it *really* happened. I just couldn't believe it.

So far, I am one of the fortunate ones. The cancer ended up in a lymph node in my neck. It was about the size of a walnut, and they took it out. I went through extensive testing and they looked everywhere for signs of more cancer. They could never find it. But I am still under the watchful eye of my doctors.

Sure, it got hard. I was used to rushing people to hospitals. I wasn't used to being hospitalized. With all that chemo and all that radiation, I couldn't keep anything down. There were times I didn't want to live anymore. But my wife would clean up the vomit. She would talk to me when I was depressed. I'm not kidding you, she was the real backbone.

I was still on duty when I got my cancer. Almost all the other guys had already retired. I got cancer in October of '92. I retired in February of '93. That was extremely tough. I spent twenty-seven years in the firehouse, and those were the best twenty-seven years of my life. I still dearly miss the fire department. I miss all the guys and the excitement.

But I had no choice. I was a pretty big guy, six-foot-one and 260 pounds, but I had deteriorated down to about 180. I didn't have the strength to do the job—dragging the hoses and carrying out the people. Just walking up stairs would tire me out.

Since I was still on duty when I got diagnosed, I filed

a workman's comp case with the city of Fort Lauderdale. It was important to me to prove a connection. That fire had so many cancer-causing agents, and so many guys who fought it came down with cancer, there *had* to be a connection. All of us felt that way.

The city of Fort Lauderdale said no. They said, "There's no correlation between the two. You got your cancer from someplace else." So, it was a fight. They kept saying it wasn't job-related. We kept saying to them, "Look at the carcinogens that were burning. Look at the numbers. Look at the facts."

They finally came back and offered me a settlement. I didn't want to settle. I wanted them to say it was job-related. We went back and forth and back and forth. Then my attorney said, "Look. They're not going to admit it. So the best thing for you to do is settle. You can pay off some medical bills. And at least we know we're making some headway."

By then the bills were really piling up. Most of my retirement pay had gone to medical treatment. Cancer is expensive. But the money part of it still didn't mean that much. I didn't know what to do.

So then I called the firefighters' union. I talked to their guys. They all told me the same thing. They said, "It's best that you settle. The city may be not saying it, but by settling they are admitting there's a connection. Anyway, it's time to start thinking a little about yourself."

So that's the way we went. But it isn't the end of this thing. We've got a bill we're trying to pass in the state of Florida. We're working nationwide within our unions, to try and help firefighters across the country. We don't want any firefighter to get cancer. But if they do, we want them to have proper medical benefits. And we want the country to know. There is a definite link between breathing all that smoke and getting cancer.

RECEIVING GRATITUDE

Being a public servant is part of the fire life. But frankly, it can get a little bizarre. You make these large sacrifices. You risk your death. And you still don't get many thanks.

For example, last year our engine company had about thirty-six hundred runs. That's fire, rescue, and medical calls. Of those thirty-six hundred calls, you figure some are false alarms, some are good working calls, some people you save and some you don't. Out of those thirty-six hundred calls, we got maybe six or eight thank-you cards last year. Every one of them went right up on the bulletin board. It happens so rarely, you never forget those people who take the time.

We had an old lady. She must have been in her late eighties, early nineties. She had a husband the same age. He fell down on the floor and stayed there all night. She kept trying, but she couldn't pick him up.

She didn't know who to call. This was a neighborhood that had once been middle-class. Then, just like any inner city, it decayed. And this old couple got trapped there. So they really didn't know anyone anymore. All the neighbors they once knew had already died.

This lady didn't have much family, either. So she tried, all night, to pick him up by herself. She didn't call us until morning. We asked her why. She said she didn't want to wake us up.

We walked in about 7:15 A.M. We picked her husband up, put him in bed and covered him up. We then turned to the lady and she was apologizing. She had tears in her eyes.

I said, "That's okay. Are you all right?"

She said, "I'm sorry. But I don't how to thank you for doing that."

We said it was no problem. That's what we do.

After a while she couldn't control herself. She really started crying. She kept saying, "I just don't know how to thank you."

This woman was poor. At that moment in her life, she would have given us anything she had. But all she had to offer us was her gratitude. That touched me more than anything on this job.

When you take a child into the emergency room, you have to relinquish that patient to the ER staff. That child should be crying, but now that child looks at you and smiles. Because she appreciates what you have just done for her.

There is nothing in the world that could ever replace that smile. It reminds you of why you wanted to be a fireman.

I remember a cardiac arrest patient. It was an older lady in her sixties. We worked her at home. Brought her back to life. Transported her in. Her family showed up at the hospital. They were very grateful. The whole bit.

Then we worked her again a couple months later.

She remembered us. She bragged to her family, "These are the two that saved me before!"

Then she referred to my partner and me as angels. A lot of old ladies do that. They call us angels.

We responded to a traffic accident. It was a seventeen-year-old girl with severe head injuries. She also had a fractured right femur, a fractured right hip, and a ruptured spleen. I mean this kid was going down the tubes.

The rescue squad extricated her from her car. When we—the paramedic team—got her, we intubated her and made a few other moves. There aren't a lot of calls where you can say this, but we saved this girl's life.

Three months later or maybe longer, we were all sitting at the station. Same shift, same crew—and there is a knock on the door. I answer the door and this guy is standing there. He's about twenty years old. He says hello and introduces himself.

Then he says, "You saved my sister's life. She wanted to come by here and say hi."

This girl walks in the door. She is absolutely fabulous-looking. She hugs my neck.

She says, "I just wanted to thank you for saving my life."

Then she gave us these little fire-hat paperweights, and she told us the whole story of her recovery. I'll tell you what, I got all welled up inside. And I looked at the faces of my partners, and they were equally moved. Because we did not even recognize this girl. The girl that we remembered was totally bloody, totally disfigured, and then this beautiful girl walks in the door, and now she has a plate inside her head, and she has scars where her hips were surgically repaired, and scars where her spleen was removed, but she's beautiful, you know, and she's alive and she's well. I don't care how many years you've got on. That's quite an emotional thing.

The fire service is real funny. When there's a rash of big fires, the public loves us. Because they get to see the commitment. They actually get to see how we fight fire. They realize it's a difficult job.

But if it's quiet for six months and we have no major fires, or no major catastrophic events, suddenly we're a burden to the tax system. We're overpaid. We're underworked. It's like playing quarterback in the NFL. They love it when you come through for them in the clutch. Six months later, it's "What have you done for me lately?"

A majority of the people like us. But some people lump us in the same category as cops. So here in New York, they talked to us about wearing bulletproof vests. It never caught on, but I do know some guys who carry guns. It's not predominant, and it's against all regulations, but there's definitely guys carrying. They say if something happens, they'll face the consequences. At least they'll be around to face the consequences.

One thing we don't appreciate is a false alarm. A guy in my firehouse got killed on one. As the rig pulled out the door, he did a back flip off the side and landed on his head. That's why firefighters are so anti–false alarm.

It isn't only firemen. On false alarms, civilians have been killed in car accidents with fire trucks.

But generally, how big an issue it is depends on where you work. Where I used to work, we would run about 35 percent false alarms. It was pretty steady around that average. So you figure one third of all the times that you go out, you are tearing through the streets and it's for naught. Now, we are public servants. When someone calls, you go. You want to do the right thing. But you get to a false alarm and you feel like an object. You're just something for them to play with.

People get very sophisticated, too. They call in with elaborate stories. They tell you the location of the apartment building. They tell you the twelfth floor and that people are trapped. We go running over there and it's nothing. There isn't even a fire. It was all for their amusement.

I guess I'm rare. False alarms in general don't bother me. I figure I'm paid to be here, and I'm paid to go on these runs whether they're important or not.

I don't know why people do it. You've got a lot of sick people out there, in all types of ways, in all degrees of sickness. Some people hate firemen. Some people just like to cause that kind of commotion.

Nobody really likes them. But it isn't just because people get killed on them. It might only be that we're watching a good movie.

THE MOVIE *BACKDRAFT*

You know where most people got their perception of firemen? From watching the movie *Backdraft*. They either saw it when it came out, or they rented the tape. Now they think that's how it really is.

Ron Howard did his best, and he was about 50, 60 percent accurate. But I think he took too much poetic license. Like the scene with Kurt Russell running into a house, where he runs right through flame and then back through flame? Without a line? That is preposterous!

Or that commercial building fire where he hollers "Dig in!" If you're in a factory that is coming apart, no, it ain't dig in. It's more like, "Let's get the hell out of here!"

The part I thought they portrayed well was the camaraderie, the esprit de corps. That was one of the truer elements of the film. Most guys do really take this job to heart, and most guys feel that they can depend on each other. The other believable thing was the pecking order. The rookies, the probies, the scrubs—whatever they called them—were made to earn their respect. It wasn't handed to them.

My own life hasn't been like the *Backdraft* movie. I have never stood in the shower with someone and said, "Hey, man! You don't know if you're going to be a great fireman, or just okay, until you face the animal!"

That's Hollywood, you know?

Real smoke, you can't breathe. The smoke in the movie, I guess you could breathe. Because these guys were running through hell without any masks!

Our union had passes for it when it premiered. I went to it and I was like, *This is weird. You don't do that. You can't see that well in a fire building. You're not hanging above the fire with three guys dangling.*

Then I started thinking, *I'm not at a training film. I'm at a movie. It's like real cops don't get shot every day and then everyone sloughs it off. If a real cop gets shot, it's a big deal. But in the movies, they got cops dying left and right.*

Once I put it in perspective—this is a piece of enter-
tainment—I enjoyed it. I have a copy of it and I still watch
it once in a while. There's certain parts I like better than
others. I think they hit the nail right on the head as far as
how firemen are. Like that retirement party they were at. I
was at that party three times. Or the way they sit around
the kitchen table and goof on each other—I was there.
And I like the positiveness that it showed for the fire
department.

But a lot of the techincal stuff we just don't do. I
would not have slid down the pole naked I don't think,
but they did it. You wouldn't have any skin left if you
did that. You wouldn't go into a fire with your coat
buckles unbuckled. You wouldn't do that because you
wouldn't survive. Anything exposed is going to get
burned. You can think you're a tough guy, but your skin
still burns at a certain temperature.

And we don't think the fire moves around walls like
an animal. We know it doesn't. We don't say, "It's in the
walls! Go get it!"

We take much more of a textbook approach.

We say, "This is balloon construction. There's a fire in
the basement, so check the attic because it probably went
up the nonfire stops past the joist to the attic."

Kurt Russell never seems to be wearing a mask. At
first that bugged me. Then I realized, *Why put Kurt
Russell in the movie, why pay him all that money, if
you're going to cover his movie-star face with a mask?*

I actually liked Kurt Russell. I think he did a good job,
even though some things were a little goofy. Like there
are a lot of brothers who are real firemen, and they don't
go around always proving things to each other. Actually,
they made us seem like we're all trying to prove things. I
mean, *all* the time. Well, we're not trying to prove anything. We're really not. We just go in and put out the fire.

Kurt Russell, though, is cool. I even watch his other movies now. But I don't know about that movie *Captain Ron*. I think he was better when he used to be a fireman.

In our department, you can't have two brothers working together. That's prohibited. It's like in the military. If something major happened and you lost a whole bunch of people, they would not want to wipe out one whole family.

Also, those guys ran around the station in civilian clothes. We wear uniforms: blue Nomex trousers with a blue Nomex shirt. Once we get a call, our turnout gear goes over that.

But special effects–wise, I did find it exciting.

I enjoyed the fire scenes. The effects were really good. They filmed it here in Chicago and I watched how they did it. They were really starting fires. This specialist they had was a little pyro.

But the story line sucked, I thought. It was terrible. It was horrible. It was corny. They could have done so much more.

That's my review. Great fires. But the story stunk.

I'm an arson investigator in Chicago, so I interacted a little bit with the cast. I talked with Robert De Niro, who played the investigator. De Niro used my tool case, my camera case. The guy's a phenomenal actor.

I would also have to describe him as intense. Even if you were just sitting at your desk, he was watching and picking up on your movements. In the movie itself, he used several things he got from real investigators. There's one scene when De Niro looks up at a lightbulb. The lightbulb is distorted, and he's mumbling to himself, "Where did you come from. Where are you hiding?"

What he means is, Where is the point of origin? That's what we call the place where the fire was set. Sometimes you get a clue from looking at a lightbulb, because a lightbulb will distort at one thousand degrees. It will hold that temperature for about ten minutes, then it will actually point to the source of the heat.

Another story I can tell you about comes from Billy Cosgrove. Billy's a friend of mine on the department. He was De Niro's personal advisor and spent forty-nine days with him.

De Niro asked Cosgrove—to show you some of this man's intensity—how a fireman puts his helmet on.

Billy said, "He takes the fuckin' thing and he throws it on his head!"

De Niro said, "No, they don't. You watch 'em. They all do it the same way."

And Cosgrove, like myself, did not believe this. But De Niro turned out to be right. About 90 percent of the time, everyone puts on a fire helmet the same way. They grab it by the top. They hold it so the opening is facing their forehead. They set the opening against their forehead. Then they slide it up to the top of their head.

Watch the very first scene De Niro is in next time. First thing he does, he reaches into his car, he picks that helmet up, sets it against his forehead, and slides it up to his head. It's pretty impressive that he could pick that up. It's also something most people probably don't take note of. But it's that little detail that makes him look authentic.

Socially, De Niro appeared to be a little indifferent. He didn't strike me as very personable. On the other hand, I see Bill Cosgrove on a regular basis, and he's never had anything bad to say about the guy. In fact, one morning on the way to work, Cosgrove got in a severe automobile accident. He fractured his back. He went through some heavy surgery. He was in a cast for a long time. This all happened after they finished the movie. And one evening, unannounced, De Niro shows up at Cosgrove's house. He just came over to sit with him for a few hours. Now, I have to think this guy is pretty busy. But he took time to sit down with someone he got to know. That probably lets you know what kind of guy he is.

I also met Kurt Russell. He's a happy-go-lucky guy. A boisterous guy. I could see him fitting in as a firefighter.

One day, they had these guys riding around with our fire companies. They had Kurt Russell, Billy Baldwin, Scott Glenn. All those guys were good guys. Anyway, they actually had them suited up in fire clothes—this was after they had them at the fire academy—so they could really see what firefighters do.

Billy Baldwin and Scott Glenn were riding with a rescue squad. Kurt Russell was on a truck company. Baldwin and Glenn went to a fire. They walk into the fire building. They're watching these firemen tearing and pulling down ceiling. They were a little bit critical of this one fireman, because he wasn't doing it the way that they had been taught to. He's pulling ceiling down on his head; timber is banging off him and everything else. All of a sudden, Kurt Russell turns around. He's the fireman they're watching.

He says, "Come on, you guys! This is a lot of fun!"

6
EMERGENCY MEDICAL CALLS

Medical calls are up and fire calls are down.

That's the trend in the fire service today. In 1980, according to the National Fire Protection Association, American fire departments responded to 2,988,000 fire calls. By 1994, fire calls had dropped to 2,054,500. In that same fourteen-year span, medical calls increased from 5,045,000 to 9,189,000. On a municipal level, the Detroit Fire Department went on 26,552 fire calls in 1994. Their medical calls numbered 132,506.

This may surprise citizens in New York, where the city's Emergency Medical Service (EMS) and Fire Department are still separate entities, and where fire calls are still the crux of the fire business. But New York is now the exception and not the standard. In a majority of places, all prehospital emergency care has been incorporated into the fire department. In some of those places, medical calls outnumber fire calls five to one.

The two trends are not related. The fire rate has dropped because America has the world's best fire-prevention technology. But despite the increasing use of sprinklers and smoke detectors, Americans still must work harder at not letting fires start. In 1994, fires still accounted for about 4,275 civilian deaths, 27,250 civilian injuries, and $8.2 billion in property damage.

As for the growth of medical calls, this has resulted in part from misuse and misunderstanding of 911. People can recognize when their house is on fire. But when does a medical problem become an emergency? When unsure, thousands of Americans dial 911 every day.

"We are like the Ghostbusters," says one captain. "If you don't feel well at night or on a weekend, when your doctor's not in his office, or if you don't have medical insurance, then who you gonna call?

"You call the fire department. And we want to help. But I've gone into people's homes and put Band-Aids on their fingers. That's not what 911 was intended for. There's only so many of us. While we're out there dealing with minor problems, other people are having life-or-death emergencies. We don't want to miss life-or-death because someone cut their finger."

For the rise in medical calls, firefighters also point to an aging population, more guns out on the street, and faster automobiles (driven by people who still choose not to wear seat belts).

With this shift in the fire service toward EMS, a majority of all firefighters are now trained as Emergency Medical Technicians (EMTs). A much smaller percentage of all firefighters are paramedics, the next level up. Nationally, the average minimum for paramedic certification is about one thousand hours of training, or about ten times as much as the average EMT. But in an extremely progressive department like Seattle's, paramedic training may cover more than three thousand hours. Most of those hours are spent in the field, riding on ambulances with senior paramedics, learning to quickly assess the severity of the problem, the necessary treatment, and if and where the patient should then be hospitalized.

"There's a big difference betweem EMTs and paramedics," says one paramedic captain. "EMTs do a great
job, but they're mostly mechanical. They can calm and
reassure a patient. They can stop bleeding. They can open
an airway. They can splint fractures. These are the things
we call basic life support (BLS).

"Paramedics are trained in advanced life support
(ALS). If you're mowing your lawn and your heart stops,
all a BLS person can do is give you oxygen or start CPR.
But with an ALS person, a paramedic, he or she will have
all the invasive skills. If your heart stops, they can come
in and start IV's, stick a tube down your throat to help
you breathe, give you cardiac drugs, and defibrillate
you—shock your heart to get it beating again. It's the
very same things they would do for you in ER."

Except in emergency rooms, hospital environments
tend to be sterile. Firefighters, in contrast, whether
they're EMTs or paramedics, must often perform in
dreadful conditions. One time, when an auto mechanic
stopped breathing, one paramedic climbed down into a
grease pit, adjusted the man's airway and probably saved
his life.

Some paramedics suffer from what they still call
"burnout." Even more than firefighter/EMTs, paramedics
see the result of ugly human behavior. It isn't like the
past, when car wrecks accounted for most of their trauma
victims. More victims come today from shootings, knifings, and beatings.

"At times I'd get so stressed out," says one urban
paramedic, "I'd feel it in my stomach. I was drinking a
case of Maalox every ten days. I mean, sometimes the
stuff we see is just relentless. And we all work these
twenty-four-hour shifts, so then you have sleep depriva-
tion. Then you have patients who don't care if they stay
alive, let alone what your thoughts are on how to treat

them. Sometimes it makes you wonder, *Is it all worth it? Why I am here in the first place?*

"Fortunately, the one time in my career I felt really burnt, I got rotated out to a slower squad. This gave me an opportunity to step back and regain perspective. Yes, our job is hard. But a lot of jobs are hard. In this one, we get to save lives."

There are all kinds of medical calls. The most encompassing would be difficulty breathing. That could be anything from the beginning of a heart attack, to any kind of allergic reaction, to a drug overdose. Then you have seizures. We get a lot of those. Included in those are febrile seizures. That's when a kid has a high temperature, and he seizes up, and he goes into something like convulsions. You have shootings, stabbings, rapes, domestic assaults. Lacerated fingers at work, at home. Falls, impacts, traffic collisions.

Then you have specialized stuff, like somebody who's been exposed to hazardous materials and needs to be deconned. That means decontaminated, which means they're getting stripped down buck naked in the middle of the street and cleaned off by a bunch of haz-mat guys wearing strange suits. "The body bag with a window"— that's what all of us who aren't in haz-mat call it. It's this encapsulated suit, with just a little window in it to see out. Hell, no, I ain't getting in that thing.

Anyway, that would pretty much cover the medical stuff.

When most of us came on the fire department, we weren't even thinking of medical calls. We all imagined dashing in the fire, grabbing the kids and the baby, and dashing back out. And that's how it was back then. You only went to fires. In between fires, you sat around playing checkers. Those days are gone.

Last year, there were 265,000 calls that came into our dispatch. Eighty-five percent of those calls were medical-related. That means some of our firefighters are not too happy. They want to go into burning buildings, which makes no sense to me, but that's why I'm a paramedic and they stopped at EMT. They're still doing the medical stuff, and they tend to be very good, but it's not what they thought the job would be.

They'll say, "I do not want to touch these patients. I don't want to start IVs. I don't want to deal with someone throwing up!"

They honestly don't like it. But that is the shift, to EMS. So they better learn to like it.

Sure, I hired on to fight fires and kick ass. But so what? The best fire is the one you never go to. I would much rather not go to a fire than to see a kid destroyed, or a home destroyed and a family turned out in the street. And the worst ones are not the million-dollar homes. That homeowner has the means to correct everything. The worst ones are the families who are poor, with five of their children all sleeping on one mattress. Everything they owned was in that apartment. Now everything they own is charred and wrecked.

So I don't have any problem with all these medical calls. Less fires the better, as far as I'm concerned.

There is a rush to medical calls, just like there's a

rush to putting out a good fire. Only a paramedic would know what I'm talking about, but when you're working a good cardiac arrest, and you start the IV and you *hit* it, and you intubate and you *hit* it, and you push your drugs and you defibrillate, and you flip your drug cap up in the air—and you're putting on this *show*—it's almost like you're performing for everyone watching.

I think there is some showmanship involved. Or I guess you could just call it showing off.

I had a call at a restaurant in Miami Beach. They were famous for their pastrami, their Reubens, that kind of stuff. So a lot of elderly people frequented there.

As a result, we could almost bet we'd get one call there each day. Often, we'd get several. To the waiters and maître d', our presence was commonplace. We'd be working on somebody having a heart attack. They would be stepping around us, seating other people in nearby tables.

We would kid about that later on, of course: "This guy just went down! We got an open table! Bring up another party!"

On this one call, a man was eating dinner with six to eight people. He swallowed a piece of steak and it went down his windpipe. He stopped talking and he started choking. By the time we got there, he was cyanotic— turning blue. He also wasn't breathing.

We tried the Heimlich manuever, but weren't able to dislodge it. Your next step then is to try and clear the airway. And using a laryngoscope, I was able to look down his throat and actually see the food blocking his airway. So with a pair of forceps, I removed it. We gave him some oxygen, assisted him with breathing. In minutes, he was breathing on his own and conscious again. Nice guy, too. Could not thank us enough.

It felt fantastic. We are trained to save lives, and in this case we did. In another five minutes, this man would have been brain-dead. Then no matter what anyone did after that, he would have ceased to be part of this world. All because he choked on a piece of meat.

A lot of calls don't need sophisticated medicine. What they require is rapid intervention. In a cardiac arrest, for example, depending on what book you read, it's three to six minutes before irreversible brain damage occurs. Well, in our fire department, we almost always respond in under three minutes. So, obviously, we have a decent chance to save that cardiac victim. That's one big reason we're known for our EMS. We can get there fast, before people slip away.

Time is our enemy. We're trying to beat the clock. We're trying to beat what's known as the golden hour.

From the moment a person gets badly injured, with trauma, to the time he or she reaches the operating room—not just the emergency room but the operating room—their life clock is ticking away. If you can get them on the table within that first golden hour, they have a very good chance of surviving.

The brain will die without oxygen in six to ten minutes. Total death, depending on how severe the wound is, may happen instantaneously. Or within a minute or two.

So let's say you have a gunshot wound. You try to stop

the bleeding. You try and put IVs in him. You try and stick a tube in his throat, so you can breathe for him. In short, you try to get him through the life-threatening stage, into an ambulance, and off to a hospital as quickly as possible. It's what we call a "scoop and run."

But it can be more complicated than it sounds. Say it's a drive-by shooting. While you're working on the victim himself, you must deal with the crowd. They are hostile and angry, because this was a drive-by shooting. There is crying, anxiety, too. All the emotions that go with somebody witnessing death. But it will be multiplied, because you may have a crowd of fifty or sixty people.

The victim may have family members there, and almost always some friends. The victim himself is crying, pulling at you, asking you not to let him die. The family and friends are hearing this as well. So they're trying to touch that person, to get a last chance to be with him and say things. Then you must deal with this kid's age. He is fifteen years old and he has been shot. So that is going through the back of your mind, too. The senselessness of it.

When you get called to a shooting, you always get the police. Because now this is a crime scene.

We got a call one time for a resuscitation, at a park where a lot of homeless people live. It's butted up to some railroad tracks and a levee. So we get there and people are pointing to one particular spot. So we go in and find this guy. He looks like hell. He has those puffy raccoon eyes, and his head has all kinds of swelling and edema. We think it is just a real bad beating. So we start to clean him up.

While we're cleaning this guy, I find a bullet hole in

front of his left ear. This was what caused the swelling. The bullet in his head.

So the cops decide it's a crime scene. They don't want us to move him. They don't want us to wipe up all the blood. They want to protect the evidence.

One cop says to me the moment I get started, "Be careful. This is a crime scene."

I say, "No, this isn't a crime scene. We're gonna save this guy's life."

That mellowed things a little; the cop wants to see him live, too. And most of the time, firefighters and cops get along fine—except when it comes to these shootings and homicides. Then the police just wig out. We're trying to save someone's life, and they're already treating it like a homicide.

We're telling them, "It isn't a homicide *yet*. Give us a chance to go to work."

I think most paramedics would agree: when you first enter the EMS arena, it's almost like a fever. You become some kind of a junkie. You're *hoping* for the bad calls.

After you've been in it about a year, that's when the sleep disturbances begin. You start having nightmares. Not about the specific patients you've seen, but about those types of injuries. Except, in your dreams, they're happening to your family or close friends. At least that's how it was for me. I began to have nightmares about my own family going through the same tragedies I'd seen.

The nightmares last for a couple months and then they dissipate. At that point, you start to adapt. Is that to say you become complacent? No. You never get complacent. But you steel yourself against the things you see.

For instance, I used to get sick at the sight of a lot of

blood. I threw up a couple times, and then it was over.
Nothing makes me sick anymore. I went from that feverish
place of adrenaline rushes, to that place of nightmares, to
the place which I refer to as adapting.

Is my head on straight today? Did I stick all my IVs
today? Did I think the right way, react the right way?
When I made my diagnostic call, did I *see* what I was
supposed to see?

A lot of that has to do with who lives and who dies. Of
course, I'd never say that in a court of law. But, yeah, our
actions have something to do with it.

Have I ever felt *godlike*? I've never thought about it.

But I have felt that I have a power. In fact, I've
flaunted that power from time to time. If I get a drunk
who's been shot in the chest, and I get him in the back of
my ambulance, and he is still conscious and fighting me,
and his blood pressure is dropping, and I know I have to
get an IV in him, and I know there's other things he
needs to stay alive, well, I have more than once grabbed
that patient by the hair, and I have told him, "Look. Right
now I control whether you live or die. You either lay
down, or I will stand here and watch you die."

And in voicing that kind of absolute control, I guess I
have felt that godlike feeling before.

You need an ego to be a paramedic. It takes an amount
of ego just to start an IV. That's what they taught us at
paramedic training: IV is a matter of attitude and ego.
Because it is one thing to start an IV in a sterile, lit environment like an emergency room. But it is something

totally different when you are in dark, cramped corners, or crouching down on the interstate with no lights on. Once you start becoming successful at that, you use it for motivation. For instance, I haven't missed an IV in seven years. I haven't missed an intubation in thirty-seven attempts. On those nonstop days when you're dragging a little bit, you use these little streaks to keep you fired up.

I went on a shooting my rookie year. This Armenian guy, for whatever reason, got in an argument with another Armenian person who lived downstairs. They're both very emotional, and one guy basically tells the other, "Fuck you." Then he starts walking downstairs toward his apartment. But he never makes it there. This other guy didn't like being cursed out. He brings out a .44 Magnum and caps him twice, once in the calf and once in the lower back. He realizes what he has done, and he takes off.

We show up, and the P.D. has everyone and their brother there. They got shotguns out and they're looking. The helicopter is up and the whole nine yards. But they never searched right there, where the guy took the shots. They assumed he was gone, because that's what the people said. They told the police this guy ran down the street.

So they set up a perimeter. They say, "How far could this guy run in the two minutes it took for us to get here?"

A block, maybe two. So they started there and worked in.

Meantime, we are down on the ground, working this patient. His tib/fib—the lower portion of his leg—has just been blown apart. He is also shot in the lower back, with a .44 Magnum large-caliber bullet. So the bullet has exploded out his front. He is a bloody mess, and I am a rookie. I'm not the squeamish type, but I haven't seen a shooting like this before.

So we're working on him, and the cops are searching around, and we're like a big yellow target. Yellow helmet, yellow jacket, yellow pants. I'm thinking about this because my brother's a policeman. I mean, there is a reason why cops wear dark uniforms.

So we're treating this guy when I hear a cop yell, "Freeze!"

I turn to my side. The shooter walks out of the bushes five feet from me. He wants to finish what he started.

I turned just in time to see him take a round from this one cop's shotgun. He took it square in the chest.

Now we had two patients to work on. The guy shot by the cops and the guy shot by the shooter. Very traumatic for me. The first shooting I've been on, a real gritty one, and I'm covered in blood from working on these two guys, and *then* we have to deal with this policeman. He has just killed his first person and he can't speak.

The city of Memphis has a more than 35 percent poverty level. Most of that is concentrated down in South Memphis, very close to the Mississippi River. That's where I worked the majority of my career.

We once had a four-year-old boy who'd been run over by a train. This little guy had followed his older brother down the train tracks. A train came by and they tried to jump on the back. The older boy made it, of course, but the little guy didn't. He fell under the train and it cut off one of his feet.

Other than the amputation, the boy ended up okay. But he was pretty hysterical when we first arrived. After calming him down, I talked to him. You know what his main concern was? That was the only pair of shoes he owned, and we couldn't find the foot that had been cut off. So he was going to be in trouble because he lost his shoe.

Once you start to get good, you start developing rivalries with other paramedics. Who can do the best work in the most adverse conditions?

We've worked people in boats that were half full and sinking. We've worked them in their cars, on golf courses, and in the aisles of airplanes. We've done EMS in mom-and-pop grocery stores, in high-rises, down in the sewer system when someone falls through a manhole.

I worked a person once on wet sand. He was drowning. We pulled him out of the water, suctioned all the fluids out of his mouth and airway, hooked up him up to the EKG and saw that his heart was not working. We went to shock him and I ended up shocking myself. I was kneeling down in the sand. The shock went right through the patient, right through the sand, and into my knee. If I had somebody lying in a puddle of water, I would have known to move them. But nobody ever told me about wet sand.

If a person codes on you—that's what a cardiac arrest is commonly called—that patient is expected to get the same treatment they'd get in ER. But when a person has a cardiac arrest in an emergency room, there are probably no less than six people there: a doctor, someone from X ray, someone from respiratory therapy, a couple of nurses and probably a couple technicians running and getting things.

In most parts of the country, only two paramedics go on a call. So from a manpower standpoint, you are under adversity every time.

Traffic accidents are adverse, when people are trapped in a twisted, broken-up car, and their bodies are mangled, and gas and transmission oil is leaking all over the place, and you don't know when something might light up and burn your ass, and the rescue is trying to cut them out of their car, and you can hear the tools popping metal apart, and the people inside are dying, and you must do something for them immediately.

Because treatment doesn't wait for extrication. If it's a delicate maneuver, extrications can last an hour. So you have to work on them while they're still trapped.

DELIVERING BABIES

We've had babies born in closets and bathrooms. We've brought them into this world on top of toilets.

Those are the fun calls. Babies are great. And I've been real fortunate. I haven't had any breeches. I haven't had any single-limb presentations. I've never been to a still-birth. I've done a lot of them, too. In the early eighties, we had all these boat people coming to the northwest. They were Cambodian refugees and Laotians and Vietnamese, and a lot of the women were pregnant. Most of these folks didn't have prenatal care. They just waited at home, knowing we would show up. We were delivering two or three babies a month.

One time we charged into an imminent birth. What we found was a captain I didn't especially care for, but a good, tough firefighter. He had already delivered this young girl's baby. He and his guys had done it in the bathroom, real tight quarters, and they had done a great job.

So we just finished it off: cleaned up all the mess, cut the umbilical cord, pulled out the placenta and got this young lady going. Well, as we're working on this young mom, her own mom and grandma walk in. Now there's *real* excitement in the house. She has never told them she was pregnant.

So Mom and Grandma come in and look down the hallway. Here's this young girl with her head out the bathroom door and her feet near the bathtub. Her mom doesn't look too happy.

So the girl looks up at her and says, "This ain't *his* baby, Mama. I ain't been messing around with no boys."

I looked at Mom and Grandma. I said, "Well, it happened in Bethlehem."

I've delivered fourteen, and it still raises the hair on the back of my neck. I even have a few babies named after me. That's always kind of neat.

But it can get a little nerve-racking, at times. We used to get a lot of teenage pregnancies. One time we had this girl who was just fifteen. She was six months pregnant, and she gave birth at school just seconds before we got there. It happened in the bathroom, while she was on the toilet, so the six-month fetus fell into the water. The mom was still standing there when we burst in, so we hurried and cut the cord. But we figured the baby was dead.

Nope. This little thing was swimming in the toilet.

I guess the cold water was keeping it alive. And fortunately, its little face was pointing out of the water.

So we pulled out this fetus, suctioned it and made certain it stayed breathing, watched it very closely, treated the mother, and got the mother and kid to the newborn center. We did that, and it lived! The baby's name was Page.

I've been pretty lucky. I delivered five babies, and all five times went relatively smoothly. The first one, in fact, was probably the best. This was this lady's seventh child. It was kind of like a Montana pass. The baby was just there.

Many of our deliveries come in the projects. Unfortunately, there's a lot of cocaine and heroin there. So with many of those babies, we get called in at the very last moment. Because the mother has taken drugs, and that has induced the labor.

One lady did crack cocaine at 2:45. They called us about 2:55. At three o'clock, the baby was born.

So you get there and it's just, "Let's get this kid out! Quick!" And the baby's just *there*, you know?

Another time in the projects, there was this man and woman on the tenth floor. We came in and they were using drugs. Her water was already broken. She was having contractions. The baby was starting to crown.

We're like, "Okay! Let's go!"

So the baby was born, and we got it crying. Cleaned out the mouth, the whole bit. And in this little OB kit that we carry, we had a little hat with little flowers on it. We put these on babies' heads so they won't lose heat through their head.

So I put this little hat on the baby's head. Then I gave the baby to the mom, and these people were really grateful. Very, very nice people. About one watch later, there is a knock at the front door of the firehouse. The two parents came in with a cake from Safeway. My name is Frank, and they had "Uncle Frank" on top of the cake.

That was the tender part. The tragic came three months later. Our engine got a call and went to the same apartment. The baby had died of crib death. So our engine brought the baby into the world, and our engine saw it out.

BEDSIDE MANNER AND HONESTY

On emergency medical calls, people are screaming, hollering, moaning, crying. So the most important thing is maintaining control. If you lose control of yourself, the patient, the family, the other people standing over you watching, you've lost control of the scene. From that point forward, it all goes into the toilet.

It's one thing if you're a doctor in a hospital. In a hospital, control is something that's given. It's not that way in the street. You have to *get* control. Sometimes that means being gruff.

When you are dealing with patients, I think your manner's *the* most important part of the job. Monkeys can do the techniques. I mean, anyone who's been trained can start IVs. Anyone can splint patients or intubate. But that technical part of the job, and the actual time you spend doing it, is minimal compared to the other part. That is dealing directly with human beings, their fear and pain and distress. It's like what they say about being a seamstress. Anyone can thread a needle. Threading the needle is easy. Putting some love in the fabric is the key.

If the patient's family is large, that can be real stressful.
We are poking needles and inserting tubes, and we're
doing this to the person they love. So you have to be sensitive to the relatives' needs, too.

But some paramedics aren't sensitive to anyone. Their
medical skills are good, but their bedside manners stink.
When you're partnered with someone like that, you tend
to play good guy, bad guy. In my case, good woman, bad
guy.

For example: We work on twenty-four-hour shifts.
If you work in a busy station, you might get twenty
calls in those twenty-four hours. If you're running
bullshit calls, like headache and stomachache, you get
a little annoyed, but you aren't all that stressed out.
Now, if you are running calls like heart attacks, difficult respirations, gunshots and knifings, and other
severe trauma, you're so stressed by the middle of
your shift, by midnight all you want to do is sleep.
And once you hit that mattress, you're kind of hoping
the phone won't ring again.

That's not likely to happen. After midnight, you
might go on another three to six runs. And when you
walk into someone's house for that 3:00 A.M. call, and
they have a stomachache, and they've had it for a week,
but they couldn't sleep tonight, so they called you, one
paramedic will handle that pretty well. The other one
wants to know, "What the hell did you call us for? It's
three in the morning!"

That's when the first paramedic has to step in.

She has to say to her partner, "Why don't you just go
into the other room? Talk to a family member. I'll get the
information from the patient."

You try to diffuse things, because once you put the
patient on the defensive, now it makes your job harder.

A couple times, I've partnered with someone who

really ticked off the patient. I mean to the point where they said, "Get out of my house! I don't want your help! Leave me alone!"

At that point you don't argue. You get out of their house. Chances are, they'll call you back in ten minutes.

Just the way we look has an impact on people. The best paramedic in the world, if he looks like a slob, will not make his patient feel secure. And that can be important, because when patients feel they're in good hands, they're not gonna panic. If they don't panic, it's easier for them to breathe.

The more severe the call, the more important your bedside manner becomes. If you're the last person they might see before they die, you don't want to be an asshole. You don't want to judge them. You don't want to mess with their last few moments in life.

Right now we're dealing with a lot of gangbangers. They might be the toughest kid on the street, but once they're shot in the belly three or four times, they're all reduced to little fourteen-year-olds. Riding in the back of the ambulance, they all got that look and they all want to know the same thing: am I going to die and where is my mother?

Sometimes I'll hold their hands on the way to the hospital. But I never lie to them. When they ask if they're gonna die, I just tell them, "Look, you're in real bad shape. But just hang in there. We're doing the best we can to get you through this. When you get to the trauma center, just do whatever they say. They're gonna be busier there than we were here with you."

If they *tell* me they're going to die, I say, "Not right now, jack. Calm down and we'll work on not having you die at all."

It reminds me of the book *Catch-22,* when one of the guys in the plane gets his belly shot off. Yossarian is telling this guy, "There, there."

That's about all you can say. But I never lie to them.

When it's necessary, I might lie. That's my personal guideline. When it's necessary.

The one I'm thinking about is these three young ladies we had. They were college-freshman age and they got hit by a drunk driver. Their car flipped into the air and smashed back down. One girl was obviously dead, trapped beneath the car with her legs sticking out. The other two girls were thrown from the vehicle on impact. One of those two girls was conscious. The other was not. She was crushed completely. She would obviously be dead very soon.

The girl who was conscious asked me, "Are my friends okay?"

One girl was dead and one was about to be. But there is a time and place for that information. This was neither one.

So I told the girl, "We haven't got to them yet. We're still working on getting them out of the car."

Obviously, it was lying. But it never bothered me later. I felt it was the only humanitarian thing.

Absolutely not. It is totally inappropriate to lie. As many emergency calls as I have been on, I can never recall a time when it was justified. Once you have lied to a patient, you have committed the forbidden sin of losing that patient's trust. You've also created a patient who may never trust the medical field again.

My first year on the job, I had a twenty-five-year-old black gymnast who was working out at the gym. The guy came off the vault and did a somersault. That's the last thing he remembered.

He landed on his neck. Broke his neck. Twenty-five years old. Tip-top shape, like gymnasts are? Nicest guy. From the shoulders down, he is suddenly a paraplegic. He's looking at me as I'm starting his IV.

He said, "I can't feel it. Are you touching me? I can't feel you."

He knows I'm touching him. He can see me doing it. But he cannot feel it. So he has to ask. That's his only hope. Maybe, somehow, I'll say, "No, I'm not touching you."

Then he said, "Do you think I'm going to be all right?"

I said, "You broke your neck. I cannot tell you how bad it is. I cannot help you if it is completely severed. To find out that, you'll need to have X rays done. What I do know right now is that you are paralyzed. I know that because you cannot feel anything. I don't know if it's going to stay that way, or if it will get better. But you can ask me whatever you want to ask me. I will talk to you, I will hold your hand, I will do whatever you need me to do."

That was all I could do for him. The guy is a paraplegic.

I never talked to him again, either. But just last year, I ran into somebody in one of the training classes I teach. Just by coincidence, she was a very good friend of this guy. He must have remembered my name and mentioned it to her.

She told me, "He's doing okay. There are days when it's hard for him, he gets real depressed, but he is going through rehab, and he's doing a pretty good job."

I will never forget that call. It *is* hard to tell them the truth sometimes.

I know some people who will lie to keep a patient from becoming hysterical. If they won't let you stick a needle in their arm—they tell you *"No"* and cross their arms—then you are losing valuable time. But, personally, I don't do it. I try and keep somebody calm with my mannerisms, my voice, but I don't lie to people. I've had motorcyclists pinned up against guardrails by car. They want to know if they're going to lose their leg.

I tell them the truth. "It doesn't look real good."

I had a girl get her foot run over by a train. I'm not gonna say her foot will be okay. That's just a lie, and she probably knows it.

Several years ago, this department had a great controversy about Sudden Infant Death Syndrome. What do you do with the kids?

A lot of guys found it very convenient just to throw the kid in the back of the rig and race off to Children's Hospital, so they didn't have to tell the parents the kid was dead. I never felt that was fair. I never thought it was fair to leave that false hope, that somehow this child will be resuscitated.

In any instance that you can name, I think honesty is your first obligation.

There's been a few times when dying people asked me, "Am I going to make it?"

I just looked at them. I did not say a word. And they looked at me and they understood. And they became at peace with it.

It's a powerful thing. You're spending the last few moments of someone's life with them.

Right after they go, I always pray for them. That's where I find my peace.

We had a lady in her mid-thirties. She had children, a family. She had been involved in an automobile accident. Had a ruptured diaphragm.

Your diaphragm separates your chest cavity from your abdominal cavity. With the diaphragm being ruptured, it means you have your bowels, your guts if you will, in your chest cavity. They don't belong there.

She was alert and everything, and of course she was going to surgery as quickly as we could get there—but we knew. When you hear bowel sounds in the chest cavity, it doesn't look too promising.

We started to talk in the back of the rig, but we never directly talked about her dying. She was young and there was hope. You never want to take away their hope.

But we began to talk about spiritual things, like God and our own beliefs. I don't really remember how it started. Maybe she had some sense of impending doom. Patients know sometimes.

We talked about the afterlife. I was able to find out that she was a born-again Christian. She was very confident about life after death, about where she would spend eternity if indeed she died.

She was an inspiration. She wasn't afraid at all.

We had a chest-pain call at a strip mall. A crowd had gathered in the middle of the day, and someone had propped up the patient against the wall of the store.

This man was certainly having a heart attack. He was still conscious and talking, but very sweaty. His color did not look good. He was in a lot of pain.

As we began treating him and talking to him, he just nodded off and went unconscious. That was not unusual. I've seen it a hundred times in cardiac cases. So of course we continued to work him.

His wife was there with him. As we started to work her husband, *she* began having chest pains. The thing is, she didn't tell us she had chest pains. She never said she felt faint. She just dropped, right there.

At first, I assumed she was fainting. But then we ran over there and she had no heart rate. She was in cardiac arrest, probably from watching *him* have a cardiac arrest. It was really bizarre.

The man and the woman both died. There were three of us there, and two cardiac arrests, and it takes all you can do to work *one* arrest. We called for the engine to come and help, but it takes a few minutes to get there. So we did the best we could, but it wasn't good enough. They both died that day, right next to each other.

I don't want to say that call still haunts me, but I'll certainly never forget it.

It got real cold in Chicago, about twenty below zero. We were called to a house in a neighborhood that was being rejuvenated. This old couple had lived there for seventy years. But their house wasn't being rejuvenated. It was just old.

When we walked in the door, both of them were frozen at their kitchen table. It was an old frame house and somehow the heat went off. They were just sitting at the table, both of them upright. And they were encased in ice.

That really stuck with me. Because you look down the block, and this whole neighborhood is getting fixed up. And here are these two old people frozen to death. They're sitting at their kitchen table, where they had probably commiserated for their whole life.

FIREFIGHTERS AND DOCTORS

Whether we're paramedics or EMTs, in Seattle we all use something called Life Pack 200's. When a patient is in ventricular fibrillation, we use the Life Pack to shock him. Inside this machine is a recording device. It not only records the heart rhythm to ensure that we are doing correct CPR, it also records our voices.

I am a firefighter and EMT. After one call we went on, I was given a note from a man named Dr. Copass. He developed the Medic One system here, which is the emergency medical care program that every fire department in the world is patterned after. Just a brilliant guy.

Dr. Copass had listened to one of our resuscitation tapes, or I should say attempted resuscitations. Because this fellow had died.

We were first in, and my partner was saying, "This guy doesn't look too good."

I said, "That's okay. We'll keep him going until the medics get here. He'll be okay."

It turned into an hour-long resuscitation. In the midst of performing CPR, I guess I said, "You're not gonna die on me, fucker." I guess I said it three or four times.

Believe it or not, there's many times when unconscious people can hear you. So maybe I said it to make this guy angry, make him try and fight a little harder.

But I definitely said it, because it was on the tape. That's why I got the note from Dr. Copass.

He said, "I appreciate the fact that you take it personally, but you need to understand that you're being taped."

On the real big calls where you have multiple patients, a doctor always seems to show up at the scene. They seem to be drawn to the calls that draw media attention.

Sometimes we utilize them and sometimes we don't. I've had doctors show up and want to start running the show.

I tell them they have to understand: "If you take the scene from me, you are totally responsible for these patients."

When you give them that, they usually back off.

When someone has mortal wounds and is close to death, but you treat them and keep them alive, and they're still alive when you drop them at ER, we call that a "save."

Sometimes when you make a save, you bring them into ER and they die on the table. It's not a prevailing thing, but it definitely does happen. It's happened to everyone. And that is very hard. Once you get them to the hospital, they're supposed to get more definitive treatment. So they're supposed to improve.

Probably the toughest is watching it happen. If you see doctors moving slow, or making a move that you wouldn't make, you might actually think you are seeing them kill that person. But that may just be your frustration, so you have to try and be fair. You have to step back and tell yourself: *They didn't kill that person. That shot-gun blast killed that person.*

We get called for a child impaled on a fence. Young girl, twelve years old, on roller skates.

So we respond to the box. The fence has spikes on top, about seven inches long. The fence is encased in a little cement wall. With her roller skates on, the girl wanted to walk on top of this cement wall. So she was holding the fence to keep her from falling.

Needless to say, the skate wheel decides it's going to flip out. The girl goes up and comes down. The spike goes in under her chin and comes out her mouth. It's sticking six, seven inches in the air. She's still holding on to this fence.

We show up and we look at this girl. She has a death grip on the fence with both her hands. She can't talk. Can't move her head. But her eyes are going a mile a minute—from side to side to side to side—just looking at all of us, as if to say, *Well, guys, what are we gonna do now?*

What a trooper. What a trooper. She was unbelievable. Super little kid, just twelve years old.

So we look at this. We size it up. We figure we'll take a torch and cut the fence. And, if we cut this fence correctly, we can also use it as a stretcher.

We start making our cuts. Last cut we make, the little girl won't give up her grip on that fence. Damn. She has to let go. We talk to her and she does. The last cut is made and we're going to lay her facedown. There's a guy there now from EMS. In New York City they have their own department. EMS guy says for whatever reason—I still don't know—to lay her *faceup*.

He says, "What are you doing? Put her faceup on her back and put her on a real stretcher."

So we look at this guy. Like he's crazy. I mean, we *all* looked together. We're going to put this girl with a spike out of her mouth on her back? She's gonna drown in her own blood.

So we just kind of told him, "This is the way she's going. Facedown."

We put her facedown, take the fence with her on it. Lay it nice and gentle onto the stretcher. Put her into the ambulance. I get into the ambulance, with one other guy from the rescue. Take off for the hospital. Notify them we're coming. Pediatric Emergency, which is a big hospital. It's part of Kings County Hospital in Brooklyn.

Get to the hospital. Wheel the girl in, facedown. Go into the emergency room, and there's a doctor there. The epitome of Mr. Cool.

He says, "Yeah, what we got?"

I say, "We've got a girl who's been impaled through the mouth with a spike from a fence."

"Yeah, okay, let me see her."

He walks around to the front where this girl is laying. He looks at her. Her two eyes are going back and forth again.

The doctor says, "Oh, my God!"

That's all he could say. And that annoyed us, because this girl doesn't need to hear this from a doctor.

He went back to this desk, where he was sitting when we first came in. Sat down at the desk and started making phone calls. Continued making phone calls. He was not able to get up, and come over there and help us.

He would say, "Have Dr. Jones get down here right away. We have a child who's been impaled."

Hang up.

"Have Dr. Williams come down here."

Hang up.

"Have Dr. Feinstein come down here."

We figured he would call his mother and father next.

We just ignored him, left him out of the picture. He wanted to act cool, but not once he saw what we had. He just wasn't able to deal with it at all.

Another doctor arrived. No phony Mr. Cool. Just a doctor.

He said, "Can we get a couple of you guys to come into the operating room with us? We decided what we are going to do. We would like your assistance."

This has been done a few times over the years in the city. The rescue company has been asked to go into operating rooms.

So we said, "Of course."

We go into the operating room. They're looking at the X rays. We're just watching this whole thing as they come to their decision.

They say, "This is how we'll do it. We will anesthetize her. We will start her IVs. We'll have all the fluids hooked up, ready to roll. When we take her off the fence, if any vital arteries, or the neck, have been punctured or cut or severed, we'll be ready to go."

So they anesthetized her, and she was out. They checked the X rays again.

They said, "Okay, we're just going to pull her off the fence. We don't need to cut. Let's see if we can just pull her off the fence."

Two doctors held her shoulders. Two doctors held the head, bracing it. Myself and my partner slowly grabbed the fence.

"Ready, ready, okay, pull."

We started pulling this fence. It didn't come easy, but it didn't come out hard either. I was surprised. It just . . . pulled out. And it was done. Then they went to work on her. Except for a little damage beneath the skin, I think she wound up losing a tooth. All in all a very happy ending.

We went back to see her later on. We brought her some candy and whatnots.

We said, "How the hell could you act so calm?"

She said, "Well, I couldn't go anyplace and I didn't know what to do. I couldn't talk. So I just figured I'd hold the fence and wait, and see what *you* guys would do."

Yeah, she was super. And those are the cool jobs. It's great to get in there and know you helped out a kid.

I worked for a long time on Miami Beach. Back in the early eighties, quaaludes were rampant there. Especially with teenagers.

The station where I worked was right off the beach. On weekends, we just went from drug call to drug call. It was not unusual to be treating one teenager and then hear two or three people calling you, "Here's another one over here! There's one over there!"

I remember one particular call. This guy was older, several years out of high school. I recognized him as soon as I walked up. I played high school football with him. He was one of the stars. He was much better than me and much more popular. But this guy took one path and I took another. Now, here we are years later. He's out of his mind on drugs and I'm trying to save his life.

The early eighties were crazy and that stuff happened a lot. I'd wind up treating people who I knew. It's a strange sensation but you have to block it out. You can't get caught up in memories when someone's life is at stake.

Also, on most drug calls, you never get a straight answer. You don't know how many pills they took, so it's hard to tell if their overdose has peaked, or if they are still going higher. The overdosed person himself is normally incoherent. So he can't help at all. If other people are present at the scene, they'll say, "He took cocaine," or "He took sleeping pills," or "He took amphetamines."

But that might be half the story. People often take several drugs at once.

It can be frustrating. You want to help them, but you can't get to the truth.

The first and the fifteenth are the biggest days for overdoses. That's when people get paychecks. On those two days each month, we will average six to eight overdoses a shift.

They're mostly using heroin. It goes into their medulla, which is a section of their brain controlling their breathing functions. The heroin basically puts the medulla to sleep, so the breathing stops and that's what kills these people. They go into what we call respiratory arrest. Their heart is still beating, but they're not breathing. Because they're not breathing, they're bringing no oxygen into their heart. After three or four minutes their heart stops beating. If they go undetected this way for, say, fifteen minutes, they will die of a heroin overdose.

Many times we get there and find the people in showers. Somebody put them there because it's the old commandment: if you stick them in the shower or throw some ice on their balls, it brings them around.

But it doesn't bring them around. So we will pull them out and start breathing for them. We breathe for them with this thing called an ambu-bag. Part of it is a mask and part of it looks like a football. The football has a tube on it, hooked to an oxygen bottle. After putting the mask over their nose and mouth, you squeeze the football. This forces the oxygen into their lungs. The oxygen goes to the heart and keeps the brain alive.

As EMTs, we can keep them alive for ten or twelve

minutes this way. Then our paramedics get there and shoot them up with Narcan. It's this magic drug the fire department uses. Boom—the Narcan reawakens the medulla. It's almost instantaneous. Three seconds after these people are on the threshold of death, they're alive and well and talking to you. Narcan is an unbelievable drug.

Even though we're getting more and more shootings, we still get a lot of car accidents. And nothing is more grotesque, nothing is more graphic, than what happens to people in major auto wrecks. It's amazing, at first, if you've never seen it before, just how swiftly the human body is mutilated. And just when you think you've seen it all, the next day you get something you've never seen before.

At one auto accident, we had three kids traveling in one car. Two boys and a girl, between nineteen and twenty-one. This was a two-lane street up on a hill. They were traveling, obviously, at a very high rate of speed. Their car went airborne for some three hundred feet.

When they touched back down on the ground, they lost control, spun around, and hit a tree. Big tree, almost four feet in diameter.

The two passengers were ejected from the car. The driver was not, but he and the car both struck the tree. It was the driver's side of the car that took the primary impact.

The boy who got ejected was dead on the scene. The girl who got tossed out was screaming and hollering. We transported her by helicopter to the trauma center. She later died of head injuries.

The thing that sticks in my mind is going to see the driver. He was still pinned in the car, with absolutely no form or shape to his head. When the car hit the tree, the force must have crushed every bone in his head. It looked like a big ball of Jell-O was sitting on top of his shoulders.

Obviously, speed kills. The faster you go, the more potential for the injury to be severe. But some people would be shocked: even with what might seem like minimal impact, it's amazing how severe an injury can be.

There was a motorcycle accident I responded to. A car backed out in front of a guy on a Harley. The biker could not have been going twenty-five miles an hour. But his bike struck the rear quarter panel of the car, and he went headfirst into the back of the car. And he was dead.

This guy had a helmet on and he still wound up dead. So even with helmets, you will have fatalities. But people should still wear helmets in my opinion. Motorcycles can be extremely hazardous. The potential for serious injury is great, greater even than driving in a car. There is no way around that. And this comes from a person who used to ride.

TREATING AIDS PATIENTS

In the old days you didn't worry too much about blood. You didn't worry much about AIDS, or hepatitis B and tuberculosis. Nowadays it enters into your mind. It enters into your process. Especially in a car accident, when you have a very difficult extrication, you have to be looking at how you can work on this victim. How can you give this person your utmost care, without exposing your own people to the blood?

We had one car accident with a Volkswagen. It was tipped onto its side. The guy inside had lost a pretty good amount of blood. Normally, our procedure is not to right the vehicle. You just leave it where it is and try taking the person out.

In this situation, I could see what would happen if we just took this guy out. We'd have a firefighter crawl through the window, and he would be lying in blood. So what we opted to do was stabilize the guy's head while he was in the car. We did this with tape and a cervical collar. Then all the firefighters got together, and we picked the car up and set it right. We were then able to open the door, and remove him without exposure to his blood. Two hours later, the information came back to us from the hospital. This person was HIV-positive.

So this was a situation where being careful paid off.

When I first became an EMT, we just waded into things. But with AIDS such an issue now—particularly here in San Francisco—handling and dealing with blood has become a large concern. Sometimes we'll hear on our radio, "Double glove up, boys." That means wear two pairs of gloves. Because the dispatch knows or believes the person has AIDS.

AIDS is a very big issue throughout our industry. I kind of resent that. I resent that some people are reluctant to treat other people because of the AIDS situation. We've had infectious diseases around forever, but now we wear all this extra paraphernalia—the gloves and the mask and the gowns and all that crap. I still have trouble putting all that on. It's a pain in the ass, especially the gloves. Many times while starting an IV, I will find myself taking my gloves off. These gloves are so sensorially depriving, I can't feel the patient's veins. So I'll take my glove off, then manipulate my finger over the vein until I find it.

It kind of saddens me, this general reluctance to treat *all* people. Hell, the chances of us getting AIDS has got to be a lot less than the chances of us dying in a fire. But we still run into burning buildings. Even with a significant exposure like a needle stick, the chances of us getting hepatitis are about a thousand times greater than the chances of us ever contracting AIDS. And yet it's got this terrible stigma about it. I understand that, I guess. Anything lethal has a stigma about it. But while I always believe in being cautious, and while I believe in good hygiene, the issue of AIDS has gone much deeper than that. It's a lot deeper than just the medical precautions. There is a definite stigma, and in some instances, I think it does affect our patient care.

For most of my career, my partner and I were stationed in a section of the city with two or three AIDS halfway houses. That's for people with AIDS who come out of the hospital and don't have anywhere to go. Because sometimes their own families don't even want them.

In a few of these places, they had some people with full-blown AIDS. They almost looked like lepers, and this was back when AIDS was first coming to the forefront. We didn't know how this thing spread. All we knew was that it was very contagious. You wore your gloves, your gowns, your face mask. You wore everything.

We wore all this, and we still didn't want to touch them. I know this is very cruel, but we actually made this one man get himself onto the stretcher. It was almost like we were saying: "This is your problem, not mine, and I don't want to *make* it my problem. If you want to go to the hospital, get on the stretcher. I'll take you there. But I'm not doing anything else."

That was many years ago. Many years ago. It was during that time when the public was uninformed, and firefighters did not have the needed training. But, yes, we were cruel. And yes, we were scared. We didn't want to bring anything home to our families.

My father died of AIDS. He died in February of 1994.

One night he called me and said he wanted to talk. He called my sister and brother and said the same thing. Before we met with our dad, we all sat down together. As part of my medical training, I had been taught to detect the possible signs of AIDS. And I thought my father had it. I had seen the symptoms and signs. I had seen his health deteriorate.

But I didn't want to admit it. I told my sister and brother it *could* be HIV. But then again, I said it could be cancer. I wasn't leading them on. I was being honest. I felt it was AIDS or cancer.

I said, "I think he's going to tell us it's HIV. But hopefully, he'll just tell us he has cancer."

My sister said she hoped so, too.

When my father told us, I handled it all right. I didn't cry like my sister and brother did. I tried to calm them down. Later, when I was away from anyone, that's when I broke down.

I took care of my dad while he was sick. My EMT training was helpful in that way. He would check into a hospital, then come home, and certain things would have to be watched on him. I would monitor his vital signs, his temperature, any blood pressure changes. My father and I had always been close. If anything, this made us closer. While he was dying, I became his nurse.

I think the experience has given me greater compassion. I know, firsthand, what people with AIDS are going through. But I am in the minority. There are still so many people who don't understand. There's even some EMTs and paramedics. They're still naive about it, so they're afraid.

When I see them acting this way around a patient, I don't get mad. I just show them there's nothing to be scared of.

I tell my partners, "You're not having sex with this patient. You won't catch the disease just by touching them. Take your precautions, yes. Wear your gloves and mask. But don't be afraid. *Show* them you're not afraid. Make them feel comfortable. That's what they need, like any other patient."

I do more than just say this to my partners. I make sure they see me touch the patient.

In this fire department, I've never seen anyone not treat a patient. But I did have a patient once who got angry at one of my partners. The patient was having breathing difficulties. We showed up and his mom told us he had AIDS. As we got ready to move him to our cart, my partner saw a little blood on his sheets. The blood came from small open sores on the patient's feet. When my partner saw this, he tried covering every little sore. Even with gloves on, he didn't want to touch this patient's feet.

I was up at the patient's head while this was going on. I looked at his face and he was getting upset. Then he said to my partner, "If you don't want to touch me, I'll do it myself. I can get up and move myself, you know."

I said, "Sir, just relax. We can handle it."

I said to my partner, "Man, you got your gloves on. Let's just move the patient."

So we moved him, and then I talked to my partner later. He's a compassionate person. He was just honestly scared. Firefighters have fears like anyone else.

EPILOGUE
"YOU'RE MY HERO"

I was working on Truck Company 9, out by Candlestick Park, where they were just getting ready to start the World Series.

The earthquake hit at 5:07 P.M. I was sitting at a table in the firehouse. Having lived in San Francisco all my life, I just figured it was another shaker. You're gonna lose a few glasses off the shelf. Maybe a mirror falls down.

Then I looked out our back door. I could see the cars in our parking lot moving. Inside our firehouse, things were crashing off the wall. Other firefighters were moving toward the doors. These guys are all native San Franciscans. They usually aren't affected by a shake. But this wasn't the average shake. It kept intensifying instead of slowing down.

Immediately, our electricity went out. So as soon as the shaking stopped, I thought, *How will we open the doors? How will we get the rigs out on the street?*

We have an emergency generator, but it would not kick on. So we went out and started it by hand. Once we opened the door, the first things we saw were a crack down the middle of our street and a broken water main, with water shooting up about fifteen feet in the air. That was an indication that this could get pretty serious. I hadn't seen that, ever, in my life.

In emergency situations, what you always do first is circle your own immediate neighborhood. There were people standing outside and wires down. There was broken glass and water running all over. But we didn't see any injuries yet. Then, as we came back around our block, our radio came on and you could hear all the traffic. Instead of waiting for the channel to clear, firefighters were running right over each other. "I'm on this street . . . I'm on this street . . . We've got a building down . . . We got a wall collapsed."

The catastrophe was starting to sink in. It was fairly clear from the people's voices. You don't hear people on the radio, especially officers, getting that excited.

At that time, they called 41 Engine and 9 Truck to Cervantes and Fillmore in the Marina. A building had collapsed. The thing of it was, we were seven miles away. San Francisco is seven miles across, and we were all the way on the other side of town.

Our Lieutenant Nolan got on the radio. He said, "Is that correct? Could you repeat that? You want 9 Truck to the Marina?"

He was told, "Correct. No other units available."

With that, everyone on our truck just kind of looked at each other. The city was dry. We were the final truck. Everybody else was already at an incident.

The ride across the city was like a science fiction movie. All the lights in the city were out. Traffic lights were out. Cars were stopped in the middle of the streets. People were standing beside them. Everything just stopped. Remember *The Day the Earth Stood Still*? Like that.

We wound up taking side streets—the freeway was not

even moving—and as we got to the top of Fillmore Street, you could begin to see the columns of smoke. There were seventeen fires going on simultaneously. On our radio now, they were talking about another building collapse. Five citizens got killed. The firemen on the radio were upset. You could hear voices cracking.

I was driving. As I started down from the top of Fillmore Street, our guys were pounding on the back window for me to slow down. I didn't realize I was going that fast. Looking down the hill into the Marina, I was looking at this huge mushroom cloud. It was coming up from a five-story building. And it was fully involved.

There were several smaller fires, too. The whole Marina was just a mess. It's located on a landfill, which is almost like jelly. You know how jelly shakes? Well, when the earthquake hit the Marina, everything twisted and broke. All the gas pipes and gas mains. And then you had pilot lights on, these open flames, and everything just took off and started burning.

As I put on the brakes, I took a few breaths. I told myself, *Okay. Now get it together.*

We took Fillmore Street to Cervantes. As we pulled up in the rig, I went right for the guy in the white helmet. That was the chief, but he was waving us through.

He was saying, "Don't stop, go right, go right."

I couldn't believe he was waving us through. I mean, we could see the building on Cervantes. It was pancaked out into the street. The upper three or four stories had cascaded down. The whole bottom floor was collapsed. All the cars in the garage were smashed flat.

But the chief just said, "Keep going, keep going, go right. We got a fire going. It's already a fifth alarm and we're losing it."

As we pulled up to Beach and Divisadero, 41 Engine

was screaming they had no water. They were hooked up to a hydrant and the hydrant was dry.

The chief there said, "We're going to lose this whole building if we don't get water."

This was that five-story building, fully involved.

So we grabbed a big line off the back of 41 and dragged it down to a high-pressure hydrant. It was about a block away, so guys were just running. We hooked into the high pressure, and as we spun the spindle nothing happened. The water main was broken. All the mains were broken in the Marina.

So we ran back to 41 and said, "No water." By this time it was really getting hot. You got a five-story fire, with flames going maybe two hundred feet in the air. So we turned our helmets around to keep the heat off our face, and we backed up behind the rig and waited for water.

We heard on the radio then, "The fireboat Phoenix is coming into the harbor. They're going to try and pump water into the manifolds in front of the Saint Francis Yacht Harbor."

I could see the Phoenix pull in and it was a welcome sight. The Phoenix started pumping water out of the bay, and the manifolds all lit up. Suddenly Engine 41 just started shooting water.

Bringing the Phoenix was actually a great move. I think it saved the Marina. By this time we already had a general alarm, which I had never seen in twenty-five years. A general alarm is a call for mutual aid. You're asking for help from companies in other cities. You're asking for help from anyone who can get there. A general alarm also means the fifth alarm didn't do it. And the fifth alarm *always* does it.

At roughly this point, our truck got assigned to rescue operations. We were sent to 2090 Beach Street. Four-story, wood-frame, old Victorian-style apartment building, directly across the street from the five-story building on fire. This particular building had collapsed. The first floor was gone. It was under the second floor. The second floor collapsed, too. It was hanging over the sidewalk, into the street. The rest of the building was tilted to the west, at about a forty-five-degree angle. It looked like something out of the fun house.

You had citizens on the scene and also PG&E: Pacific Gas and Electric. They told us they were trying to shut down the gas main. Until they did, they were warning us to stay out of the buildings. If there's a spark, they said, there's going to be an explosion.

We understood that this was a real danger. It was why the fifth-alarm building took off so fast. When the gas got thick enough there, the pilot light lit it up, and it blew all the windows out of the building. That's why it was going from top to bottom by the time we got there. And that's why two people there had gotten killed. It happened so fast, they had no chance to get out.

But we didn't have a choice. We had to go into this apartment building. We knew there were people inside.

All the glass was out, so some guys went in through the windows. Some guys went in anywhere there was an opening. We just tried to crawl in as far as we could. Then we just kept yelling for people.

First, some guys found two women and got them out. As we took these two women down to an ambulance, a citizen said to me, "I think I heard a voice around the corner. Somebody else is in there."

I went up to my lieutenant and I told him. He said they wanted us to wait before going in again. They wanted to shore up the building, make it a little more stable. They also wanted to wait for PG&E to get the gas shut off.

But I told my lieutenant again, "Supposedly there's somebody inside there."

He said, "Well, I can't tell you to go in, and I'm not going to tell you to stay out."

So I went in.

I could see a V shape where a wall had split. So I got on my hands and knees and crawled through there. When I got in a little bit, I saw a four-poster bed. The posts of the bed were holding up the ceiling. So I crawled up and over the bed and started yelling. All of a sudden I heard this woman say, "I can hear you! I'm in here!"

I crawled back outside and said, "There's somebody in here."

There was a captain and a chief standing on the sidewalk. The chief was saying he didn't want anyone in there.

I just said, "I'm going to need some stuff."

The captain said to our other guys, "Get some blocks and jacks. We've got to make sure there's an egress out of here."

When I crawled back in, I could hear that some people outside were still not real happy. In fact I heard people yelling, "Get the hell out of there!"

But by then, I had kind of a dialogue going with her.

I told the lady, "Keep yelling and I'll go toward your voice. But you're also going to hear a lot of noise. I have to cut all these floor joists."

I could barely hear her reply, so I knew then I was pretty far away.

I started cutting a tunnel with a chain saw. The floor joists were about two inches by fourteen inches. I would cut all the way through, about the width of my shoulders. Then I'd knock the thing out and crawl to the next one. It got a bit claustrophobic going through all this rubble. At times the crawl space would narrow, and I didn't have enough room to get my shoulders through. So I'd kind of wedge in sideways, then straighten back out when I could.

At this point you're thinking, *Shit. How will I turn around and get out of here?*

But you keep telling yourself, *Don't think about it. Keep cutting. It ain't your time.*

Well, just when I thought that things couldn't get any worse, our building caught on fire. First, a building across the street completely collapsed. It fell forward into the street, with all its burning debris. The debris flew into our building and caught it on fire.

I was aware of it right away. It got real bright inside there and real hot. Then I guess the guys from 41 or 28 got up on a building next door. They started spraying water onto our building. The water started coming down on us. It was leaking through the floors. This lady kept saying to me, "What is that water? What's going on?"

I'd say, "That's just a precaution. It's water running off from the building next door."

I never told her our building was on fire. I wanted this rescue to be successful. So I didn't want her to panic. I wanted her calm. And she was fantastic that way. If she was grabbing at me and hysterical, it would have changed everything.

When this building had first collapsed, the woman had been in her hallway outside her bedroom. I was now through her bedroom and into this hallway, but there was a big, old, wooden support beam between us. By then I'd probably been in there about an hour. The saw was pretty much finished. The blade was shot, from cutting through all the nails in the floor joists. So I had to crawl back to the bed.

The bed was like the point of no return. If the rest of this place came down, it would've been tough for me getting past that big bed. So we had three other guys who were working there. They would go to the bed and slide in these big blocks. Then they would use our jacks to shore it all up. Well, as I went back to get another saw, they were telling me all these good things that they had going.

They said, "We got this part of the bed blocked up over here, and we got these jacks over there . . . "

And everything they were telling me was bullshit! It was funny, talking to those guys later on. Because I was telling things to this woman in there, and they were telling me things back at the bed. But if there was another shake, it was all over. This whole place was coming down.

I crawled back in with the new saw, to start on that big beam. It went about two feet by two feet. I still couldn't see her yet, so I said, "How you doing there?"

Because all this water was still pouring down on us.

She said, "I'm getting drenched. They're drowning me."

I yelled back for them to shut the water down. Not only was she getting soaked, the floor was starting to drop from the weight of the water. I also took off my turnout coat at this time. Then I reached in with my coat and slid it under the beam.

I said, "Grab my coat. I'm going to cut this beam and there's going to be splinters. Just put it over your face and head. It will keep out the water, too."

And as I reached under the beam, she grabbed my hand.

She said, "Don't leave me. I don't want to die in here."

I said, "I won't leave you. I promise. I got this beam I have to cut, and in a little while, we'll be out of here having a cup of coffee."

She put the coat over her head and I started cutting the beam. I was lying flat on my stomach. I had my elbows on the ground, with the saw extended directly in front of me. When I cut through one side of the beam, I was able to lift the thing up. I looked underneath it and I could see her face with my coat pulled up to her nose. I could also see one arm and one shoulder. The rest of her was trapped beneath her bedroom door.

The sun had gone down by then, so I shined my flashlight on her. Then I handed it to her. She grabbed it and held the light right up to her face. It was pitch-black in there. It was like she'd finally gotten her hands on the daylight.

Then she grabbed my hand again and I said, "It's okay. We're going to be all right."

She said, "What's going on out there? Where's the water from? I can taste salt."

I still hadn't told her our building was on fire. I said, "They're pumping water out of the bay. They're keeping the fire off us. Off of this building."

Her eyes got wide open then. There was a wall directly across from her. It started getting bright orange and she said, "What's that?"

I said, "It's a reflection from the building across the street."

It wasn't the truth. When I told those guys before to shut the water down, the heat inside the building had picked back up. So now it was a race. The building was on fire. I had to cut and move the last piece of beam. Then I had to get the door off of her. There was a lot to do, and I didn't know how much time there was to do it. There was a moment or two when I thought we might not get out. But I never let on to her. I knew she was watching everything I was doing.

I got the beam cut, moved it to the side and kept on talking to her. I asked her name and she said it was Sherra.

I said, "Sherra, I'm going to cut the door."

She said, "I'm right under this door, you know."

I said, "Well, I was a woodsman. I'm an expert with this saw."

No . . . that wasn't true either.

But I did believe I could do it. I just thought I'd need some luck. The door was a half inch thick, and here's a body laying right underneath it with nothing on but a nightgown. So I put one of my hands under the door— under the door and right on top of her stomach. I wanted to feel the blade coming through the door, to make sure I wouldn't cut her.

I've got to tell you, it went *real* well. There was a *lot* of luck involved in this thing. The door just cut in half, and at this point Rich Allen, the head of the Rescue Squad, came crawling in with a stretcher. I was just really, really glad to see him.

Rich said, "Let me check her out before we move her."

Rich crawled ahead of me, then crawled right back.

He said, "I think her hip's broken."

We both agreed we couldn't wait for splints, or anything else, because now the place was cooking. So I crawled back in and took Sherra by her shoulders. She was grabbing my arms and she was just yelling.

I said, "I know it hurts, but you gotta hang in there."

She said, "Then let's go, then let's just go!"

So we slid her onto the board and started crawling out.

Once we got through the narrow space where we had tunneled in, we handed her on the stretcher out to the street. I take a little peek out, and there's 250 people cheering and yelling. There's ambulances, the police, TV cameras and flashbulbs going off. A Channel 5 helicopter is overhead.

I was like, *What the hell?*

I had no idea this stuff was going on. It was pitch-black inside that building. And we were probably in there for two and a half hours.

When I saw all the lights and the commotion, I just handed the bottom of the stretcher to a paramedic, and I stayed where I was. It's just a habit you get. When you see cameras and stuff, you just kind of turn away.

Then the paramedics carried her through the crowd, and everybody was clapping. I waited until the cameras started to follow the stretcher. When everyone's back was turned, I got out and stood up. The lieutenant up on the roof, a guy named Pete Cornyn, jumped down and started patting me on the back.

Pete said, "Great job, but don't let it go to your head. If we knew it was you in there, we wouldn't have gone through all this trouble."

I was just standing there, glad to be out. I was thinking about my family. I've got a wife and two kids.

Then all the sudden this ambulance driver walks up.

He said, "You gotta come up. She won't let us close the doors. She won't get into the ambulance until she gets your name."

So I walked through the crowd and she reached up and pulled me down by my neck.

She hugged me and said, "You're my hero."

Then she asked my name.

I said, "My name's Jerry."

She said, "Thanks. I had to get your name."

I said, "I owe you a cup of coffee."

She said, "I owe you more than that."

Then she took off. They closed the doors and away they went. It felt real good. Unbelievably good. You know, when you first hire on, you think you're gonna save every last person. And then you don't. Some people die. So you stop phoning the hospital to check up. It just gets too depressing when people don't make it. So, yeah, it felt fantastic when this rescue worked.

We ended up staying in the Marina until seven o'clock the next morning. Then they let us go back and eat and put on some dry clothes. That morning we got a call from the chief's secretary.

She said, "The *Examiner* has called, the *Chronicle* called, KPIX called."

I'm going, *What the hell?*

Up until that point, I hadn't really thought much about the rescue. It might sound corny, but I really was just doing my job. It's what they pay you to do. We got fourteen hundred guys here who would do the same thing. They'd do it in a heartbeat.

So the chief's secretary said, "They're all going out to the hospital to interview this woman. Had you planned on going by?"

I said, "Well, I'm working."

She said, "Why don't you go ahead if you feel like it?"

I said, "Yeah, it sounds great. I'd love to see her."

So I went by and she gave me another hug. That night, she said, they were going in to fix her pelvis. They found out it was crushed. She also had cuts and abrasions on her face and arms. Some of the cuts on her arms were real deep. She was all bandaged and taped. But she was doing great. Upbeat. Not worrying. Glad to be out of that building. Happy to be alive. And she must have already talked to some other firemen there—firemen who had been injured. Because she started kidding me.

She said, "Jerry, I heard you weren't a woodsman."

I said, "Well . . . practically a woodsman. I've done a lot of work with a saw."

She even told the reporters, "I believed him the whole time. I believed everything he said. I didn't find out until later that he'd been lying. It doesn't matter, either. I would still believe anything he told me."

It was a nice moment. A great moment. Then I said good-bye and went back to the firehouse. The other guys were saying, "Don't let this media crap go to your head. Get in there and do the dishes. You're still a bum in here."

I don't know if you remember, but right when the earthquake hit, the World Series game was just about to start. That game and the whole Series was interrupted. Then they waited another month to replay it. They wanted a mourning period. I mean, sixty-seven people were lost in that earthquake. They didn't feel it was right to play baseball games the next week.

So they waited a month and then they said, "Okay. San Francisco's come out of this before. It's time for us to resume living. We are going to finish the World Series."

A few days before the game, the chief's office called again. They asked if I'd like to throw out the first pitch.

I said, "Are you kidding? Of course I'll throw out the first pitch."

Then once I got out there and saw the crowd, I was scared to death. It was just overwhelming. I'm walking out on the grass at Candlestick, and the PR man for the Giants is handing me the ball.

He's saying, "Here you go. Now remember there's fifty million people watching."

So he gave me the ball. And I'm thinking about these guys back at the firehouse. There's a lot of ex-ballplayers there. This one guy, Lonnie, had told me, "Hey, you better put some mustard on that thing. Don't give us any lame throws."

So I went into my windup. Then I almost threw it over the backstop. Yup, it came in a little high. I guess I had just a little adrenaline going.

A few of the Giants came up to me right after. Brett

Butler gave me a ball and said, "God bless you. We heard the story."

Craig Lefferts said, "I saw you on TV. My wife and I were in tears."

I couldn't believe these guys. They're waiting to play the World Series and they're walking up to *me*. I figured they'd be thinking, *Let's get this thing over with. Let's get this guy out of here and play ball.*

I got to bring my family with me, too. They were in the VIP box watching. It was one of those once-in-a-life-time things.

But the biggest thrill of all was winning the Scannel Medal. It was named after the chief at the time of the 1906 quake. They've only given it out a handful of times since then.

There was a ceremony here. A couple of hundred firemen showed up. They gave a standing ovation. I still remember looking into the crowd, seeing these captains and chiefs I'd worked for standing and clapping. It was like a dream. When you get it from your peers, somehow it's different.

Sherra and I, by the way, have stayed friendly through all this stuff. I'd never done that before, but it was just something that kind of naturally happened. I would call her up to check on her. Then she'd call me to see how I was doing.

Sherra was in the hospital a long time. On the day she got out, they were having a going-away party for her. The news media were all there, taking pictures of her and congratulating her. After she got out and things had kind of died down, my wife and I knew that Christmas was coming up. We thought Sherra might be alone in her new apartment. So me and my wife and our kids went over there on Christmas. We brought Sherra dinner and a tree. It was a good day. A very good day.